Vegging Out

The Taste of Plant Based Eating

By Richard Church

All words and pictures Copyright © Richard Church 2018

This book is dedicated to Katherine, Charlotte and Morgan.
300g of love, mixed with 600g of chaos and insanity.
The best recipe ever…

*****

Also by Richard Church
Going Vegan
Available to buy on Amazon now.

A massive thank you to all of my family and friends in helping create this book, and to my wife, Samantha, for her never-ending support.

Visit my website for more recipes: www.richardchurchuk.com
Facebook: https://www.facebook.com/richardchurchuk/
Instagram: https://www.instagram.com/richardchurchuk/

Table of Contents

Let's Talk About Eating………………………………………4

Using This Book………………………………………7

Recipes

Beans and Pulses………………………………………8

Local Delicacies………………………………………34

Pasta and Rice………………………………………77

Root Vegetables………………………………………97

Squashes………………………………………117

More 'Meaty' Things………………………………………137

Nuts………………………………………154

Breads, Pastries and Batters………………………………………178

Warmer Climate Food………………………………………212

Chocolate………………………………………242

Let's talk about eating...

No, not the mandatory daily function of putting food in your mouth in order to live. I'm not talking about that. I'm talking about the pleasure derived from eating. The sensation that occurs when a fresh, ripe blackberry explodes between your teeth, sending its luxurious juices along its journey over your tongue and down your throat. The way chocolate clings to your mouth as you chew, sweet, thick and warming, a feeling you never want to end. Perhaps the joy from that first crunch of a hot roast potato, or the gravy that oozes from a well-baked Yorkshire pudding. These, in my mind are real pleasures and, if you're reading this book, then I can assume that the very act of eating holds a certain resonance with you too.

From our first mouthfuls as an infant, when we are introduced to solid food, we explore taste as a new adventure. Sometimes pleasurable, sometimes not, each bite is a milestone of either delight or discomfort.

There were not many foods I disliked as a child. I was the kid who ate all his meals and asked for seconds. I didn't understand the sickly-looking face the other children pulled in the dinner hall at school, when they were presented with their mashed potato or semolina pudding. I wasn't raised in any great culinary environment. My mother's cooking was inadequate at best and my father, though working long hours, put a lot of the food on the table. Being a man of simple tastes, the meals he served were often repetitious, though always nourishing and plentiful. Certain taste experiences did not come to me until later in life. Aubergines and asparagus were an adult discovery, and I was already working as a chef before I understood the pleasures of pine nuts and avocado.

At different times in our lives we unearth new tastes, be they precious stones or lumps of bitter clay that stain our tongues with unpleasant and clinging memories. I have been lucky. I have not encountered much that has made me wish I'd never opened my mouth. Not that every morsel has been something worth remembering. Sometimes, quite simple, we just eat.

Foodies think about food perhaps more than others do. We analyse the act of consumption as if it were a Shakespearean play. Flavours and textures are ingested and stored for future evaluation. They are broken down, reassembled and either repeated or discarded. But they are not forgotten.

As a former chef, a food writer, and a generally hungry person, I think about the act of eating a great deal. From chomping down on an apple to concocting an elaborate meal, eating is rarely an absent-minded task for me, or a thing that I just do because I have to. Nor is it always an occasion. I don't put a lot of thought into everything I eat, but I do put in some thought. Even if I'm just having instant noodles.

Good food is all around us, if we are willing to seek it out. It lies in the eclectic, in the combination of seemingly banal things that transform when put together. It is the bunch of bananas in the corner of the kitchen and the espresso maker that needs dusting off. It's the swede at the back of the fridge and the half-empty jar of Marmite in the cupboard. It's the dried beans that we bought six weeks ago on a whim and haven't got around to opening yet, and the frozen vegan chorizo sausages, still in their box in the freezer. Good food is contrast and balance, harmony and disorder. Black, white and every shade of grey in between. But first, we must know how to look.

Thankfully, generations of intrepid human beings have done a lot of the work for us. They've already tasted the good and the bad. They've thrown together things out of both curiosity and necessity, they've compared and contrasted the results and passed them on down the line. We know that the aforementioned banana and coffee work well together because somebody, somewhere along the way has told us. Of course, it doesn't work for everyone (coffee-haters will not go near the combination), but on the whole, it is a success. The same with the not-so-famous chilli and chocolate duo, and many other culinary pairings, some with more notoriety than others. With this foundation of knowledge as a good starting point, we can then rely on our own tastes and experiences. Peanut butter and jam (or jelly in the US) is a celebrity marriage familiar to everyone, but I have discovered that peanut butter and chocolate spread is so much more exciting. It is not as much a marriage as it is an illicit affair in a dimly-lit hotel room. It clings to your mouth and doesn't want to let go.

Our tastes also change over time. Up until recently I wouldn't touch Marmite, or any other brand of yeast extract. In the last year, however, I've really come to appreciate its culinary charms. Added as a base for many sauces, also as a marinade for things like sausages, it can add a real depth of flavour. Though it'll still be a cold day in hell before I put it in a sandwich. Olives were another food that I had no appreciation for as a child. Now I'll happily work my way through a bowlful of good quality olives and then go back for more. Many a parent has despaired over the unwillingness of their child to eat the most basic of vegetables only to find that, later in life, they hold no such reserves. My own son is very difficult to feed at the time of writing, but I know this will change in the future.

Food is such an integral part of our lives that it is no wonder certain tastes trigger memories. Eating blackberries always takes me back to autumn trips through the woodland areas just beyond my grandparents' house, where we would pick them until our bowls were full. The area has since been built upon and my grandparents have passed, so the taste of a fresh, ripe blackberry is a strong link to a magical childhood moment. I was recently trying to introduce my son to celery. It was a logical step as he is already very much into cucumber. While taking a bite to show him how good it was, I was immediately transported back to weekends at the same grandparents' house, where sandwiches would be laid out on a Saturday afternoon. Sticks of celery would always be stacked on a plate, next to batons of carrots, cucumber and a glass salt cellar. Sliced tomatoes would be in the sandwiches themselves. My grandmother would slice them so thin you could see through them. I remember helping her with that once, and it became a mission of mine to get them as thin as I possibly could. Though they were probably not as good as hers, I remember feeling very proud of the results. Perhaps, while trying to feed my son, I became too caught up in nostalgia, because I couldn't get him to go for the celery. Not this time, at least. Tastes can trigger different times in our lives. Some, perhaps, we would rather forget, but most of these recollections are pleasant.

Sometimes, for whatever reason, we want to trigger our own nostalgia. Perhaps we want a quick visit to our youth, or go back to a certain place and time where we remember things being good. Cooking can help us do that. Let's say you were eating this great tiramisu at a restaurant on holiday when your partner proposed to you. Eating another good tiramisu is a way of sending you back to that place and time, if only for a short while. I have my own dishes for this, and both are desserts. Trifle always reminds me of times at my other grandmother's house – my father's mother. My sister and I would stay there every Friday night and leave again Saturday afternoon, and there was a point in our childhood when we lived with her. Most of the food she made for us I no longer eat: a fried egg sandwich for breakfast and those packets of fish in sauce for lunch, with mashed potatoes and peas. It was the same every Saturday and I never wanted it any different. But from time to time she would make a trifle, especially when there were more people coming to visit. She was the only member of my family who made one, so it was a real treat. When I make trifle now I get such an incredible sense of being in that place and time: a small boy standing on the stone floor of her kitchen, waiting to be served a bowl of this most precious dessert. The other dish I make for reasons of nostalgia is semolina pudding. I have no specific memory that I am trying to revisit when I make it. It is just something I used to like as a kid. I have a recipe for semolina pudding in my first book Going Vegan.

I am a plant-based eater. A vegan. But my books are not just for vegans.

Vegetables and plant-based foods in general are something we could all eat a little more of. I am not an obsessively healthy eater. I am not always looking to lower my fat intake. I don't say no to an extra slice of cake (and if you're looking for me down at the gym, don't trouble yourself. It's too early in the morning and I haven't had anywhere near enough coffee to be doing that), but I do try to make sure I get my fair share of fruit and vegetables on a daily basis.

This, in essence, is what this book is all about. It's about taking advantage of the endless choices of fruit and vegetables available to us in this modern world. You might not be vegan or vegetarian, but if you want to increase your consumption of veg, then you've come to the right place.

I think vegetables get a bad rap. From our parents' first struggles with trying to get them into us as young children, to our teenage years of passive resistance, right through to adulthood, which we often view as a licence to avoid veg whenever we feel like. In fact, we are so bad at it that, even as grown-ups, we are still having to be told to eat our greens. The government recommends five portions of fruit and veg a day (no, ketchup doesn't count) and social media is constantly pointing out to us the health benefits of chomping down on carrots and broccoli.

If I had to guess at why this is, I would say it was due to the same four or five, grossly-overcooked vegetables being shoved unsympathetically onto the side of our plates when we were growing up. I can't speak for everyone, but I know I got sick of the sight of discoloured mushy peas that had cooled just enough to form an unappetising skin over the top, and please don't even get me started on Brussels sprouts!

For fear of doing my childhood a disservice, I want to state that it was not all bland vegetables, cooked to destruction and served unceremoniously. There was much love at our dinner table, in addition to plenty of colour and flavour. My father, the sole cook in my house after my parent's divorced when I was seven, went through a period of culinary experimentation, and interesting things started to appear on our plates. I remember pizzas being a thing for a while. There would be a selection of vegetables, most of which seemed to be peppers, stacked high on a pre-made pizza base (the kind that are essentially solid discs, almost like biscuits). Some of the peppers would be browned at the edges and there never seemed to be much in the way of cheese with them. They were almost like warm salads on plates made of bread. We ate these with reverence, my sister and I, because they were something different, something away from the routine of roast dinners and fish and chips.

There were casseroles and hotpots too, but of course, always meat-based. Sausages, lamb, or leftover chicken would be the feature of these dishes. Like most of us, I grew up believing that meat was centre stage and that vegetable were a necessary accompaniment. My own reading has led me to understand that this is very much a western way of eating. I was recently admiring a social media post by a famous food photographer on the subject of Marrakesh. The photographer had captured the astounding colours and variety of Moroccan cuisine in this series, and I was taken immediately by how many of the dishes were just vegetables: broccoli and spinach, tabbouleh and potatoes, roasted squash with whole garlic cloves and fresh, seasoned beetroot. About 90 per cent of the food in these photographs were dishes containing only vegetables, and the colours were amazing.

Fruit and veg liven up a meal in a way nothing else can. The vastness of their colours, textures and flavours is so great that you can make endless combinations and be constantly eating different food. Don't assume that fruit and vegetables need to be separated. Yes, they are more common apart – fruit for dessert and veg for savoury – but they also sit exceedingly well together in a plethora of meals. This book is littered with examples of not only their juxtaposition, but also their incredible harmony.

Whether you are vegan, vegetarian or meat-eater, it is my hope that this book will get you thinking about fruit and vegetables in a whole new way. If you are new to cooking, I would advise following the recipes word-for-word until you get a feel for what you are doing. If you are a well-honed kitchen adventurer then, by all means, let the recipes here guide you and inspire you to take leaps in directions you might not have previously considered. For the most part, recipes are not written in stone. They are one of many possible combinations that are only limited by your knowledge and imagination. I encourage you here to use that imagination. To take the knowledge gained from this book and run with it to create your own stunning meals in ways that only you can, using ingredients that are special to you.

Now let's get out our pans, cooking knives and roll up our sleeves. We've got some work to do…

Using This Book

Come on in. Pull up a chair. Let's chat a little while longer. The recipes are coming, I promise.

Before we get into the cooking, I want to go over some aspects of this book so that you can easily find your way around. I'm not going to tell you how to use a recipe book, because I think you've got that down (read recipe, cook recipe. If you either burn, mush, dry, singe, drop or cataclysmically explode said recipe, cook recipe again). I just want to show you how this cookbook is laid out.

I started writing Vegging Out with the intention of showing just how versatile fruit and veg can be. I wanted to come up with a range of dishes that emphasised the limitless options available to you, the vegetable-eater. It was easier than I thought it would be, because there really are endless combinations out there. Over 150 recipes later, I believe I have a good range of ideas to get you consuming more fruit and veg on a daily basis.

The book is divided into 10 recipe chapters, grouped into the type of food featured most prominently in the ingredients. For example, Beans and Pulses features recipes rich in black beans, borlotti beans, lentils, and of course tofu. Local Delicacies is concerned with food often grown closer to home, such as mushrooms, apples and pears. There is a chapter on root vegetables, as well as squashes. There is a chapter on meat replacements and alternatives, as well as a section containing mostly bread, in which you will find my 5 Ways with Pizza. There is also, at the very end of this book, a chapter devoted entirely to chocolate, and there are desserts and sweet dishes throughout the book, enough to keep any sweet tooth satisfied.

Gluten- Free Recipes.

As with my first book Going Vegan, there are many gluten-free recipes here, and there are some that can be easily converted to gluten-free. I have labelled all recipes accordingly, so that it is easy to see, at a glance, which ones are suitable for those with a wheat intolerance. A lot of my readers have no such intolerance, and so I have chosen to make recipes gluten-free where it will not affect the integrity of the dish. It is my hope, by doing this, that I have made Vegging Out as inclusive as possible.

That Blurb at the Top of the Recipe.

I have dispensed with as much unnecessary waffle as I can in this book, while still (hopefully) making it entertaining for the reader. That being said, there are a few stories sprinkled amongst the chapters, as well as plenty of information on the best ways to cook a particular dish. These are usually contained at the top of the recipe, in the blurb a lot of readers like to skip. I urge you to at least glance over them to make sure you are not missing any important information regarding the recipe you intend to cook.

The vast majority of ingredients in this book you can get from any large supermarket, with most, if not all of the vegetables also being available at your local greengrocers, whom I urge you to support as much as possible. Supermarkets are wonderful, convenient places to shop, but please remember that local independent sellers cannot compete with them and therefore struggle to make a living. For some of the ingredients in this book you will need to go to either health food shops or shop online, particularly Vital Wheat Gluten, Agar Agar and Braised Tofu, which comes in a small can. There are also Spring Roll Wrappers and Dumpling Wrappers, which can be purchased at any Chinese supermarket. Xanthan gum, a powder that helps gluten-free flour to bind, can now be bought in the Free From section of most large supermarkets.

I have tried to make sure that the items you buy are used several times throughout the book, so that you don't end up with something gathering dust at the back of your cupboard. Should that be the case, however, I encourage you to study the techniques in this book and use those items to create your own exciting dishes. For example, agar agar can be used in a variety of cheesecake-style fillings to make them solid. It is used in sweet dishes a lot in Japan. You just need to put a teaspoon or two into the mix and simmer it for about 5 minutes for it to set solid when cooled.

Above all, have fun with these recipes. There are plenty to choose from and give you a whole load of inspiration to get creative in your kitchen. Play about with them. As I've said before, recipes are for the most part a guide and not a blueprint, so make some changes where you feel it's appropriate. If you're unsure of what you're doing, experimentation can come later. Now, let's get cooking…

Beans and Pulses

Vegan Quiche Lorraine

Shredded Spring Greens with Red Kidney Beans and Teriyaki Sauce

Spice-Marinated Tofu Curry

BBQ Chickpeas with Braised Tofu

Sweet Potato and Three Bean Nachos

Smoked Tofu in Coconut Milk Soup with Rice Noodles

Roasted Pumpkin with Lentils and Vegan Feta

Braised Tofu Kebabs

Mung Bean and Aubergine Dal

Oven Roasted Kale with Spiced Lentils and Mango

French-Style Aquafaba Omelette with Vegan Cheese and Tenderstem Broccoli

Chickpeas with Lemon, Parsley and Vegan Feta

Borlotti Bean Chilli with Rice

15 Minute Thai-Style Lentils with Green Beans and Coconut Rice

Fried Tofu with Rice Noodles and Black Bean Sauce

Lentil, Spinach and Coconut Curry

Aquafaba Mango Mousse with Raspberries

Vegan Quiche Lorraine

For most of us in our pre-vegan days, the enjoyment of a quiche came from the packaged variety bought from the chilled section of the supermarket, its top wrinkled from the cold and the pastry soft. Rare was the opportunity to taste a quiche fresh from the oven, with crisp, browned pastry and a filling dense with flavour. Making one yourself is, of course, the most obvious way of achieving this and now, as vegans, this is currently the only way I have encountered of tasting this historically French dish.

This recipe, understandably, has been adapted from the original Quiche Lorraine, using only plant-based ingredients. Most of them are readily available in the supermarkets, but you may have to hunt further afield to get the vegan bacon slices.

Fresh tomatoes are not a part of the original recipe, but I have used them here to add additional colour and flavour. If you are not keen on tomatoes, then you might prefer to substitute for another vegetable like mushrooms or even spinach. I would advise frying the mushrooms first if you are going to do this. It is important to allow the baked quiche to cool completely before cutting into it to allow it to set properly.

Prep time: 30-40 minutes. Cooking time: about 1 hour 15 minutes.
Makes 1 x 9 ½ inch quiche.

Ingredients:
For the Pastry:
300g plain flour
1 tsp baking powder
1 tsp salt
2 tbsp gram flour
150g vegan margarine, plus extra for greasing
100ml plant-based milk

For the Filling:
1 tbsp oil
1 pack (about 100g) vegan bacon, chopped into small pieces
½ block (200g) firm tofu
250ml vegan cream
200g humous
100g vegan cream cheese
2 tbsp nutritional yeast
Splash of plant-based milk (if required)
Salt and black pepper to taste
1 ripe tomato, cut into thin wedges
30g vegan parmesan cheese
Drizzle of oil
Pinch sea salt
About 1 tsp dried oregano.
You will also need a 9 ½ inch loose-bottomed tart tin.

Method:
First you want to make your pastry. Place the flour into a mixing bowl and add the baking powder, salt and gram flour. Put the margarine, a spoon at a time in with the flour, then use your fingers to work the flour mix and margarine into fine bread crumbs. This will take about 5 minutes. Once this is done, pour in the milk and mix together using an ordinary table knife. When it has formed large lumps it is ready to bring together. Use your hands to work the dough together into a large ball and then bring it out onto a lightly floured surface. Knead gently for just a minute or so to make sure it is fully combined. When this is done, place into a container with a lid and chill for 20-30 minutes.

While that's chilling you can fry the bacon. Heat the oil in a frying pan and add the bacon pieces. Fry for 8-10 minutes, stirring often, until they are slightly crisp and browned. When they are done, transfer them to a small bowl and set aside.

Now preheat the oven to gas 6/200C/400F and grease the inside of the tart tin with a little margarine.

Roll out the pastry on a floured surface to a couple of inches beyond the size of the tart tin. Place it in the tin and press into all the sides. Trim the pastry with scissors to just a little over the lip of the tin, so that if it shrinks it will still be level with the edge of the tin. Place a sheet of greaseproof paper over the pastry and trim to size. Fill this with baking beans or dried rice, then place in the middle of the oven and cook for 10-15 minutes, until firm.

While the pastry is baking put the tofu, cream, humous, cream cheese and nutritional yeast into a blender and blend until completely smooth. If the consistency seems too thick, you can add the splash of plant-based milk to loosen it up a touch. Season with the salt and pepper to taste and then blend again for a moment. Pour the mixture into a bowl.

Remove the pastry from the oven and take out the baking beans and paper. Set aside.

Turn the oven down to gas 5/190C/375F.

Put the vegan bacon and tomato wedges into the batter and stir to mix. Spoon the mixture into the pastry base and shake a little to even out. Grate the parmesan cheese over the top and then place the sliced tomatoes on top of that. Drizzle with some oil, season with sea salt and then sprinkle over the oregano. Place the tin on a baking tray and then put it in the bottom part of the oven. Bake for 50 minutes to 1 hour, until firm and browned on top.

Once cooked, remove from the oven and set aside to cool completely and set. Slice and serve.

Vegan Quiche Lorraine

Shredded Spring Greens with Red Kidney Beans and Teriyaki Sauce

This is a quick and easy mid-week supper that's bursting with flavour. Like all stir-fries, everything is cooked quickly on quite a high heat, so that the edges are seared and softened, but there is still a lot of bite to the meal. There is plenty of goodness and colour too, making this a quick meal that's worth getting excited about.

Prep time: 5 minutes. Cooking time: 15 minutes.
Gluten Free
Serves 2

Ingredients:
1 tbsp sesame oil
1 tbsp vegetable oil (or other flavourless oil)
1 red onion, cut into thick wedges
1 can red kidney beans, rinsed and drained
2 cloves garlic, sliced
1 head of spring greens, washed and cut into thin strips
2 medium tomatoes, cut into wedges
2 tbsp tamari
3 tbsp teriyaki sauce
2 tbsp cider vinegar

Method:
Heat the two oils in a large frying pan or wok and fry the onions for 3 minutes. Add the drained beans and cook for 3 minutes more, then throw in the sliced garlic. Cook for two minutes, stirring often.

Now put in the spring greens and cook for about 4 minutes, until the greens have started to wilt, then add the tomato wedges and give the whole dish another couple of minutes. The tomatoes should be softened but not turned to mush.

Now, with the heat still going, you can make up the sauce by simply adding the tamari, teriyaki sauce and cider vinegar. It will start to sizzle immediately, and the liquid will begin to evaporate, so add these and stir them in as quick as you can. Cook for 2-3 more minutes on a high heat and then serve straight away with rice or noodles.

*****

Spice-Marinated Tofu Curry

I bought a tofu press at a vegan fair, having heard that they dry the tofu out a lot better than the customary (and rather precarious) balancing of pots and pans on top of the towel-wrapped bean curd. This is the first dish I made with my new gadget, and I have to say that it did get a lot more water out and produce a firmer, and therefore more robust, tofu.

Of course, you might not have a tofu press, and so this dish can be made just fine with the heavy weight pressed upon it for 20 minutes or so (as with all of my other tofu recipes), though I did press my tofu for a few hours with this one. If you don't have one, put a press on your Christmas list. They are worth having.

Prep time: 15-20 minutes, plus pressing time. Marinating time: 30 minutes. Cooking time: about 30 minutes.
Gluten Free
Serves 3-4

Ingredients:
1 x 400g block firm tofu, pressed for 3 hours in a tofu press, then diced (pressed for 15-20 minutes under pans is also fine)

For the Marinade:
¼ tsp cayenne pepper
1 tsp onion granules
½ tsp ground ginger
2 tsp ground paprika
2 tsp ground coriander
1 tsp garam masala
½ tsp salt
75ml oil
3 tbsp tomato puree

For the Curry:
2 tbsp coconut oil
1 red onion, diced
1 red pepper, diced
100g button mushrooms, quartered
3 cloves garlic, chopped
300g natural, dairy-free yoghurt
100ml vegan cream
2 tbsp tahini
Salt and pepper to taste

Method:
First put all of the marinade ingredients into a mixing bowl and mix together. Stir in the tofu, until it is fully covered, and then leave for about 30 minutes.

When the time is up, heat 1 tablespoon of the coconut oil in a large pan or wok and fry the tofu, on quite a high heat, for about 15 minutes. Empty out the pan into a bowl, including all of the marinade, and then wipe the pan clean.

Now heat the remaining tablespoon of coconut oil in the pan and fry the onion, pepper and mushrooms, again on a high heat, for 7-8 minutes. Turn down the heat a little and put in the chopped garlic, cooking for another 2-3 minutes, stirring often.

Put the tofu, as well as all of the marinade, back in the pan and cook for another 3-4 minutes.

Now pour in the yoghurt, cream and tahini and mix thoroughly. Simmer for about 5 minutes, until you have a thick and rich curry sauce. Season with the salt and pepper if required and serve with rice.

*****

BBQ Chickpeas with Braised Tofu

This is sort of a much quicker and vegan version of Boston Bakes Beans. The original is slow-roasted over pork, but here we're using canned chickpeas and braised tofu to produce a similar, but cruelty-free effect. You can use any canned bean you want with this (borlotti beans would work particularly well), or you can make them out of the dried variety, as long as you soak and cook them properly beforehand. Once they are done, you can serve them with whatever you like as a side. My personal preference is with fried potatoes, but rice will do just as well.

Prep time: 15 minutes. Cooking time: About 30 minutes
Serves 4 as a side dish

Ingredients:
2 tbsp flavourless oil, such as groundnut
1 can braised tofu, drained and finely shredded
1 large onion, diced small
1 red pepper diced small
3 cloves garlic, chopped
1 can chickpeas, drained (about 240g drained weight)
300ml veg stock
1 can chopped tomatoes

4 tbsp soft brown sugar
75ml tomato ketchup (make sure it's gluten-free)
2 tbsp liquid smoke
3 tbsp American style yellow mustard sauce (make sure it's vegan and gluten-free. 2 tsp Dijon mustard will also do fine if you can't find this)
Salt and pepper to taste

Method:
Heat the oil in a large pan and fry the braised tofu for 4-5 minutes on a medium-high heat, until it is starting to brown. Add the onion and pepper and cook for 3-4 more minutes, stirring often. Now put in the garlic and the chickpeas and cook for a few minutes more.

Put in the rest of the ingredients, bring the whole dish to the boil and simmer for about 15 minutes, stirring from time to time, until you have a thick and fairly dry mix.

Serve immediately with fried potatoes or rice.

*****

Sweet Potato and Three Bean Nachos

I really can't remember when I first discovered nachos. It was probably at a restaurant I worked at that had them on the menu. I know I didn't have them growing up, and I was certainly into adulthood before I'd tasted them. Whenever it was, I've gone back for more many times since. As a vegan they can be a little more elusive when eating out. I did have some at the Download festival recently, but I've yet to come across them anywhere else. Thankfully, this recipe will guarantee that you can have tasty nachos whenever the fancy takes you.

The recipe makes two large platefuls, which is enough for four people sharing, and don't worry if you're gluten intolerant as the only wheat is in the tortillas. Just swap them for a gluten-free variety and you're good to go. I've used beetroot tortillas for this, which I got for the colour, but you can use any variety you like. I made a video of this one so that you can follow along. The video is on YouTube, so please subscribe to get more as they come in.

Prep time: 20 minutes. Cooking time: about 35-40 minutes.
Serves 4.
Easy to Make Gluten-Free

Ingredients:
For the Sweet Potato:
2 tbsp olive oil
1 medium sweet potato, peeled and diced
Pinch sea salt
1 tsp garlic granules
50ml cold water

For the Tortillas:
8 beetroot tortillas (or other variety)
Enough oil to coat them

For the Chilli Sauce:
1 medium red onion, sliced into rings
2 Romano peppers, sliced into rings
2 cloves garlic, finely chopped
1 can red kidney beans, drained
1 can Borlotti beans, drained
1 can haricot beans, drained
200g cherry tomatoes, halved
A handful of chopped parsley
1 tbsp mild chilli powder
1 tbsp dried oregano
Sprinkle of black pepper
3 tbsp tomato puree
2 tbsp sriracha sauce

Juice from ½ lime
3 tbsp tamari
1 can chopped tomatoes
½ can cold water
2 tbsp soft brown sugar

For the Nacho Cheese Sauce:
1 heaped tablespoon vegan margarine
1 tbsp gram flour
300ml plant-based milk
75g vegan cheese, grated
2 tbsp American style mustard sauce
1 tbsp sriracha sauce
A little water to thin
1 tbsp nutritional yeast
Salt to taste
A splash of white wine vinegar (about 2 tbsp)

To Garnish:
Sprinkle of chopped parsley
1 red chilli, finely sliced

Method:
Preheat the oven to gas 6/200C/400F

To cook the potatoes, heat the oil in a saucepan that has a lid and fry the potatoes for about 3 minutes. Add the salt and the garlic granules and stir in. Pour in the cold water and then put the lid on the pan. Turn down the heat and cook gently for 10 minutes, stirring occasionally, until cooked through. Set aside when done.

To make the tortilla chips coat each side of all the tortillas with the oil using a pastry brush and then cut, first in half, then into quarters. Then cut three wedges from each quarter. Separate them and place on a baking tray. Cook in the oven for about 15 minutes, making sure to move them around halfway through cooking to prevent the top from burning.

While they are baking you can make the chilli sauce. Heat the oil in a large saucepan or wok and fry the peppers and onion for 4 minutes. Add the garlic and fry for another minute. Pour in the three beans and cook for another two minutes, then add the cherry tomatoes. Cook for about 5 minutes, stirring often and then put in the chopped parsley. Add the rest of the chilli sauce ingredients and bring the dish to the boil. Simmer for 15-20 minutes, until the sauce has reduced and thickened. Now you can add the cooked sweet potatoes. Stir them in and then set the chilli sauce aside.

To make the nacho cheese sauce, melt the margarine in a pan and whisk in the gram flour. Add the milk, a little at a time, making sure you get all the lumps out before adding any more. Mix in the cheese, mustard and sriracha sauce and bring to a gentle simmer. Add a touch of water to thin the sauce just a little and then add the rest of the ingredients. Simmer for 2-3 minutes, whisking often.

To assemble, divide the tortilla chips between 2 large plates, spoon over about half of the chilli sauce onto each and then pour over the nacho cheese sauce. Garnish with the parsley and the sliced chillies, then serve immediately.

Sweet Potato and Three Bean Nachos

*****

Smoked Tofu in Coconut Milk Soup with Rice Noodles

This is a Thai style soup using smoked tofu, which infuses deliciously into the coconut milk to produce an unbelievable flavour. The smoked tofu you get in packets is so firm that it holds up very well to something like this without breaking up, and the smoked, nutty flavour makes this a very memorable dish.

I've put in some dried whole chilli, but I've kept this optional and would certainly urge caution when doing so, as it can easily overpower the dish.

Prep time: 10 minutes. Cooking time: 20-25 minutes.
Gluten-Free
Serves 2-3

Ingredients:
1 tbsp coconut oil
120g fresh green beans
1 red pepper, large diced
3 cloves garlic, chopped
1 tsp ginger paste (or ½ inch piece ginger, minced)
Juice of 1 lime
2 tbsp madras curry powder
½ tsp ground cumin
1 tsp ground coriander
300ml veg stock
1 can coconut milk

1-2 dried whole chillies (optional)
1 block smoked tofu, diced
A handful of baby spinach leaves
1 pack ready-cooked rice noodles, or dried rice noodles soaked in hot water for 10 minutes and drained

Method:
Melt the coconut oil in a large saucepan and cook the green beans and pepper together for 6-8 minutes. Add the garlic and ginger and cook for 2 minutes more, stirring frequently.
Squeeze in the lime juice and then stir in the spices. Now pour in the veg stock and coconut milk and bring to the boil. Add the chilli, if using, and the smoked tofu and simmer gently for 8-10 minutes to really allow the flavours to infuse.

Stir in the spinach leaves just prior to serving and ladle the soup into bowls, over the rice noodles.

*****

Roasted Pumpkin with Lentils and Vegan Feta

You can get vegan 'Feta', or 'Greek-Style Cheese', as it is often known, in a couple of the supermarkets, as well as from online suppliers. A quick internet search will lead you straight to it. It's usually served in a 200g slab, some dry and others in liquid, the latter being my own personal favourite. They all differ in texture and taste, so if you're not keen on the one you've tried, please try a different one before giving up entirely. The vegan feta goes exceptionally well with pine nuts, though walnuts make an alternative, but equally scrumptious pairing, so switch to those if it's more convenient for you.

Pumpkin, again, can be traded for another squash if it's not in season, so there's no need to wait until October to make this recipe. The lentils don't have to be soaked first, but it does make cooking them a lot quicker, so I would recommend it for this dish. You'll want to soak them for at least three hours. You can also leave them in water in the fridge overnight.

Alternatively, you can soak them in the morning before going to work and they'll be ready for cooking by the time you get home.

Prep time: 25-35 minutes, plus at least 3 hours soaking time. Cooking time: 1 hour.
Serves 3-4
Gluten Free

Ingredients:
800g fresh pumpkin (about ½ medium-sized pumpkin), peeled and deseeded
300g dried lentils, soaked in cold water for at least 3 hours, or overnight
3 tbsp olive oil
A generous pinch of sea salt
½ tsp ground cinnamon
A pinch of mild chilli powder
2 more tbsp olive oil
2 celery stalks, sliced
1 red or orange pepper, sliced
2 tsp garlic puree (or 2 chopped cloves garlic)
Juice and zest of 1 lemon
3 tbsp tamari
3 tbsp tomato puree
¼ tsp mild chilli powder
A pinch of salt
A handful of pine nuts
100g vegan feta cheese, cut into small squares
A drizzle of balsamic vinegar

Method:
Preheat the oven to gas 7/220C/425F.

First cut the pumpkin flesh into 1-inch thick strips along its length, then cut those long strips in half. Put them into a mixing bowl and add the 3 tablespoons of olive oil, the salt, the cinnamon and the chilli powder. Mix with your hands until the pumpkin is thoroughly coated, then tip the slices out onto a baking tray, making sure they are not piled on top of each other. Roast in the oven for about an hour, until they are browned and tender.

While the pumpkin is cooking, wash the soaked lentils in cold water, then tip them into a saucepan. Cover with fresh water to about one and a half inches over the top of them and bring the saucepan to the boil. Simmer for 15-20 minutes. You will need to skim the foam off the top at the beginning of the simmer. Don't be tempted to stir it in as this is the dirt and impurities coming off the lentils.

Once the lentils are cooked, drain them and set them aside.

Heat the 2 tablespoons of olive oil in a frying pan and fry the celery and pepper for 5-7 minutes, stirring often. Add the garlic puree and fry for a minute more, then add the lentils and cook for 3 minutes on a high heat, stirring constantly, to get rid of any excess moisture.
Add the lemon juice, tamari, tomato puree, chilli powder and a pinch of salt if required, then cook for 5 minutes, until quite dry.

Once the pumpkin is cooked, fry the pine nuts gently in a little oil, stirring often, until they are just starting to brown, but don't let them burn. Remove from the heat as soon as they are done and set them aside.

To serve, spoon some of the lentils onto a plate, place some of the roasted pumpkin on top then top with a few cubes of the cheese and some toasted pine nuts. Drizzle on a little balsamic vinegar at the end.

*****

Braised Tofu Kebabs

I was the guy who stumbled drunkenly at one in the morning into the kebab shop and ordered the nastiest greasy donner I could get my hands on. I always felt like crap afterwards, but I never learned my lesson. I would get drunk again and I would once more be swaying in a queue of other tired revellers, propped up against the glass cabinet of wilted salad and chilli sauce for support. Eagerly waiting to punish myself all over again. Veganism and quitting drinking finally put paid to all that, and I haven't entered one of those places since.

But let's not discredit the kebab, because when done right, it is truly a wonderful thing. Though typically a meat dish, vegan versions can be made with an array of produce available at most supermarkets, health stores or online. My ingredient of choice for this recipe is braised tofu, which can be shredded and fried with spices to make a delicious and succulent filling. I've also used aubergine, red onion and tomatoes to accompany the braised tofu and spices. The dressing is a quick version of Tzatziki, which can be knocked together in about 2 minutes right at the end of cooking. I bought the flatbread from my local market, which is Turkish and sells the bread perfect for this dish. Any flatbread or wrap will do fine, however.

Prep time: 15-20 minutes. Cooking time: 20 minutes.
Makes 4.

Ingredients:
For the Spiced Braised Tofu:
2 tbsp coconut oil
2 cans braised tofu, drained and cut into thin strips
1 tsp cumin seeds

1 tbsp tandoori masala curry spice mix (or whichever blend you have)
1 tsp garlic granules
1 tsp mild chilli powder
2 tbsp lime juice
Salt and black pepper to taste

For the Vegetables:
2 tbsp olive oil
1 aubergine, cut into batons
1 red onion, sliced
2 medium tomatoes, cut into wedges
3 tbsp tamari (gluten-free soy sauce)
1 tbsp chipotle chilli sauce (or other not too hot chilli sauce)

For the Tzatziki:
5 heaped tablespoons dairy-free plain yoghurt
2 tbsp olive oil
¼ cucumber
1 tsp Dijon mustard
Salt and black pepper to taste

4 Flatbreads
4 small handfuls of lettuce leaves.

Method:
Heat the coconut oil in a large frying pan or wok and fry the braised tofu on a medium-high heat for 8-10 minutes, until reasonably crisp, but not burnt. Add all the spices and pour over the lime juice, then cook for another couple of minutes for the tofu to take on the flavours.
Empty the cooked tofu into a bowl, clean out the pan and then heat the 2 tbsp of olive oil.

Fry the aubergine and red onion together for 5 minutes, stirring often, then add the tomato wedges and cook for a further 4 minutes. Pour in the tamari and chipotle sauce and let that cook for a couple more minutes. Mix the vegetables and the tofu together.

Once that's done, quickly make the tzatziki by putting the yoghurt and olive oil into a bowl and stirring until fully combined. Grate the cucumber into the bowl, add the Dijon mustard and season with the salt and pepper. Mix again to fully incorporate.

Warm the flatbreads briefly in the microwave or the oven. Spoon a quarter of the tofu and vegetable mixture in a line across the centre of the flatbread. Spoon the tzatziki over that and then place the lettuce on top. Roll and serve as desired.

*****

Mung Bean and Aubergine Dal

You don't need to use yellow or red split peas to make a dal. Happily, there are a whole range of beans, pulses and legumes that you can use to make this incredible Indian dish. I've used mung beans in this recipe and have adopted a more traditional method of cooking the beans in with spices and making the vegetables in a separate pan to add later. Soaking the beans overnight will help them to cook more quickly, as well as making them more easily digestible, so it is a good idea to plan this meal a day in advance.

Prep time: 20 minutes. Cooking time: 1 hour 20 minutes
Gluten-Free
Serves 4

Ingredients:

1 cup (200g) dried mung beans, soaked overnight
2 litres water
2 tsp vegan bouillon (also gluten-free, if needed)
1 whole dried chilli
2 bay leaves
3 cardamom pods
2 tsp ground turmeric
2 tbsp coconut oil
1 large (or 2 small) aubergines, diced
4-5 cloves garlic, chopped
250g baby plum tomatoes, halved
1 tsp mild chilli powder
2 tsp ground coriander
1 tsp garam masala
1 tsp ground cumin
A generous pinch of sea salt
4 tbsp natural vegan yoghurt
Additional salt to taste

Method:
Drain and rinse the soaked beans, then put them in a saucepan with the 2 litres of water. Bring the water to the boil and gently simmer for a few minutes, skimming the foam off the top of the water as it rises.

Once the foam has gone, add the bouillon, dried chilli, bay leaves, cardamom and turmeric to the water, partially cover the beans with a lid and gently simmer for an hour to an hour and 10 minutes. After this time, remove the lid and mash the beans slightly with a potato masher, then cook for a further 10 minutes with the lid off to reduce some of the liquid.

While your beans are simmering, heat the coconut oil in a large frying pan or wok and cook the aubergines on a high heat for 10 minutes or so, until soft and browned. Add the garlic and the tomatoes and cook for another 5 minutes, stirring frequently to prevent burning. Now stir in the spices and the sea salt and cook for another 3-4 minutes, then turn off the heat.

Once the mung beans are cooked, add the spicy aubergines to the bean pan and mix thoroughly. To finish, stir in the yoghurt, add more salt if you need to and serve.

Mung Bean and Aubergine Dal.

Oven Roasted Kale with Spiced Lentils and Mango

This is a quick meal that's ideal for the middle of the week, when you really don't want to be doing too much cooking. The lentils come in a can and all the other ingredients are quick to cut up and cook. Follow this recipe and you can have a tasty meal for two in about 20 minutes.

The curry is mildly-spiced, with the hottest thing I use being a teaspoon of mild chilli powder, which is entirely optional if you want to leave it out. I have found the dark mild chilli powders are usually available in the supermarket spice section, and are typically their own brand. If you are using a hotter chilli powder, then make sure you at least half the amount to keep it from overpowering the dish.

Try to get your kale as dry as you can after washing it, otherwise it won't become crispy after cooking it in the oven. You can use a towel if you like to pat it dry, but I simply gave it several good shakes and plenty of draining time. As with all cooking involving mangos, make sure that your fruit is ripe. Unripe mangoes are hard, have no flavour and are really not worth your time. A ripe mango will give a little when you squeeze it with your fingers.

Prep time: 10 minutes. Cooking time: about 20 minutes.
Gluten-Free
Serves 2-3

Ingredients:
4 fresh kale leaves, washed, dried and roughly chopped

2 tbsp olive oil
A pinch of salt
1 tbsp coconut oil
1 red pepper, sliced
1 ripe mango, peeled and cut into strips
2 medium tomatoes, cut into wedges
2 cloves garlic, chopped
1 can green lentils, washed and drained
1 tsp cumin seeds
1 tsp ground turmeric
2 tbsp tandoori curry powder (or other mild curry powder)
½ tsp mild chilli powder (optional)
Salt to taste
150ml vegan cream
A handful of coriander leaves to garnish

Method:
Preheat the oven to gas 5/190C/375F.
Put the dried kale into a mixing bowl and add the olive oil and the salt. Mix with your hands and then spread out onto a baking tray and cook in the middle of the oven for about 15 minutes. Keep an eye on it so that it doesn't burn.

While the kale is cooking, heat the coconut oil in a large frying pan or wok and fry the peppers for 4 minutes, until starting to brown. Add the mango and fry for another 3 minutes, stirring often. Add the tomato wedges and garlic and cook for about another 4 minutes, until the tomatoes have softened and begun to create a sauce, then pour in the lentils.

Stir the lentils in and then add all the spices and salt. Cook for a minute more then pour in the vegan cream and bring to a gentle simmer. Simmer for 2-3 minutes, stirring often, until the sauce has thickened, then turn off the heat.

Divide the kale onto 2-3 plates, spoon the spiced lentils on top and then sprinkle over the coriander leaves. Serve with rice or any other grain.

French-Style Aquafaba Omelette with Vegan Cheese and Tenderstem Broccoli

Whipping up some aquafaba to firm peak stage just to have an omelette might seem like a bit of a chore (not to mention the washing up) but, when you try this omelette, you'll know why you went the extra mile. This is, without a doubt, the lightest and fluffiest vegan omelette I've ever eaten, and I really want you to have the pleasure of it too.

This is still a tofu-based dish, only it has the addition of a gram flour batter, with the aquafaba folded into it. This makes for an extremely light and airy omelette. Vegan cheese is placed in the middle and then the omelette is folded over to a half-moon shape, just like the classic French version. It is served with tenderstem broccoli, that has been steamed, then sautéed with garlic. Finally, a quick cheese sauce is poured over the top, making this a meal to remember.

Prep time: 30 minutes. Cooking time: 20 minutes.
Serves 2-4
Gluten-Free

Ingredients:
For the Omelette Batter:
1 can chickpea water (the chickpeas reserved for something else)
1 tsp cream of tartar
50g gram (chickpea) flour
200ml plant milk
2 heaped tbsp nutritional yeast
1 tsp Dijon mustard
Salt and pepper to taste

For the Broccoli:
200-250g tenderstem broccoli
2 tbsp olive oil
2 cloves garlic, sliced

For the Omelette:
4tbsp olive oil
1 x 400g block firm tofu, drained until as dry as possible and cut into small cubes
100g vegan cheese, grated

For a Quick Cheese Sauce:
100ml plant milk
75g vegan cheese
1 tbsp nutritional yeast
Salt and pepper

Method:

First make your aquafaba. For the best results, pour the chickpea water into a saucepan and simmer until it has reduced by one third, then allow it to completely cool before whisking it. You can skip this step if you are short on time, but you'll get a more robust aquafaba if you do it.

Now pour the chickpea water into a mixing bowl and add the cream of tartar. Whip with an electric whisk on a medium setting for between 5 and 8 minutes or so, until the aquafaba is thick and meringue-like and you are able to tip the bowl upside down without it spilling out. Set aside until you are ready to use it.

Put the chickpea flour into another mixing bowl and gradually add the plant milk, whisking continuously until you have a smooth batter. Add the nutritional yeast, mustard and salt and pepper and whisk again, then gently fold in the aquafaba, trying to retain as much air as possible.

Bring a pan of water to the boil and steam the broccoli for 4-5 minutes, with a lid on. Drain and cool immediately in cold water. Drain again and set aside.

To cook the omelette, heat half the olive oil in a non-stick frying pan and add the tofu. Fry for about 10 minutes, until starting to brown. Mash up the tofu using a potato masher, then remove half from the pan and set aside. Add a little more oil if necessary, then pour half the omelette batter into the pan and stir it in with the tofu. Use a spatula to form a large round with the cooking batter before it completely sets, then sprinkle half of the cheese along the middle of it.

Now gently fold the omelette in half, so that the cheese stays in the middle. The omelette might break up while doing this, but you can press it back together using the spatula.
Cook on the one side for a couple of minutes, using the edge of the pan to help give it a crescent shape, then flip it over and cook the other side for the same amount of time.
Remove the cooked omelette and keep warm, then repeat the process for the second omelette. You can cut each cooked omelette in half and serve them as four smaller portions if you wish.

Now finish the broccoli. Heat some more olive oil in the frying pan and fry the broccoli for 3-4 minutes, until just starting to brown on the edges. Add the sliced garlic and cook for another minute, then serve with the omelette.

To make the quick cheese sauce, heat the plant milk in a small saucepan and put in the rest of the sauce ingredients. Whisk and simmer for 2 minutes, then pour over the omelette. Serve immediately.

French-Style Aquafaba Omelette with Vegan Cheese and Tenderstem Broccoli

Chickpeas with Lemon, Parsley and Vegan Feta

Just like in the previous recipe, I had some chickpeas left over from using the aquafaba. I tend to keep them in a storage bag in the freezer until I need them, then pick what I want from the bag. This time I was in the mood for something with a real lemon taste that could be served cold. I had some vegan feta style cheese in the fridge that I had recently discovered and wanted to use that as well. What I came up with was sort of a chickpea salad, much in the style of a potato salad, using vegan yogurt and mayonnaise as the base. The lemon in this is quite strong, but it can be adjusted if you prefer something lighter. You can either halve the amount of lemon going in, or you can add more mayonnaise. You can also do both if you prefer.

As you're frying the chickpeas to start with, it helps to get them as dry as possible. Wash them first and let them drain, then tip the drained chickpeas onto a towel to allow it to soak up as much of the excess moisture as possible. If they are too wet, they will simply steam in the pan instead of frying. I've used the equivalent amount of chickpeas as from 3 cans, to make a good family-sized portion. You may not want this much, so consider halving the recipe if this is the case.

Lemon and parsley go so well together that it was, in my opinion, the only herb choice for this dish. I've used a lot of it to really take advantage of its robust and earthy flavour. This is not a dish where you need to be strict with the ingredients. I have orchestrated this one to suit my desires at that particular moment, and I suggest you do the same. If you don't want loads of parsley, just use less of it. The same goes for the lemon.

Prep time: 10 minutes, plus draining time. Cooking time: 10 minutes, plus cooling time.
Serves 4-6
Gluten Free

Ingredients:
For the Fried Chickpeas:
3 tbsp olive oil
Chickpeas from 3 cans, washed, drained and dried as much as possible
3 cloves garlic, finely chopped
The zest from 2 lemons
Salt and pepper to taste

For the Dressing:
6-8 tbsp vegan natural yoghurt
The juice from 2 lemons
4 tbsp vegan mayonnaise
50ml olive oil
Generous handful of roughly chopped parsley leaves. Hold some back to garnish
Salt and pepper to taste
100g vegan feta-style cheese, roughly chopped

Method:
Heat the olive oil in a large frying pan and fry the chickpeas on a high heat for 10 minutes, stirring often, until they have browned a little. Add the garlic, lemon zest and a little salt and pepper and cook for 2-3 more minutes. Set aside and allow to cool.

To make the dressing, put all the dressing ingredients into a bowl and mix until thoroughly combined. Add the cooled chickpeas and mix again, then garnish with the extra parsley, cover and store in the fridge until ready to use.

Chickpeas with Lemon, Parsley and Vegan Feta

Borlotti Bean Chilli with Rice

There is a chilli recipe in my last book *Going Vegan*, and I wanted there to be another one in this book, because chilli is something most of us enjoy at some point. Also, in my opinion, you can't have too many chilli recipes.

This one, as the title suggests, uses borlotti beans as its main ingredient and, like my other chilli recipe, it makes use of the incredible depth of flavour that chocolate provides, albeit in the form of cacao nibs here.

A quick note on the rice: If you ask 10 chefs how to cook the perfect rice you will get 10 different answers, so I'm not going to say that this is how to cook the perfect rice. All I'm going to say is, the recipe written below produces a nicely-cooked long grain rice using the correct amount of water to rice ratio. I am satisfied with the results, but there is always room for adjustment, with perhaps adding a little water if needed, or cooking for less time. Try this method if you don't have your own, and only change it if you feel you need to. I also never salt rice while I'm cooking it as I personally find it unnecessary. I like the contrast of very simple tasting rice with a more extravagantly-flavoured dish.

Prep time: 20 minutes. Cooking time: 30-35 minutes
Gluten-Free
Serves 4

Ingredients:
2 tbsp coconut oil
1 medium red onion, diced
2 celery sticks, thinly sliced
½ bulb garlic, peeled and roughly chopped
2 cans borlotti beans, only 1 can drained
1 medium carrot, grated
1 tbsp dark, mild chilli powder
1 tbsp ground cumin
2 tbsp ground paprika
½ tsp harissa paste
3 tbsp liquid smoke
2 ½ tbsp cacao nibs
1-1/2 tsp salt
3 tbsp tomato puree
2 cans chopped tomatoes
½ can water
Salt and pepper to taste
3 tbsp natural, dairy-free yoghurt

2 cups (350g) long grain rice, washed in a few changes of water and left to drain
600ml cold water

Method:
Melt the coconut oil in a medium to large saucepan and gently fry the onion, celery and garlic for 6-8 minutes, until soft.

Pour in the borlotti beans, along with the brine from 1 can, and cook on a high heat for 8-10 minutes, stirring often, until most of the liquid has evaporated. Now put in the carrot, the spices, the liquid smoke, the cacao nibs and the salt and stir thoroughly, letting the spices cook through for a minute or so.

Add the tomato puree, canned tomatoes and ½ can of water, stir in and bring to the boil. Simmer for 30-35 minutes, until you have a thick and deeply-flavoured chilli sauce.

While the chilli is simmering, put the washed rice in a saucepan that has a lid. Pour in the water and bring to a gentle boil. Now cover the pan with a tea towel, being careful to keep the edges of the towel away from the flames or cooker hob, and put the lid on the saucepan. Fold any excess of the towel over the lid of the saucepan to keep it out of the way. Turn the heat down to minimum and cook the rice, without lifting the lid, for 15 minutes. Once the fifteen minutes are up, remove the pan from the heat (but do not take off the lid) and allow to rest for another 5 minutes. Finally lift the lid off and gently fork through the rice.

Once the chilli has finished cooking, season it to taste, then turn off the heat and stir in the yoghurt. Serve with the rice.

*****

15 Minute Thai-Style Lentils with Green Beans and Coconut Rice

Cooking healthy food when you're tired is no easy task. Work and/or looking after the children all day can leave you in no mood to spend yet more time in the kitchen. It can be so tempting to open a packet of frozen vegan burgers and to hell with the nutritional value. There are certainly plenty of choices when it comes to ready-made items that you just have to throw in the oven and wait for 20 minutes. No work, no fuss, but hardly any vitamins either. Also, fibre tends to be overlooked when we eat like this (and we *all* eat like this from time to time). Processed foods usually contain simple carbohydrates, which have very little nutritional value, not to mention the high salt and sugar content.

On occasion we all want to eat well without slicing and dicing, and we want to do it quickly so that we can get on with the twenty other things that are going on at the same time. The good news is that you can make a delicious, healthy and, most importantly, quick, meal for the family using frozen or ready-prepped veg, a couple of things in cans and jars and a microwave. If you're organised, this dish takes 15 minutes to make and you won't have to break a sweat. Also, if you use the same ingredients listed here (all of which are found at the supermarket), the only thing you'll need to use a knife for is to cut a lime in half.

To do it in time I'd recommend gathering all your ingredients together first (there aren't many), including putting the correct amount of spices into a small dish, ready to pour into the pan at the right time. You're going to use your microwave as the timer here. The microwave is what you're going to cook the rice in, so when you press the start button on that, you're going to cook the rest to finish at the same time.

Ready? Here we go…

Prep time: 2-3 minutes. Cooking time: 15 minutes.
Gluten-Free
Serves 4.

Ingredients:
1 can green lentils
275g (1 ½ cups) white basmati rice
600ml (3 cups) cold water
50g creamed coconut (1 sachet, or cut 50g from a block)
1 tbsp flavourless oil, such as groundnut
1 cup frozen diced onions
170g (1 small pack) ready-trimmed green beans (fresh veg section)
2 tsp minced garlic from a jar (world food section)
1 tsp minced ginger from a jar (as above)
1 tbsp cumin seeds
1 tbsp ground coriander
1 tsp ground turmeric

1 ½ tbsp hot madras curry powder
1 veg stock cube, broken up so that it dissolves more quickly (make sure it's vegan and gluten-free)
½ tsp harissa paste
Juice of 1 lime
1 can coconut milk.

Method:
Before you start, drain and wash the canned lentils in a sieve and set aside until you need them.

Put the rice, water and creamed coconut into a microwavable bowl that's large enough to allow the rice to expand. Put a wok, or saucepan on the stove and turn on the heat, then put your rice in the microwave with no lid and set it on 80% power and the cooking time for 15 minutes. Hit that start button!

Put the tablespoon of oil into your hot pan and fry the onions and the green beans together for 4 minutes. Add the garlic and ginger and fry for another 30 seconds, stirring continuously. Pour in the spices, stock cube, harissa paste, and lime juice and give it another 30 seconds. You should have about 10 minutes left on your microwave time by this point. Add the green lentils and pour in the coconut milk. Bring to the boil on a high heat and then turn down to a simmer for the remaining time.

When the microwave has finished the rice should be perfectly cooked. Fork it through to break up the grains and mix in the coconut, then put a plate or lid over it and leave it to stand for a couple of minutes. Your lentil curry will have thickened to a delicious thick sauce by this point. Serve into four bowls and squeeze some extra lime over if you like.

*****

Fried Tofu with Rice Noodles and Black Bean Sauce

Noodles with black bean sauce has always been one of my favourite Chinese dishes. I used to eat it on Shaftsbury Avenue when I was in my early twenties, in those Chinese restaurants that were permanently busy and where they would cram you in at tables next to complete strangers to eat your food (It was a good way of meeting new people). I've made this one using fried tofu and tenderstem broccoli, in addition to red peppers and onions. Stir-fries are a good way of cooking vegetables while retaining their nutritional value. Cooking the sauce at the end helps finish off the veg (particularly the broccoli, which can be underdone when stir-frying alone).

The tofu for this is deep-fried, so it is important to get it as dry as you can beforehand. If you don't have a tofu press, the best way is to wrap the tofu in a towel and put some heavy weights on top for at least 10-15 minutes. The water will absorb into the towel, leaving you with a much drier tofu. To get it extra dry, you can always unwrap it and wrap it again in either a dry part of the towel, or with a fresh one. Remember to never fill your pan for deep frying more than half-full of oil, as it rises significantly when you put something in it to cook. If you have small children, always put the deep-frying pan at the back of the stove for cooking.

The only item in this recipe that is not gluten-free is the dark soy sauce. Switch for tamari if you need to.

Prep time: 20 minutes. Cooking time: 15-20 minutes, plus 12 minutes for the tofu to fry.
Easy to make gluten-free.
Serves 3-4

Ingredients:
1x400g pack of firm tofu, fully drained using the method described above, and cut into large squares
Enough vegetable oil for deep frying
1 can of black beans, washed and drained
2 tbsp sesame oil
2 red peppers, large diced
1 large onion, large diced
100g tenderstem broccoli
2 tsp garlic puree

1 tsp ginger puree

For the Sauce:
250ml hot vegetable stock
4 tbsp dark soy sauce
¼ - ½ tsp hot sauce, depending on how hot you like it (it should be a background flavour)
30ml cider vinegar
4 tbsp brown sugar

To Serve:
1 pack pre-cooked rice noodles
1 red chilli, finely sliced to garnish

Method:
First heat the deep-frying oil so that it is hot enough to fry the tofu. You can test it by putting a piece in. It will bubble immediately when it is ready. Deep-fry the tofu for approximately 12 minutes, stirring from time to time to ensure even cooking. The tofu will be brown all over and crisp when it is done. Drain on kitchen paper and set aside.

While the tofu is frying, wash and drain the black beans, so that they are quite dry by the time you come to cook them.

Heat the sesame oil in a wok or large frying pan and fry the peppers and onions together for about 4-5 minutes. Add the broccoli and cook for 4 minutes more, stirring often.

While this is cooking, make the sauce by putting all of the sauce ingredients into a jug or bowl and mixing together. Set aside until ready to use.

Add the black beans to the other vegetables in the wok and cook for 3 more minutes, then add the garlic and ginger. Give it another 2 minutes and then pour over the sauce. It will begin to bubble and reduce immediately. Allow to reduce on a high heat for 3 minutes or so, then put the fried tofu into the dish and heat through. Finally, add the rice noodles and stir until completely mixed.

Serve into bowls and top with the sliced chilli if desired.

*****

Lentil, Spinach and Coconut Curry

This is a curry suitable for lazy, mid-week cooking, or when you don't have much time. Canned lentils, as well as canned spinach are easy to get hold of in most supermarkets and will make life a hell of a lot easier when you need a stress-free meal in a hurry.

Prep time: 10 minutes. Cooking time: 25 minutes.
Gluten-Free
Serves 3-4

Ingredients:
2 tbsp coconut oil
1 medium onion, diced
1 green pepper, diced
100g chestnut mushrooms, quartered
3 cloves garlic, chopped
1 knob ginger (about ½ inch), chopped
3 medium tomatoes, cut into wedges
2 tbsp curry powder
1 tsp turmeric

1 tsp cumin seeds
½ tsp ground cinnamon
1 vegan stock cube (make sure it's gluten-free, if needed)
1 can green lentils, drained
1 can coconut milk
A handful of coriander leaves, chopped
1 can spinach leaves, well drained (press against the sieve to remove as much moisture as possible)
Salt and pepper to taste

Method:
First heat the coconut oil in a large pan or wok. Stir-fry the onion, pepper and mushrooms for about 8 minutes, until they start to brown, then add the garlic and ginger and cook for 2 more minutes, stirring often. Put in the tomatoes and cook for 3 more minutes before adding the spices.

Put in the curry powder, turmeric, cumin seeds, cinnamon and the stock cube and mix until fully incorporated. Keep that going for 2 more minutes to cook all the spices through.

Now add the drained lentils and let them cook for another couple of minutes. Pour in the coconut milk and bring to the boil, then simmer for 5 minutes or so, until you have a thick curry sauce. Now sprinkle in the chopped coriander and stir in the spinach. Give the whole dish a final two-minute blast, then season with the salt and pepper, if desired. Serve with rice or flatbread.

*****

Aquafaba Mango Mousse with Raspberries

If you're a little fed up with making chocolate mousse out of aquafaba, this mango mousse is a refreshing alternative. The mango you choose for this must absolutely be ripe, so that it will blend well, and for the flavour to come through properly.

As with my omelette recipe, the aquafaba is best heated in a saucepan and reduced by one-third volume for a firmer, more stable mix. This generally takes about 10 minutes of simmering time. It is then cooled completely prior to whipping. If you are going to reduce it then use about 1 ½ cans of chickpea water to allow for the loss in volume. If you are not planning on reducing it, just use 1 can and skip the first step.

The coconut cream is chilled overnight, so that it is firm and easy to separate from its water content. Removing the water and just using the cream makes for an excellent vegan whipped cream that has a whole host of uses. I always put them straight in my fridge whenever I buy them, then I don't have to plan the recipe too far in advance.

Prep time: 30 minutes, plus 2-3 hours cooling time.
Gluten-Free
Serves 4

Ingredients:
For the Aquafaba:
1 ½ cans chickpea water (just 1 can if you are not reducing first)
2 tsp cream of tartar
3 tbsp icing sugar

For the Mango Filling:
1 mango
100g icing sugar
½ tsp vanilla extract
1 carton coconut cream, chilled overnight so that the cream becomes solid
2 tbsp icing sugar
150g raspberries, cut in half

For the Raspberry Topping:
150g raspberries, plus extra for garnish
3 tbsp icing sugar
3 tbsp cold water

Method:
Pour the chickpea water into a saucepan and bring to the boil. Simmer for about 10 minutes, until the mixture has reduced by one third. Take off the heat and allow to cool completely (you can speed this up by pouring it into a jug and standing the jug in a bowl of iced water).

Once it has cooled, transfer to a large mixing bowl and add the cream of tartar. Using an electric whisk, whip the aquafaba for 5 minutes, until you get reasonably firm peaks. Add the sugar to the remaining aquafaba and whip on a higher speed for another 5 minutes or so, until you reach the stiff peak stage. (you can tell when you get there because you can tip the bowl upside down and it won't move). Set aside.

To make the mango filling, put the mango, the 100g icing sugar and the vanilla extract into a blender and blend twice, until completely smooth. Gently fold this in to your aquafaba until it is fully combined.

Open the carton of coconut cream and drain away the water (it will have separated as it cooled, as mentioned above). Put the remaining coconut cream into a separate mixing bowl and add the 2 tablespoons of icing sugar. Start mixing with a spoon to loosen it, then use the electric whisk to whip it up into a thick cream. Add the mango mixture and the halved raspberries and gently mix together. Pour the mixture into four serving glasses and freeze or chill for at least 2 hours.

Once the desserts have set, blend the topping ingredients until smooth, then pour over the top. Add a couple of raspberries on top to garnish and then chill until ready to serve.

Aquafaba Mango Mousse with Raspberries

Local Delicacies

Woodland Mushroom Tempura with Garlic and Lemon Mayo

Cavolo Nero and Dill Falafel

Sam's Vegan Rhubarb Crumble

Summer Green Vegetable Quiche

King Oyster Mushrooms with Tomatoes and Pesto

Rhubarb and Red Onion Chutney

BBQ Baked Spiced Apples

Whole Wheat Mushroom and Kale Tartlets

Braised White Cabbage with Sugar Snap Peas and Cherry Tomatoes

Vegan Parsley Sauce

King Oyster Mushroom and Black Bean Dumplings

Rice Noodles with Portobello Mushrooms and Green Beans

Creamy Vegan Mushroom Soup

Cherry and Cranberry Pies

Cajun Spiced Broccoli Bites

Easy Chestnut Mushroom, New Potato and Leek Pie

Carrot and Red Pepper Soup

Vegan Leek and Cheese Parcels

Pan Fried Cinnamon Pears

Mulled Pears with Vegan Whipped Cream

Blackberry Panna Cotta

Caramelised Pear Crostini with Haloumi-Style Cheese

Pan-Fried Pear Tart with Greek-Style Cheese and Redcurrant Jelly

Deep-Filled Apple Pie

Woodland Mushroom Tempura with Garlic and Lemon Mayo

Japanese batter is a little different from the milk-based versions we are used to using. Containing just flour, water and salt it is, without needing to change anything, already vegan-friendly. It is also a lot thinner than we are perhaps used to. Tempura is not much more than a kiss of batter over raw vegetables, and it is therefore common to see the colours of the veg protruding from inside the finished dish.

The varied shape and texture of woodland mushrooms makes an enticing subject for tempura. They are perfect, once doused in a little flour, for gripping the thin batter and holding onto it for frying. As is often the case with my fusion style of cooking, I have eschewed the more tradition Japanese dipping sauces and favoured a European-influenced garlic and lemon mayonnaise, which I believe complements this dish particularly well. The dip is extremely easy to make, so I hope you will try it out along with the tempura.

Prep time: 15 minutes. Cooking time: 10-12 minutes per batch
Serves 3-4

Ingredients:
300g woodland mushrooms (I used shitake, oyster and eryngii)
150g plain flour for dusting
Salt and pepper

For the Batter:
250g plain flour
500ml cold water
1 ½ tsp salt
Dash of black pepper
4-5 ice cubes

Enough oil for deep-frying

For the Garlic Mayo:
150g vegan mayonnaise
2 tbsp lemon juice
1 clove garlic, minced or grated on a micro plane
A pinch of cayenne pepper
A pinch of salt

Method:
Put the mushrooms in a bowl of cold water and leave them soaking.
Put the 150g plain flour in a bowl and add a good amount of salt and pepper. Set that bowl to the right of the mushrooms.

Now mix the batter in a third bowl with a whisk by adding the water gradually to the flour. It doesn't matter if it has a few lumps, as this is quite customary in Japanese batter. Season with the salt and pepper and then drop in the ice cubes to keep it cold.

Fill a medium-sized saucepan half-full with oil and bring up to frying temperature. Don't fill the pan more than half full as the oil will rise during frying. You can test the oil is ready for cooking by dropping a little batter into it. The batter will rise and sizzle immediately.

Take a few of the mushrooms out of the water and shake or gently squeeze any excess water off. Drop the mushrooms in the seasoned flour and shake until they are completely covered. Now put them into the batter and again cover them completely.

Carry the batter bowl over to the pan of oil and gently drop each battered mushroom into the pan. Cook for 10-12 minutes, stirring occasionally to prevent them from sticking together. Remove them when they are light brown and crisp, and drain them on some kitchen paper or a tea towel. Repeat this process until all of the mushrooms are used up.

You can keep the cooked mushrooms warm in a low oven while you are finishing the others.
To make the garlic mayo, mix all of the mayo ingredients in a small bowl and chill until ready to use.

Woodland Mushroom Tempura with Garlic and Lemon Mayo

Cavolo Nero and Dill Falafel

I did a falafel recipe in my last book, *Going Vegan*, but I've made this one quite different both in colour and flavour from that version. This one predominantly uses Cavolo Nero kale to give it a stark green colour and vibrant taste. Dill is also used, which adds a real freshness to it. Try to get your canned chickpeas as dry as you can. I do this by washing them under cold water, draining them for about 10 minutes and then wrapping them in a towel for a good 10-15 minutes to ensure that most of the water is removed. I use this same technique when frying chickpeas, as it prevents mushing.

These can be made up to a couple of days in advance if you want to use them for something special, and they can also be frozen once you've cooked them. Just wrap them up well to protect from freezer burn.

Prep time: 30 minutes. Cooking time: 8 minutes per batch.
Gluten-Free
Makes about 18-20

Ingredients:
350g (2 cans) chickpeas, washed, drained and dried (you can use the chickpea liquid for any of the aquafaba recipes in this book, such as Aquafaba Mango Mousse – page 31)
50g walnuts
3 Cavolo Nero kale leaves, washed, stalks removed and leaves torn
4 spring onions, sliced
Generous handful fresh dill leaves
2 garlic cloves, peeled
Zest of 1 lime
½ - ¾ tsp salt
A dash of black pepper
2 heaped tbsp gram flour, plus extra for dusting
3 heaped tbsp dairy-free natural yoghurt
1 tsp ground cumin
¼ tsp mild chilli powder
Enough oil for shallow frying

Method:
Put all of the ingredients, up to and including the black pepper, into a food processor and blitz until fully chopped and combined. Transfer the mix to a large bowl.

Now add the rest of the ingredients, apart from the frying oil, and mix thoroughly. Roll the mix into small balls, using gram flour to help you, then set aside.

Preheat the oven to gas 5/190C/375F.

Heat enough oil for shallow frying in a large frying pan, until quite hot, and fry the falafel balls, in batches, for about 8 minutes, until lightly browned all over. Transfer the cooked falafel to an oven tray.

Once all of the falafel are cooked, put them in the oven to finish off for 10 minutes.

*****

Sam's Vegan Rhubarb Crumble

When I first tried this crumble, I was immediately smitten. Not with Samantha (that had already happened), but with this beautifully sweet and oaty dessert. Her mother taught her how to make it, where, as rumour has it, the rhubarb was cut from the home garden before being tossed into the pan. As fresh as you please.

Samantha has graciously given us her recipe to be included in this book, and I am excited to be sharing it with you. Do give it a try. With its subtle hints of ginger and its oaty, crunchy topping, you won't be disappointed.

Prep time: 20 minutes. Cooking time: About 1 hour 15 minutes.
Serves 6-8

Ingredients:
For the Filling:
800g fresh rhubarb
8 heaped tbsp golden caster sugar
100ml water
4 tsp ground ginger

For the Crumble Topping:
150g self-raising flour
75g rolled oats
100g golden caster sugar
130g vegan butter

Method:
Top and tail the rhubarb and wash under cold water, then cut into 1-inch pieces. Put it into a large, heavy-based saucepan, then add the sugar and the water. Bring to the boil, then simmer gently for 20-30 minutes, until you have a soft, shredded pulp. Stir in the ground ginger and then turn off the heat and set aside.

Preheat the oven to gas 5/190C/375F.

To make the topping, put all of the topping ingredients into a large mixing bowl and work between your fingers, until you get a clumpy breadcrumb texture.

Pour the rhubarb mixture into a suitably-sized oven dish, to a depth of about 3cm (1 ½ inches), then sprinkle the crumble mixture over the top, being sure to get it into all the corners and to create an even layer.

Put the crumble straight into the middle of the oven and cook for 40-45 minutes, until the top is golden brown and crispy. Allow to cool for 10-15 minutes before serving.

Sam's Vegan Rhubarb Crumble

Summer Green Vegetable Quiche

This is a great little quiche to have in the spring or summer time. Hearty and full of nutrition, with a lovely creamy, vegetable taste. Chilled, it is ideal to take on picnics or other afternoons out. It is perfect served with a mixed salad and eaten in the garden on a sunny day with friends and family. Hot, it is a gorgeous lunch to have with a few crisps or fries and a good book open in front of you. If there's just one or two of you, it'll keep nicely in the fridge for four or five days, so you can pick at it at your leisure. Serve it as a centre piece at a dinner party and it will be annihilated in short order. You can use ready-rolled pastry, as in the recipe, but there's also nothing to stop you from going all out and making your own. I've provided a recipe for vegan parsley pesto in this book (page 114), or there are a couple of brands that you can buy ready-made.

Prep time: 20 minutes. Cooking time: 1 hour 10 minutes, plus setting time.
Makes 1 x 9-inch quiche

Ingredients:
For the Pastry:
1 tsp vegan margarine for greasing
1 sheet ready-rolled shortcrust pastry

For the Filling:
1 head spring greens, thinly sliced
1 head broccoli, cut into small florets (halve, or even quarter the bigger heads)
100g cashew nuts, soaked in hot water for 20 minutes
1 x 400g block tofu, drained
150ml vegan cream
300ml plant milk
1 vegan stock cube
¼ tsp ground nutmeg
1 tsp Dijon mustard
2 tbsp nutritional yeast
A dash of black pepper
2 courgettes, 1 roughly diced, one left whole
1 clove garlic
Salt to taste

For the Cheese Sauce:
150ml plant milk
2 tsp vegan pesto (see my parsley pesto recipe)
65g vegan cheese, grated
1 tbsp nutritional yeast
Salt to taste

Method:
Preheat the oven to gas 5/190C/375F.

Grease a 9-inch, loose-bottomed tart tin and line it with the ready-rolled shortcrust pastry. Trim any edges that overlap, and then line the pastry with greaseproof paper. Fill with dry rice or baking beans and then bake in the middle of the oven for 15 minutes, or until just cooked.

While the pastry is baking, set a steamer to boil and steam the sliced greens and broccoli for 6 minutes, until *al dente*. Put the greens immediately into cold water to stop them from cooking further, then drain and set aside.

Put the rest of the filling ingredients, apart from the courgette that you left whole (keep that aside), into a blender jug and blend until smooth. Pour the resulting batter into a mixing bowl.

Use a vegetable peeler or mandolin to cut the whole courgette into long, thin strips, then put these into the batter. Put the steamed broccoli and greens into the batter as well, then mix in.

Pour the vegetable batter into the cooked pastry case and set aside.

In a small saucepan, heat all of the cheese sauce ingredients until the cheese has melted and the sauce thickened. Pour the sauce on top of the quiche, so that it sits just below the rim of the pastry.

Turn the oven down to gas 4/180C/350F.

Place the tart tin on a baking tray and cook in the middle of the oven for 45 minutes, or until the filling has set and the top is nicely browned. If you need to you can transfer the quiche to the top of the oven for an additional 10 minutes to brown further.

The quiche will fully set once it has cooled.

*****

King Oyster Mushrooms with Tomatoes and Pesto

This is a nice and quick stir-fry type of dish that you can serve with rice, pasta or mashed potatoes if you like (someone told me they put it on toast). The whole point is that it's a tasty mid-week meal that can be done in about 25 minutes, and then served with whatever you happen to have lying around. It uses the slightly more expensive king oyster mushrooms, but you can use any mushroom you like. I chose the king oysters for this because of their firm texture. You can also use any vegan pesto you like, and there are a range to choose from these days. There is an aubergine and walnut pesto recipe in this book (page 157), in addition to parsley pesto (page 114), either of which would go very well with it.

Prep time: 5 minutes. Cooking time: 18-20 minutes
Gluten Free
Serves 2

Ingredients:
3 tbsp olive oil
3-4 king oyster mushrooms, sliced lengthways
2 cloves garlic, peeled and sliced
2 medium tomatoes, cut into wedges
3 heaped tbsp vegan pesto (make sure it's gluten-free, if needed)
3 tbsp tamari (gluten-free soy sauce)

Method:
Heat the oil in a frying pan, until quite hot, and fry the mushrooms on quite a high heat for 6-8 minutes. Keep them moving to prevent burning, but you do want them nicely browned.
Turn down the heat just a little and add the garlic, then cook those for another two minutes, stirring often. Now throw in the tomato wedges and cook for 5 minutes more, until they have softened but not turned to mush.

Spoon in the pesto and tamari and cook for another 3 minutes or so, until you have a sauce texture. Serve immediately.

*****

Rhubarb and Red Onion Chutney

Chutneys are not something I make that often, and when I do they are usually the quick variety that don't require hours of cooking. This one is somewhere in the middle. The cooking time is about 90 minutes, the majority of which is just gentle simmering that frees you up to get on with something else. I write this in rhubarb season, at a time when I have several pots of tiny rhubarb seedlings just poking their young heads out of the soil, that I can look forward to harvesting at a later date. For now, I have shop-bought bunches of reddish-green stems that I am eager to cook with.

A rhubarb chutney struck me as an interesting and timely choice, and red onion makes the perfect accompaniment to give it the sweetness and depth it deserves, as well as adding to the richness of colour. It is better to make this the day before you want to eat it, to allow for full flavour infusion and a properly chilled preserve. It'll keep in the fridge for up to 4 weeks without proper canning. There's enough in this recipe to last you that long, and even enough to give some to a friend.

Prep time: 15 minutes. Cooking time: about 90 minutes, plus overnight chilling time.
Gluten Free
Make about 1kg

Ingredients:
2 tbsp olive oil
6 medium red onions (about 500g) sliced
2 mild, red chillies, deseeded and thinly sliced
3 large cloves garlic, chopped
600g rhubarb, cut into 1-inch pieces
400g golden caster sugar
300ml water
¾ tsp ground ginger
1 tsp ground cinnamon
½ tsp salt

Method:
Heat the oil in a large saucepan and gently fry the onions for about 10 minutes, stirring often. Add the sliced chillies and the garlic and cook for another 5 minutes, stirring a little more frequently as they begin to cook through.

Now put in the rhubarb and the rest of the ingredients and bring the pan to the boil. Simmer gently for about 1 hour 20 minutes, stirring it from time to time to prevent sticking, until you have a thick and reduced chutney. Allow to cool before transferring it to a storage container, then refrigerate overnight.

Rhubarb and Red Onion Chutney

BBQ Baked Spiced Apples

When barbeque season is in full swing, it can be difficult sometimes to know what to shove on the coals. Burgers and sausages are always great, but we do want a little variety on our summer plates. Desserts are particularly tricky. Barbecued pineapple steaks are an obvious choice, but there are other things we can do as well. Tin foil opens up a whole new avenue in outdoor cooking if you haven't used it before. You can marinade and cover all kinds of food in foil, and then leave them to bake over the coals while your sausages are browning.

These baked apples are one of many possible ideas. You can wrap them up tightly and just leave them for 20 minutes or so off to the side of your barbecue (making sure there are some hot coals underneath, of course). You will want to turn them about half-way through, which will not only help them cook evenly but also ensure proper distribution of the sweet sauce inside the parcel.

Prep time: 10 minutes. Cooking time: about 20 minutes.
Makes 6 baked apples.

Ingredients:
6 medium apples (I used pink ladies)
6 tsp vegan butter
6 tbsp maple syrup
6 pinches of ground cinnamon
About 10 raisins per apple
You will also need an apple corer and 6 sheets of tin foil.

Method:
Heat your barbecue coals up in the usual way.

Remove the core of each apple and then cut them in half. One apple at a time, lay out your sheet of tin foil. Grease the apple and the inside of the foil with 1 tsp of the butter. Pour 1 tbsp of the maple syrup over the flesh side of the apple, sprinkle on a pinch of cinnamon. Put about 10 of the raisins in the groove of the apple where the core used to be, and then put the two halves together.

Wrap the foil tightly around the apple and then repeat the process with the rest.
Cook the apples either at the side of the barbecue, where there is less heat, or on a top rack away from the direct heat if you have one. After about 10 minutes turn them over. Cook for around 20 minutes in total and serve when ready.

*****

Whole Wheat Mushroom and Kale Tartlets

These are a great little party piece if you're having a buffet, or some other social gathering. The recipe is for whole wheat pastry, which you can make from scratch. If you're short on time, or if you want to make them gluten-free, then you can always use the pre-made pastry of your choice. Like most buffet food, they can be served either hot or cold, and they are the perfect size for a couple of bites of deliciousness. Give them a practice run and see how you get on.

Prep time: 20 minutes. Cooking time: about 50 minutes, plus chilling time.

Easy to make gluten-free.
Makes approximately 12 tartlets.

Ingredients:
For the Pastry:
250g whole wheat flour
2 tsp baking powder
½ tsp salt
125g vegan margarine, plus extra for greasing
4 tbsp plant milk

For the Filling:
3 tbsp olive oil
4-5 chestnut mushrooms, finely diced
2 cloves garlic, chopped
4-5 fresh kale leaves, washed, stalks removed and finely chopped
200ml vegan cream
1 tsp wholegrain mustard
100g humous
60g vegan blue-style cheese
Salt and pepper to taste
A little oil for brushing

Method:
First make the pastry. Put the flour, baking powder, salt and margarine into a mixing bowl and crumble between your fingers until you have a breadcrumb texture. Stir in the milk and then bring together with your hands. Knead into a dough, but don't overwork it. Cover and chill for 30 minutes.

While the pastry is cooling, you can make the tart filling. Heat the olive oil in a frying pan and fry the diced mushrooms for about 5 minutes, until they are slightly browned and most of the moisture has evaporated. Add the garlic and fry for a minute more.

Add the chopped kale and cook for another 3 minutes, then put in the rest of the ingredients, apart from the brushing oil. Cook for 3-4 more minutes, stirring often, then turn off the heat and allow the mixture to cool.

Preheat the oven to gas 6/200C/400F and grease a 12-hole tart tin (the kind you would use for mince pies) with margarine.

Roll the chilled pastry out onto a floured surface to about 5mm thick and use a round pastry cutter to cut out small circles from the dough. Cut out twelve in total, enough to fill each hole in the tin. You will have to roll the pastry out a few times to do this.

Place each pastry round into the tin and press down into shape. Put about 1 ½ tsp of the filling mixture onto the centre of the pastry, then press down slightly with the back of the spoon. The mixture won't really spread out as it cooks, so you can add a little more if you feel you need to.

Once you have your 12 tartlets, brush them all with a little oil and then place the tart tin in the middle of the oven and cook for 15-20 minutes, until the pastry is golden brown and cooked through.

Serve either straight away or chill for later.

Whole Wheat Mushroom and Kale Tartlets

Braised White Cabbage with Sugar Snap Peas and Cherry Tomatoes

This is sliced white cabbage braised in a light stock with a few other vegetables. It makes a nice and easy mid-week supper when you're really craving a healthy option.

Prep time: 15 minutes. Cooking time: about 30 minutes
Gluten Free
Serves 2

Ingredients:
2 tbsp olive oil
½ white cabbage, thinly sliced
50ml cold water
100g sugar snap peas
200g cherry tomatoes, halved
2 cloves garlic, chopped
2-3 leafy greens, washed and cut into 1-2 inch pieces
100g frozen peas
200ml vegetable stock
Salt and pepper to taste

Method:
Heat the oil in a large frying pan or saucepan that has a lid and sweat the cabbage for 5-6 minutes to cook down a little. Add the water, put the lid on the pan and cook for a further 10 minutes, until the cabbage is tender.

Remove the lid and add the sugar snap peas and the cherry tomatoes. Cook on a high heat for 3-4 minutes, then throw in the garlic and give it 2 minutes more, stirring often.

Put in the leafy greens, the peas and the veg stock and bring to the boil. Cover again with the lid and simmer for 10 more minutes. If you want, you can remove the lid to cook some of the stock off. Adjust seasoning and serve.

*****

Vegan Parsley Sauce

I grew up loving parsley sauce, so I wanted to make sure I had a recipe to hand if I ever felt like making it. This is that recipe. You can use either regular or gluten-free flour, depending on your preference.

Prep time: 5 minutes: Cooking time: 10 minutes.
Easy to make Gluten-Free
Serves 3-4

Ingredients:
40g vegan butter
2 tbsp plain flour (or gluten-free)
600ml vegan milk
4 tbsp natural vegan yoghurt
2 tsp vegan vegetable bouillon (gluten-free if needed)
½ tsp Dijon mustard
A large handful of parsley leaves, finely chopped
Salt and pepper to taste

Method:

Melt the butter in a pan and whisk in the flour to create a roux. Gradually whisk in the vegan milk, making sure you get out any lumps before adding more. Now add the yoghurt, veg bouillon and mustard and bring to the boil, whisking constantly.

Turn down the heat to a gently simmer and add the parsley. Simmer for 5 minutes, whisking often, and then season to taste. Serve immediately.

*****

King Oyster Mushroom and Black Bean Dumplings

King oyster mushrooms are perfect for shredding. You can either tear them apart with your fingers, or use what I think is the better method, which is two forks that you drag through the flesh of the mushroom, pulling it apart as you go. This method tends to give you a better shred, which is ideal for making things like vegan pulled 'pork'.

It's also great for these dumplings, as its fine shred means it can be used in small amounts. You can buy dumpling wrappers in Chinese supermarkets (they are usually in the freezers with the spring roll wrappers). There typically come in a pack of 20, so you will need two packs to use up all the filling in this recipe, which makes about 35-40. You can oven-bake these dumplings just fine (brush some oil on them first), but I have a real liking for fried dumplings and so that is what this recipe calls for.

Prep time: 20 minutes. Cooking time: 30-40 minutes.
Makes 35-40

Ingredients:
2 tbsp sesame oil
1 tbsp groundnut oil (or other neutral oil)
1 green or red pepper, very finely diced
3-4 king oyster mushrooms, shredded using the methods described above
2-3 kale leaves, washed, stalks removed and the leaves very finely sliced
1 can black beans, washed and drained
1 ½ tsp garlic paste
1 tsp ginger paste
½ tsp Chinese five spice powder
¼ tsp mild chilli powder
50ml tamari (or regular light soy sauce)
2 tbsp dark soy sauce
2 tbsp cider vinegar
3 tbsp hoisin sauce
2 tbsp unrefined sugar

40 dumpling wrappers, defrosted
Enough oil for shallow frying

Method:
Heat the 3 tbsp of oil in a large frying pan or wok, until quite hot, and then fry the diced pepper for 3-4 minutes, stirring often. Add the mushrooms and the kale and cook for another 5 minutes or so. Now add the black beans, keeping the heat quite high to cook off any moisture, and give it a few more minutes.

Now add the rest of the ingredients, apart from the dumpling wrappers and the frying oil, and stir together. Cook until all the moisture is evaporated (about 5 minutes), then turn off the heat and let the mixture cool.

To wrap the dumplings, have a small bowl of water beside your wrappers. Dip the entire circular edge of one wrapper in the water, so that the centre remains dry, then place it onto a flat surface. Put about a teaspoon to a teaspoon and a half of the cooked mixture into the centre of the dumpling wrapper and then fold it over to a semi-circle. You really cannot fit much filling in these and attempts to do so will result in it spilling out of the sides.

Now press down firmly with the tines of a fork around the entire edge of the dumpling where the join is. This will seal the wet pastry ends together so that they hold during cooking, as well as make them look attractive. Set the dumpling on a plate and continue until you have used up all of your mix.

Now heat a good amount of frying oil in a clean frying pan (about 5mm deep) and fry your dumplings, in batches, for about 4-5 minutes each side, until crisp and golden all over. You can either keep the ones you have already cooked warm in a low oven, or serve at room temperature.

King Oyster Mushroom and Black Bean Dumplings

Rice Noodles with Portobello Mushrooms and Green Beans

If you want a fast stir-fry after a hard day's work, then this is a good place to start. Done in 25 minutes, so that you can get on with the rest of your evening without worrying about slaving over a stove or having tons of washing up to deal with.

You can buy rice noodles that are ready-cooked in a pack in most supermarkets, or you can use the dried ones and soak them for 10 minutes in hot water. The recipe also makes use of a few ready-made sauces, i.e. tomato ketchup and sweet chilli sauce. If you're gluten intolerant, remember to make sure these sauces are gluten free.

Prep time: 5 minutes. Cooking time: 20 minutes.
Gluten-Free
Serves 2

Ingredients:
2 tbsp sesame oil
170g (1 pack) trimmed green beans (frozen is also fine)
200g Portobello mushrooms, quartered
3-4 spring onions, sliced
3 cloves garlic, sliced
50ml tamari
3 tbsp tomato ketchup (make sure it's gluten-free)
2-3 tbsp white wine vinegar
2 tbsp sweet chilli sauce (make sure it's gluten-free)
50ml water
360g pre-cooked rice noodles
A handful of salted peanuts

Method:
Heat the sesame oil to a medium-high temperature in a wok or large frying pan. Stir-fry the green beans for 4 minutes (a little less if you're using frozen), stirring often, then add the mushrooms and cook for 4 minutes more. Now toss in the spring onions and garlic and cook for 2-3 more minutes before pouring in the sauce ingredients: the tamari, ketchup, vinegar, chilli sauce and water.

Boil the sauce for 2 minutes and then stir in the rice noodles and peanuts until fully combined. Cook for a few more minutes to make sure everything is heated through, then serve.

*****

Creamy Vegan Mushroom Soup

A light soup is a welcome meal even in the warmer weather. I'm not talking about heavy stews with tons of ingredients, served thick enough to keep upright the proverbial spoon, but something much thinner, gentler on the pallet. Something suiting a lazy afternoon in the sunshine. There are probably a whole host of soups that would rise to the occasion, but I have settled upon a very simple mushroom variety. It is both light and creamy, with a subtle flavour that doesn't leave an aftertaste, making it not only ideal as a light lunch, but also as a starter to something more robust.

I've used gram flour as a thickener in order to keep the recipe gluten free, which also serves to add a tiny amount of colour to the dish. If you have no gluten issues use whatever flour you have at hand. I have also chosen the most basic closed-cup mushrooms that you get in packs at the supermarket. If you have a taste for something more exotic, then by all means experiment. Remember that different mushroom will affect the colour and flavour of the final soup. Flat or field mushrooms that are much darker in colour will show up as such in your finished dish. Oyster or shitake might be an exciting alternative. Just remember to cut your mushrooms up small, so that you or your guests are not chewing on big chunks.

Prep time: 10 minutes. Cooking time: 15-20 minutes.
Gluten-Free
Serves 2-3

Ingredients:
40g vegan butter
3 cloves garlic, finely chopped or crushed
250g closed cup mushrooms, finely diced
2 tbsp gram (chickpea) flour. You can put in a little more if you prefer a thicker soup.
2 tbsp nutritional yeast
1 litre hot vegetable stock, using two stock cubes (make sure they're gluten free)
150ml vegan cream
Salt and pepper to taste

Method:
First melt the butter in a medium-sized saucepan. Add the garlic and fry for 2 minutes, then put in the mushrooms and fry, stirring often, for a further 5-7 minutes, until they are soft and coloured, but not burnt.

Add the flour and nutritional yeast and mix well, then pour in the vegetable stock, a little at a time, stirring constantly with a whisk to prevent lumps from forming. Once you have used all the stock, bring it to the boil and simmer gently for about 10 minutes, stirring from time to time.

After 10 minutes, turn down the heat and stir in the cream. Heat the soup back through to just about boiling point, but do not boil as the cream will split. Season with salt and pepper to taste and serve immediately with your favourite crusty bread.

Cherry and Cranberry Pies

Not everybody likes mince pies, so I wanted to make something that could be an alternative to them. Something very much *like* mince pies, but at the same time not. I came up with these cherry and cranberry pies, which are a delicious substitute for when you're having guests over. These are also vegan and gluten-free, so everybody can enjoy them. This recipe makes quite a lot, so you can always half it if you don't want so many. Just so you know, all of mine went within 24 hours. Again, if you don't want to make the pastry, or have no gluten issues, you can use a pre-made sweet shortcrust pastry.

Prep time: 20 minutes. Cooking time: 35 minutes for the filling, plus 15-20 minutes per batch for the pies. Resting time: about 1 hour.
Gluten-Free.
Makes about 40

Ingredients:
For the Pastry:
300g buckwheat flour
200g coconut flour
2 tsp baking powder
2 tsp xanthan gum
½ tsp salt
75g golden caster sugar
300g vegan margarine, plus a little extra for greasing
200-250ml dairy-free milk (make sure it's gluten-free)

For the Filling:
700g frozen cherries
300g fresh cranberries
400g golden caster sugar
Zest of 2 oranges
1 tsp ground cinnamon
2 tbsp marmalade
Plant milk for brushing
Icing sugar for dusting

Method:
First make the pastry. Put the flours, baking powder, xanthan gum, salt, sugar and margarine into a large mixing bowl and rub together between your fingers, until the texture resembles fine breadcrumbs. Add the plant milk, 50ml at a time, and stir with a knife or spoon. Put in enough milk to be able to bring it all together as a dough (between 200 and 250ml). When you have your pastry dough ball, cover and chill in the fridge for 1 hour.

Now make your pie filling. Put all the filling ingredients into a saucepan and bring to the boil. Simmer, stirring from time to time, for 30-35 minutes, until you have a thick, jam-like consistency. Turn off the heat and allow to completely cool and thicken up.

When you are ready, preheat the oven to gas 6/200C/400F and grease a 12-hole pie tin, the same kind you would use for mince pies.

Break off about a third of the pastry dough and roll it out on a gluten-free floured surface (I used the buckwheat flour for this). Take a circular cookie cutter and either a smaller star cutter or a smaller circular cutter. Use the larger circular cutter to cut out the pastry bases and line each hole in the tin with them. You will have to roll out the pastry several times to do this. Now fill the pastry bases with about 2 tsp of pie filling. Use the smaller cutter to cut out a top for the pie and place these on top of each one.

Brush the top of each pie with plant milk and then place in the oven for 15-20 minutes or so, until the pastry is cooked and browned. Allow them to cool for a few minutes and then use a spoon to take them out of the tin and onto a serving plate.

Prepare and cook your next batches in the same manner, until you have used up either all the filling or all the pastry.

If you have filling left over, keep it in the fridge as it will make a great alternative cranberry sauce.

Once all the pies have cooled, dust with the icing sugar and serve.

Cherry and Cranberry Pies

Cajun Spiced Broccoli Bites

I'd been mulling this idea over in the back of my mind for some time, while working on a host of other recipes. I'd seen plenty done with cauliflower in terms of seasoning with spices, and I wanted to try something with broccoli. I've always had a fondness for Cajun spice. There's an earthy sweetness to it that juxtaposes with the heat. It's a spice blend normally associated with meat and fish, and I don't think vegetarian and vegan cuisine gets anywhere near enough of a look in.

This is the kind of dish we wish we could see on the menu of our local pub. It's battered, it's deep-fried, and it's spicy. On top of all that it's vegan and gluten-free, neatly checking all the boxes on our fast food wish list. These bites are best served straight away but you can, if need be, reheat them in the oven (please don't microwave them, unless you want soggy mush for dinner). Serve them either with fries or rice, or you may find them quite adequate on their own with a dollop of ketchup or barbeque sauce, they really are quite filling.

When cooking, the oil must be hot enough to bubble and seal the batter right away, as this is what makes them crispy. It must not be too hot, however. It is quite easy to burn the outside batter without fully cooking the broccoli inside. A medium heat should be enough, just watch for the oil temperature dropping with the more broccoli you add. It must always bubble and seal the batter from the outset.

Prep time: 20 minutes. Cooking time: 6-8 minutes per batch.
Gluten Free

Ingredients:
For the Batter:
200g gram flour
2 tsp salt
¼ tsp black pepper
1 tsp baking powder
2 tsp dark, mild chilli powder
1 ½ tsp Cajun spice mix
1 tsp dried oregano
3 heaped tbsp vegan natural yoghurt
Juice and zest of 1 lemon
2 tbsp nutritional yeast
3 tbsp tomato puree
250ml cold water

For the Broccoli:
3 fresh heads of broccoli, cut into florets and soaked in enough cold water to submerge them
About 200g gram flour for dusting
Salt and pepper to season flour
Enough sunflower or vegetable oil for deep-frying

Method:
To make the batter, put all the batter ingredients into a large bowl and either whisk or blend until completely smooth. If the batter seems too thick, you can always add a little more water. Allow about 30 minutes for all the flavours to infuse.

Now set up your three bowls. Have your water-soaked broccoli on the left, a bowl with the 200g of seasoned gram flour in the middle, and the batter on the right.

Fill a saucepan no more that half-full with the oil and bring it up to temperature. You can check when it is ready to fry by dropping a little bit of the batter into it. The oil will bubble, and the batter will float straight away.

When it is ready, take about 6-8 heads of broccoli from the water on the left and dip them straight into the gram flour. Shake the bowl to cover the broccoli and then drop the heads into the batter, making sure to shake off the excess flour first. Once the broccoli heads are fully coated, take the batter bowl over to the hot oil and gently place each head into the oil one at a time. Allow then to fry for about 30 seconds, then give them a gently stir with a slotted spoon to separate any that have stuck together. Fry for 6-8 minutes, until golden brown but not burnt.

Use the slotted spoon to transfer the cooked broccoli bites onto a baking tray and transfer them to a low oven to keep warm. Continue this process until all the broccoli has been used up. Serve immediately.

Cajun-Spiced Broccoli Bites

Easy Chestnut Mushroom, New Potato and Leek Pie

I've created this pie with ready-to-roll pastry to make it as easy and non-time-consuming as possible. You can, of course, make your own pastry if you prefer, but the idea behind this is to keep it simple.

Chestnut mushrooms are easily accessible and a perfect size for a chunky pie, when cut either in half or quarter. The same with new potatoes, just halve or quarter them before cooking to get the right size. I've also kept the ingredients to a minimum to make it fuss-free, making this a pie you can throw together and be eating before you know it.

If you want to make this gluten-free, just switch to your favourite gluten-free pastries and change the flour to a gluten-free brand.

Prep time: 15 minutes. Cooking time: just under an hour.
Can be made gluten-free
Serves 4-6

Ingredients:
A knob of vegan butter for greasing
1 block of ready-made shortcrust pastry
Flour for dusting

For the Pie Filling:
500g new potatoes, cut in half
3 tbsp olive oil
600g chestnut mushrooms, cut in half
1 large leek, sliced
1 vegan stock cube
2 tbsp fresh chopped thyme
A good dash of black pepper
4 tbsp nutritional yeast
2 tbsp plain flour
400ml vegan cream
Salt to taste

To Top:
1 block ready-made puff pastry
A little vegan milk for brushing
A sprinkle of sea salt
A sprinkle of dried oregano
A sprinkle of ground paprika

Method:
Preheat the oven to gas 6/200C/400F and grease a large pie dish with the vegan butter.

Bring a pan of water to the boil to cook the new potatoes.

While the water is coming to the boil, dust your work surface with some of the flour and roll out the short crust pastry to allow it to fill the bottom of the pie dish, as well as up the sides. Line this with greaseproof paper and then fill with dried rice or baking beans. Bake the pastry base in the middle of the oven for 15-20 minutes, until just cooked.

While the pastry is cooking, boil the new potatoes for about 8-12 minutes, until tender but not falling apart. Drain them when they are ready and set them aside.

To make the filling, heat the oil in a large frying pan or wok and fry the mushrooms, on a high heat , for about 10 minutes, until browned all over. Add the sliced leek and cook for 5 minutes more, then stir in the stock cube, thyme and black pepper.

Now add the cooked new potatoes to the mix and cook them for another 3-4 minutes. Stir in the nutritional yeast and the flour, until fully mixed, and pour in the vegan cream.

Bring to a gentle simmer and continue simmering for 4-5 minutes, stirring often, until you have a thick sauce. Now turn off the heat and adjust the seasoning if desired.

Allow the filling to cool a little, then pour it into the cooked pastry base and set aside.

Roll out the puff pastry on a floured surface to the size of your pie dish, then place it on top of the pie filling. Press down the edges to seal them, then pierce the pastry a little with a sharp knife and lightly score diagonal lines into it.

Brush with the milk and sprinkle the salt, oregano and paprika on top. Bake in the middle of the oven for 35-40 minutes, until risen and browned. Allow to cool for 5 minutes or so before serving.

Easy Chestnut Mushroom, New Potato and Leek Pie

Carrot and Red Pepper Soup

Soups have long been favoured by us Brits but, for reasons that I can't quite figure out, we get a lot of it processed in cans. I never buy canned soup. I didn't before I became vegan, and I don't now that I am vegan. I have fond childhood memories of canned soup provided by my grandmother, but when I learned how easy it was to make it, and to make it *better* than the processed stuff, I never did anything else.

Ok, making a soup from scratch does take a little longer than opening a can and microwaving the contents. It also takes a bit more effort. On the plus side, you can get exactly the soup you want, and in the quantities you want it. Nobody ever makes homemade soup for one. Even if you're living by yourself, it's sensible to make a batch of it and freeze what you're not going to eat straight away. At home, we use old ice cream and takeaway containers to freeze portion sizes of soup. That way, if I'm coming home late from work, all my wife has to do is pop one in the microwave (just like you would with a can, only better).

Soups, of course, can range in their difficulty, and some are a lot more involved than others. This one is definitely on the easy scale, as it's all done in the one pan and then blended at the end. The whole thing takes about 45 minutes to make, so you have time to do it even if you've been at work all day.

Prep time: 10 minutes. Cooking time: 35 minutes.
Gluten Free
Serves 4

Ingredients:
2 tbsp flavourless oil, such as groundnut
600g carrots, peeled and diced
2 sticks of celery, sliced
1 red pepper, diced
1 small onion, diced
3 cloves garlic, peeled and smashed with the flat of a knife
3 medium tomatoes, cut into wedges
2 heaped tbsp ground paprika
2 tsp Dijon mustard
1 litre veg stock (made with 2 stock cubes – make sure they're gluten-free)
250ml vegan cream
Salt and pepper to taste
A handful of grated vegan cheese to top

Method:
Heat the oil in a large saucepan and sweat the carrots for about 10 minutes, until they are soft. Add the celery, pepper and onion and cook for another 5 minutes, stirring often. Add the garlic and give it two more minutes then put in the tomato wedges, paprika and mustard.

Pour in the veg stock and bring everything to the boil. Simmer for 20 minutes, stirring from time to time and then blend until completely smooth. If you're using a jug blender, make sure that steam can escape. I use a handheld blender for all my soups and blend it in the pot it's cooking in.

Put the soup back on the stove and add the vegan cream. Stir in and allow to simmer gently for a minute or so. Season with the salt and pepper to taste and then serve into individual bowls. Top each bowl with a little grated vegan cheese.

Vegan Leek and Cheese Parcels

If you want to impress at a party, or you're thinking about a Christmas starter, you could do a lot worse than these vegan leek and cheese parcels. Pan-fried leeks with garlic and cheese, wrapped in a crunchy filo pastry parcel and dipped in a luxurious forest fruit dipping sauce. If you're having family over, then this is guaranteed to impress.

You can make these a day in advance, just be sure they are tightly covered so that the pastry doesn't dry out. They take fifteen minutes to cook in the oven, but you do need to keep an eye on them as the ends start to burn very quickly. These parcels might seem complicated to look at, but they're really not that difficult to make. I would advise being careful when pulling the parcel together, as this can sometimes split the pastry and cause the filling to leak out of the bottom a little. Some of them split while I was making mine, but I carried on regardless and there was no major disaster.

Leek and cheese are just one of endless options to fill these parcels. Replacing the leeks with mushrooms would be a great alternative. You could also switch to more east Asian ingredients and dip them in some tamari with lime juice. Indian style cooking would also suit them well, where you could dip them in homemade mango chutney (you can find a recipe for that in my book *Going Vegan*). Try this recipe first. Once you've got that sorted, you can begin to experiment.

Prep time: 30 minutes. Cooking time: about 40 minutes, plus cooling time.
Makes up to 25.

Ingredients:
For the Dipping Sauce:
200g frozen forest fruits
75ml orange juice
1 clove garlic, bashed with the flat of a knife to crush it
100g sugar
Pinch salt
½ tsp harissa paste
2 tbsp redcurrant jelly

For the Filling:
3 tbsp olive oil
3 small, or 1 ½ -2 large leeks, thinly sliced
2 cloves garlic, chopped
150ml plant-based milk
1 tsp wholegrain mustard
220g vegan cheese, cut into small cubes
Salt and pepper to taste

For the Pastry:
1 pack ready-made filo pastry (make sure it's vegan)
Plant milk for brushing
Oil for brushing

Method:
First make the dipping sauce by putting all the ingredients into a saucepan and bringing to the boil. Simmer for about 15-20 minutes, until the sauce easily coats the back of a spoon. Allow to cool a little and then pass it through a fine strainer to get a smooth sauce. Set aside or chill until ready to serve.

To make the parcel filling, heat the oil in a frying pan and then sauté the leeks for 8-10 minutes, until they are soft. Add the garlic and cook for a minute or two more, then add the milk, mustard and cheese. Stir in and bring to a simmer. Season with salt and pepper to taste and simmer for 2-3 minutes, until you have a thick sauce. Set aside to cool.

Preheat the oven to gas 6/200C/400F and line a baking sheet with greaseproof paper.

Lay out a single sheet of filo pastry, cut it in half and then half again. This will still be too large, so now fold this piece in half, so that you have a double square sheet of pastry. Brush with a little pant milk and then put about 1 ½ tsp of the filling onto the middle of the pastry. Bring all the edges of the pastry up around the filling so that they all come together at the top. Do this gently to avoid splitting the pastry at the bottom as best you can. When all the ends are together, give them a slight twist to form a sort of flower shape, then squeeze gently with your fingers in the middle to press it together. The milk should hold it in shape.

Place it on your lined baking sheet and then repeat the process until you have used up either all the pastry or all the filling. The parcels don't have to be far apart on the tray, but you don't want them touching. You should get about 25, so you may need to cook them in batches. Gently brush all the parcels with oil.

Place the sheet of parcels in the middle of the oven and cook for about 15 minutes. Keep an eye on them towards the end so that the tips of the pastry don't burn too much. A little colour is good though.

Serve hot or cold with the dipping sauce.

Vegan Leek and Cheese Parcels

Pan Fried Cinnamon Pears

Prep time: 10 minutes. Cooking time: 15 minutes.
Gluten-Free
Serves 2-3

Ingredients:
1 knob vegan butter
1 tbsp olive oil
4-5 pears, peeled, cored and quartered
A pinch of salt
A pinch of mild chilli powder
½ tsp ground cinnamon
Juice of ½ lemon
3 tbsp unrefined sugar
A splash of cold water

Method:
Heat the butter and olive oil in a frying pan, to quite a high heat, and then add the pears. Cook the pears for about 10 minutes, stirring often, until they are soft on the inside and seared on the outside.

Now sprinkle on the salt, chilli powder and cinnamon and stir until the pears are fully coated. Add the lemon juice, the sugar and the water and cook for another 2-3 minutes, until you are left with a small amount of thick syrup. Serve hot or cold with vegan cream or ice cream.

*****

Mulled Pears with Vegan Whipped Cream

This is a great Christmas dessert, or something you can have any time of year, especially if you're having dinner guests. Poached pears have long been a favourite of mine, so this time I wanted to do something with them that captured the essence of the winter season. Mulled pears seemed the obvious choice, using pretty much the same seasoning as for mulled wine and poaching the pears in that. I don't drink anymore, so I've used red grape juice instead of red wine for my recipe. You can use wine if you prefer, or perhaps two thirds wine and one third water. Whatever you use, you must make them the day before you want to eat them to allow the flavours and colour to fully infuse. You must also chill the coconut cream the night before, so that the cream separates from the water, which will give you that thick, whipped cream consistency.

If you plan ahead, this dessert will be quite the show-stopper. The recipe makes 6 pears, but there is enough liquid to cover up to 8 pears, if they are not too big. Just make sure they are fully covered in the fridge when you leave them overnight. There is plenty of syrup left over, so you can pour as much as you like onto your final dessert. I kept mine sparse for the aesthetics of the photograph, so don't think you have to throw it away because it isn't in the picture.

Prep time: 20 minutes. Cooking time: 45 minutes, plus overnight for chilling
Gluten-Free
Makes 6 Pears

Ingredients:
For the Mulled Pears:
1 litre red grape juice (or 2 parts red wine:1 part water)
1 orange, cut into 6 pieces
2 cinnamon sticks
2 bay leaves
¼ tsp ground nutmeg
½ tsp ground allspice

220g golden caster sugar
6 pears, peeled but stalks left on

For the Vegan Whipped Cream:
1 carton coconut cream
2 tbsp icing sugar
¼ tsp ground nutmeg

Method:
The day before you want to eat it, put all the mulled pear ingredients, apart from the pears themselves, into a large saucepan and mix together a little. Add the 6 pears and bring the pot to the boil. Simmer for 40-45 minutes, until the pears feel tender when you stick a small, sharp knife into the flesh. Allow the pears and syrup to completely cool, then store the whole lot in a container and chill overnight.

Put the carton of coconut cream in the fridge at the same time.

The next day the pears will be fully infused. Open up the chilled carton of coconut cream and pour out the excess water, leaving just the solid coconut cream behind. Put this into a bowl with the icing sugar and nutmeg and whip up with a hand whisk until light and fluffy.

To serve, cut a small piece off the base of the pears so that they stand upright and serve one on each plate. Pour a spoonful or two of the syrup over the pears and then add a spoonful of the whipped cream. Serve with slices of orange if desired.

Mulled Pears with Vegan Whipped Cream

Blackberry Panna Cotta

Chef moulds or rings can help you make all kinds of attractive dishes, such as this Blackberry Panna Cotta, which makes full use of the chef ring to create this two-part dessert.

This panna cotta incorporates both frozen and fresh blackberries. You can use the combination, as I have, or keep it to either one or the other, depending on the season and how available fresh blackberries are. Thankfully, supermarkets stock the frozen kind all year round. The recipe also features agar agar, which is our vegan gelatine replacement and the ingredient that holds the dessert together. Just like gelatine, you need to simmer the agar agar to activate it. It will then thicken as it cools. If you are using moulds, you will have to make sure that the Panna Cotta is cooled enough to be quite thick before you spoon it in, otherwise it will simply (and rather frustratingly) pour out from underneath the mould, leaving you with a sticky mess and no dessert. You don't *have* to use moulds to make this, dessert dishes will serve you just as well. The mould just makes it look fancy.

Prep time: 25 minutes. Cooking time: 30 minutes, plus cooling time.
Gluten-Free
Makes 4

Ingredients:
For the Panna Cotta:
450g (2 punnets) fresh blackberries, leave a few aside for garnish
100g sugar
50ml orange juice
1 tsp vanilla extract
400ml vegan cream
4 extra tbsp sugar
1 ½ tsp agar agar powder

For the Blackberry Compote:
400g frozen blackberries
180g sugar

Method:
To make the Panna Cotta, put the blackberries, sugar and orange juice into a saucepan and bring to a gentle simmer. Simmer for 10-15 minutes, until it has thickened.

Allow the mixture to cool a little and then pass it through a sieve into another bowl to produce a fine, strained sauce. Use the back of a spoon to press against the berries to pass as much through the sieve as possible.

Clean out your saucepan and pour the strained sauce back into it, then bring it back to a simmer. Add the rest of the Panna Cotta ingredients, bring them all to a simmer again and then cook for about 3-4 minutes, whisking continuously. This will activate the agar agar. Turn off the heat and set aside to cool. This should take about 30 minutes and you'll need to keep coming back to whisk it as it thickens to prevent lumps from forming.

While it is cooling you can make your blackberry compote base. Put the frozen berries and sugar into a saucepan and bring to the boil. Simmer rapidly for about 15 minutes, stirring often, until you have a thick, jam-like consistency. Turn off the heat and allow to cool for 10 minutes.

If you are using moulds, line a baking sheet with greaseproof paper and then place 4 moulds on top. If you are using dishes, then just lay 4 out ready for use.

Spoon a little compote into the bottom of the moulds or dishes. Allow to set for 5 minutes or so and then spoon the Panna Cotta mixture on top. Fill to the top of the moulds or dishes, then allow to set fully in the fridge or freezer for at least 2 hours. You can freeze them entirely if you like, just give them 30 minutes or so to thaw before serving. Top with fresh or frozen blackberries to serve.

Blackberry Panna Cotta

Caramelised Pear Crostini with Haloumi-Style Cheese

Prep time: 15 minutes. Cooking time: about 50 minutes.
Easy to make Gluten-Free
Serves 4

Ingredients:
For the reduction:
50ml olive oil
50ml white wine vinegar
75g unrefined sugar
50ml water

For the Pears:
4 pears
2 tbsp olive oil
150g halloumi-style cheese, cut into centimetre cubes
75g walnuts, roughly chopped
4 slices bread, or gluten-free variety

Method:
Preheat the oven to gas 6/200C/400F.

Put the reduction ingredients into a small saucepan and bring to the boil. Simmer for about 10 minutes, until the liquid has reduced by about half, then set aside.

Cut each pear into quarters and then cut out the core. Put them into a roasting dish and pour over the reduction. Roast in the oven for 35 minutes, turning them a couple of times throughout cooking, until the pears are softened and caramelised.

Heat the olive oil in a frying pan and sauté the pears with the cheese for 4-5 minutes, until the cheese has browned and softened slightly. Add the walnuts and cook for a minute more.
Toast the sliced bread and then cut each slice into two triangles. Serve the bread onto four plates and then spoon a quarter of the pear mixture onto each slice of toast. Drizzle on the remaining syrup from the roasting pan and serve.

*****

Pan-Fried Pear Tart with Greek-Style Cheese and Redcurrant Jelly

This is a straight forward but great looking dish that you can make with ready-made puff pastry. Pears and cheese go very well together, in a salad as well as in something like this. This tart is sweet enough to almost be a dessert, but the savoury tanginess of the Greek-style cheese pulls it back into its place. If you're doing three courses, then this is an ideal starter as it is small, light and full-flavoured. Plus, the way it looks is guaranteed to impress your dinner guests.

I've used a breakfast bowl to cut out the round shape. A 500g block of pastry will give you four servings, but you will have to fold the pastry back on itself to use it up. A word of caution here: don't mix the leftover pastry up and roll it out again. You can do this with shortcrust pastry but not puff. Puff pastry is made up of layers that must be kept intact. What you want to do is *fold* the pastry back onto itself and then roll it out again. This way you are not disturbing the layers and it will still rise.

I have used coconut nectar as the sweetener, but if you can't get hold of this then brown sugar, or even golden syrup will do fine. The redcurrant jelly is the standard type you can buy in the supermarket. It costs about 80p and is usually with the cranberry sauce.

Prep time: 15-20 minutes. Cooking Time: 25-30 minutes.
Serves 4.

Ingredients:
2 conference pears
½ tbsp coconut oil
1 ½ tbsp coconut nectar (or brown sugar)
1 x 500g block ready-made puff pastry
3 tbsp redcurrant jelly
200g white Greek style vegan cheese, cut into 1cm cubes
4 tbsp olive oil for brushing
Black pepper
Handful of fresh rocket leaves for garnish
8 chives for garnish

Method:
Preheat the oven to gas 5/190C/375F and line 2 baking trays with greaseproof paper.
Peel the pears, cut them in half, remove the core and then slice them lengthways. Heat the coconut oil in a frying pan and then fry the pear slices for 6-8 minutes, stirring often, until they start to brown and soften. Add the coconut nectar or sugar and cook for another two minutes, until they start to caramelise. Set aside to cool.

Roll out the pastry (I cut my block in half and did it in two stages) to about 5mm thick. Take a small breakfast bowl, about 15 cm in diameter, and place it on the pastry. Use a sharp knife to cut around the bowl and produce a perfect pastry circle. Put the circle on the lined baking tray and then cut out the other three. Remember to fold your pastry rather than knead it if you have to roll it out again.

Once you have your four pastry circles, use a small, sharp knife to score another smaller circle about 1 ½ cm from the edge of each pastry, to create a sort of inner-ring. This does not have to be perfect, and make sure you don't cut all the way through the pastry. This will create the puffed edge of your tart.

Soften the redcurrant jelly slightly in the microwave, then use a teaspoon to spread it onto the centre of your pastry rounds. Don't go beyond your scored edge. Layer a quarter of the pears on top of the jelly and then put a quarter of the cheese cubes on top of that. Brush the cheese and the edges of the pastry with the olive oil and sprinkle with black pepper. Repeat this for all four tarts and then cook in the oven for 25-30 minutes, until the tarts have risen and browned. Top with a little of the rocket leaves and two chives each. Add a little redcurrant jelly to your plate and then serve immediately.

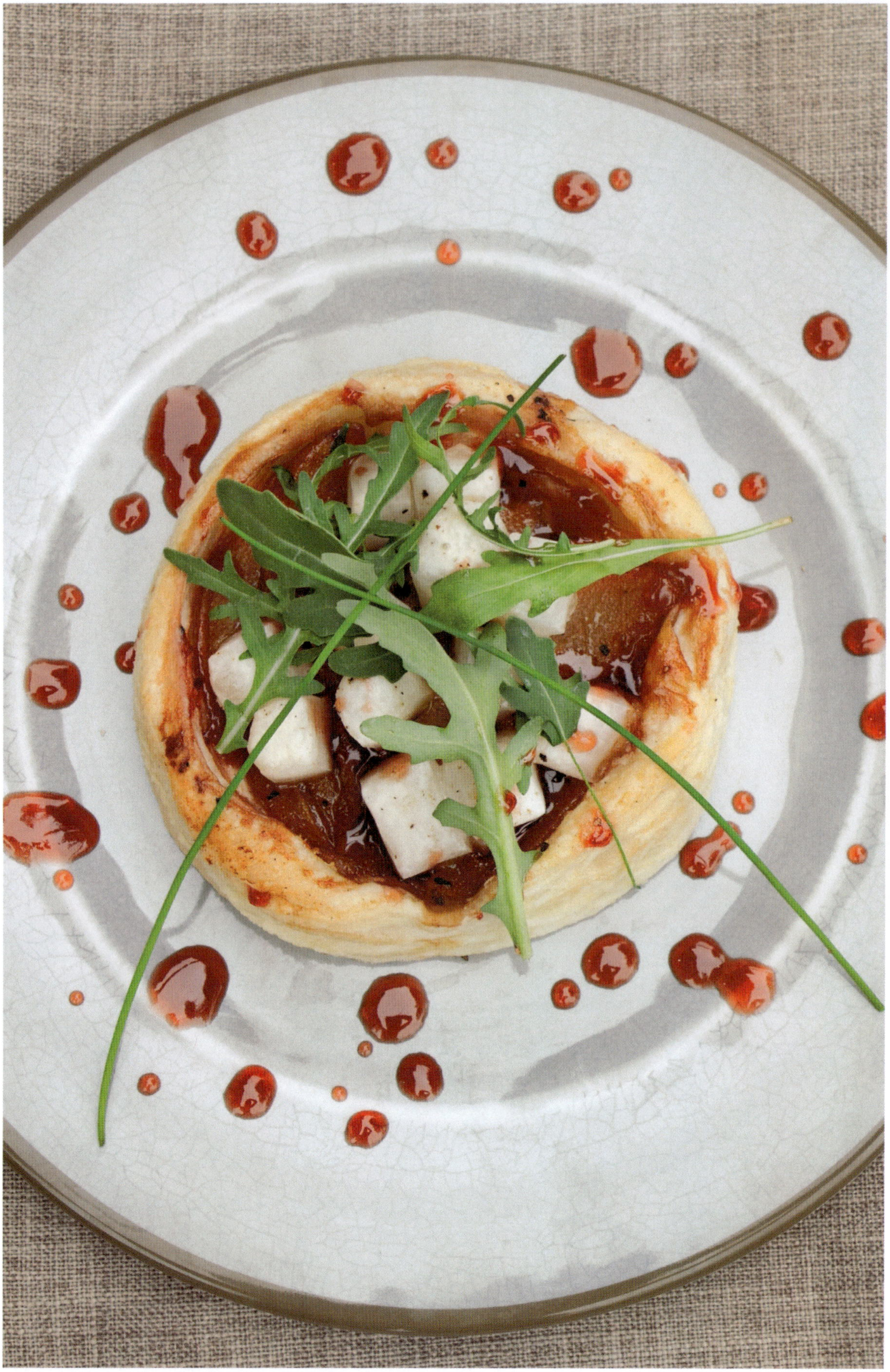

Deep-Filled Apple Pie

This is my favourite kind of apple pie: thick pastry, with a really deep apple filling that is just perfectly sweet without being overly so. Pie like this, I can't get enough of. I have a preference for chilled fruit pie with a splash of vegan cream, and I am particularly fond of it at breakfast time. I have no idea why this is, only that it seems to start my day particularly well on the occasions when I am able to have it in this way.

Prep time: about 30 minutes. Cooking time: 1 hour 20 minutes, plus cooling time.
Serves 6-8

Ingredients:
For the Pastry:
450g plain flour
1 tsp baking powder
½ tsp salt
100g unrefined sugar
75g gram (chickpea) flour
200g vegan margarine, plus extra for greasing
150ml plant milk, plus extra to glaze the pie

For the Filling:
2kg Bramley apples, peeled, sliced and soaked in water
25g vegan margarine
300g unrefined sugar, plus extra to top the pie
½ tsp ground cinnamon

Method:
First make the pastry by putting all the pastry ingredients, apart from the milk, into a mixing bowl and rubbing together between your fingers, until the mixture resembles fine breadcrumbs.

Add the plant milk and bring the mixture together with your hands. Knead for a couple of minutes to form a dough and then cover and chill in the fridge for 1 hour.

While the pastry is chilling, drain the apples, then melt the butter in a wide but shallow pan. Add the drained apples and cook for 15-20 minutes on a medium-high heat. The apples will release a lot of water, which we want to get rid of before putting them into our pie. Drain any excess water that hasn't cooked off at the end of the time. You want the apples to be slightly soft but not mushy. Add the sugar and the cinnamon and cook for another minute or two. Allow to cool.

While the apples are cooling, preheat the oven to gas 5/190C/375F and grease a suitable deep pie dish with margarine. Roll out just under two-thirds of the pastry large enough to line the pie dish and go up over the sides. Fill the pie dish with the pastry and press down gently, leaving a slight overlap at the rim of the dish. Line the pastry with greaseproof paper and then fill with dry rice or baking beans. Bake in the oven for 15 minutes, or until the pastry is cooked through but not browned too much.

Remove from the oven and take out the rice and paper, then fill the cooked pastry with the apple filling

Turn the oven down to gas 4/180C/350F.

Roll out the remaining pastry to a suitable size for a lid, then place the lid on top of the pie. Cut away any excess pastry with a table knife and then press down the edges with either your fingers or a fork. Use a sharp knife to cut two slits in the top of the pie to allow steam to escape. Now roll out any remaining pastry to create shapes on top of your pie (I used a small star-cutter for this) and stick them on with a little brushed milk. Now brush the entire lid with plant milk and sprinkle sugar on top. Place the pie onto a baking sheet and then bake in the middle of the oven for 40-45 minutes, until the pastry is cooked and golden brown.

Allow to cool a little before serving, or chill completely and enjoy cold.

Deep-Filled Apple Pie

76

Pasta and Rice

Artichoke Risotto with Vegan Haloumi and Crispy Red Onions

Awesome Spaghetti Sauce

Black Bean Spaghetti with Garlic-Braised Cabbage and Peanuts

Mac n Cheese with Asparagus and Tomato

Quinoa with Broccoli and Cashew Nuts

Brown, Red and Wild Rice with Courgettes, Peppers and Tomatoes

Brown, Red and Wild Rice with Sugar Snap Peas and Woodland Mushrooms

Creamy Kale Polenta with Roasted Tomatoes

Beetroot Risotto

Roasted Red Pepper and Aubergine Pasta Sauce

Baked Spaghetti with Tomatoes and Parmesan

Quinoa, Beetroot and Date Burgers

Brown Rice Salad with Edamame Beans and Toasted Cashews

Fettuccine with Mushrooms, Vegan Haloumi, Sundried Tomatoes and Pesto

Red Lentil Pasta with Purple Sprouting Broccoli and Garlic Dressing

Artichoke Risotto with Vegan Haloumi and Crispy Red Onions

This risotto might seem a bit fancy, but it's no more difficult to make than any other, which is not difficult at all. You do have to use a couple of extra pans to make the topping, so this isn't the one-pot-wonder that many people find so appealing about this dish. You can forego the toppings, of course, but they really do make it special and so I urge you to include them. The artichokes hearts in this recipe come pre-cooked in a can. I'm not a fan of the brine they store the canned artichokes in, so I always wash mine first to remove that taste. Remember to drizzle a little lemon juice over your artichokes when storing them out in the open, as they will quickly discolour if you don't.

Prep time: 20 minutes. Cooking time: 35 minutes
Gluten-Free
Serves 3-4

Ingredients:
For the Risotto:
2 tbsp olive oil
2 sticks celery, thinly sliced
3 cloves garlic, chopped
350g Arborio risotto rice
1.25 litres veg stock (make sure it's vegan and gluten-free)
2 cans cooked artichoke hearts, washed, drained and cut in half. Sprinkle with lemon juice to prevent discolouration.
Salt and pepper to taste
50g vegan butter

For the Crispy Onions:
Enough oil for deep-frying
2 red onions, very thinly sliced

For the Haloumi:
2 tbsp olive oil
200g vegan haloumi, cut into strips

Method:
To make the risotto, heat the olive oil in a large frying pan or wok and gently cook the celery for 3 minutes, being careful not to burn or colour it too much. Add the garlic and cook for another 2 minutes, stirring often. Now put in the risotto rice and stir in for 2 minutes, until all the grains are covered in oil. Pour in the veg stock, about 100ml (1 ladleful) at a time, making sure that the rice has absorbed most of the previous liquid before adding more. This process will take about 20 minutes.
Add the drained artichokes with the last ladleful of stock and gently stir in. Cook until a lot of the water has gone but the dish is still quite wet, then stop cooking. Season with the salt and pepper and then add the butter. Cover the risotto and rest for 10 minutes. Stir in the butter just prior to serving.

While the risotto is still cooking, make the crispy onions by heating the frying oil in a small saucepan (no more than half-full) until it is at frying temperature. Deep fry the onions for 6-8 minutes, until they are browned and crispy, then remove from the oil and drain on some kitchen paper.

At the end of cooking, while the risotto is resting, cook the haloumi. Heat the olive oil in a frying pan, until quite hot, then fry the haloumi strips for about 4 minutes each side, until they are golden brown all over.

To serve, spoon the risotto into the centre of your plates. Put a few strips of the haloumi on top of the rice and then top with a generous pinch of the crispy onions. Serve immediately.

*****

Awesome Spaghetti Sauce

I've called this awesome spaghetti sauce because, not only is it delicious, but it's also easy to make. My wife, Samantha, wanted a cream-based tomato sauce for pasta one night, so I came up with this one. This recipe is for about 8 people, but I suggest you make the full batch and portion and freeze what you don't use for a later date. That way you've got it to hand on nights when you don't feel like cooking. I've used vegan crème fraiche for the creaminess, because it has a nice little tang to it. If you can't get hold of it then regular vegan cream will do in a pinch. Not quite the same but still good.

Thyme and basil give this sauce its herby balance. Fresh, of course. The only dried herb I tend to use is oregano, or mixed Italian seasoning. Everything else comes as it was intended. You can use a micro plane for the garlic, or simply roughly chop it. I wanted a full infusion and so went for the grater. It's going to be blended until smooth later anyway, so you won't have to worry about lumpy bits.

Prep time: 10 minutes. Cooking time: 30 minutes
Gluten-Free
Serves 8

Ingredients:
50ml olive oil
1 medium onion, small diced
3 cloves garlic, micro planed or chopped
4-5 tbsp tomato puree
2-3 sprigs fresh thyme leaves
2 cans chopped tomatoes
1 can water
1 tsp sea salt flakes
A handful of chopped basil leaves
1x200ml tub vegan crème fraiche
3 tbsp nutritional yeast
Salt and pepper to taste

Method:
Gently heat the olive oil in a large saucepan and cook the onions for 5 minutes, stirring often, until they are soft and translucent. Add the garlic and cook for 2 minutes more. Stir in the tomato puree and the fresh thyme and cook that for another couple of minutes, then pour in the tomatoes, the water and add the salt.

Bring to the boil and simmer for 20 minutes, or until the sauce has been reduced by one third. Add the basil leaves about halfway through the cooking time.

Finally stir in the crème fraiche and the nutritional yeast and gently simmer for another 5 minutes or so. Season to taste and then allow to cool down. Blend until completely smooth and either use straight away or portion into batches and freeze.

*****

Black Bean Spaghetti with Garlic-Braised Cabbage and Peanuts

You can buy black bean spaghetti at a number of supermarkets. It is a thin pasta made entirely of black beans, and therefore is high in protein and has a very dense texture. Because of its density you don't need that much of it to satisfy your hunger, so one packet will adequately feed four people.

I've kept this dish simple and given it a South-East Asian feel. It uses half a white cabbage, which you can pick up anywhere. The cabbage is braised in stock for about 20 minutes, until it is tender with just a little bite to it. You can substitute it for other vegetables if you prefer, but you would have to adjust the braising time accordingly. You can use just regular salted peanuts from a packet to top this, unless you don't want the salt content, in which case get the raw kind.

Prep time: 10 minutes. Cooking time: 30 minutes.
Gluten-Free
Serves 4

Ingredients:
2 tbsp olive oil
Half a medium-sized white cabbage, cut into thin slices
3 cloves garlic, chopped
600ml hot, light vegetable stock (made with 1 stock cube – make sure it's gluten-free)
2 tbsp miso paste
1 tsp Dijon mustard
1 tsp yeast extract
1 packet (200g) dried black bean spaghetti
2 tbsp tamari

To Garnish:
2 tbsp sesame oil
100g peanuts
2 tsp hot sauce
A handful of chopped coriander

Method:
Heat the olive oil in a large frying pan or wok and fry the cabbage, on a medium heat, for about 5 minutes, stirring often. Add the garlic and cook for 2 minutes more.

Pour the vegetable stock into a measuring jug or bowl and whisk in the miso paste, mustard and yeast extract. Now pour the stock over the cabbage and bring to the boil. Simmer for 15-20 minutes, until most of the liquid is gone and the cabbage is tender.

While this is simmering, bring a large pot of water to the boil and cook the black bean spaghetti for 6-7 minutes, until al dente. Drain, wash and set aside.

When the cabbage is ready, add the drained pasta to it and pour over the tamari. Mix until fully incorporated and the pasta is hot.

In a separate frying pan, heat the sesame oil and fry the peanuts for 2 minutes, stirring often to prevent them from burning. Add the hot sauce and cook for 30 seconds more.

Serve the spaghetti and cabbage into bowls, then put some of the toasted peanuts on top and sprinkle with a little chopped coriander.

*****

Mac 'n' Cheese with Asparagus and Tomato

We eat macaroni and cheese a lot at home because the basic recipe is simple and, after a day's work, we're all about simple cooking. I do tend to mix it with other ingredients, not only to make it a little more interesting, but also to add nutritional value; something I try to do with every meal. This recipe has asparagus and tomato, which is sautéed separately. This is then topped with crispy fried onion rings to add some real crunch. The macaroni in this recipe is not gluten-free, but everything else in the recipe is. You can get gluten-free macaroni at a few supermarkets, or online, so switch it for that if you are intolerant.

Have fun with this and change up the veggies as much as you want. Mushrooms are a great substitute, and courgettes and red peppers would also work well. There's a little bit of Sriracha chilli sauce in this, which you can leave out if chilli isn't for you.

You can cook the pasta beforehand if you want to free up some time. I tend to chill it down anyway and let the cheese sauce heat it back up prior to serving. I use that technique for this recipe because keeping pasta warm is difficult without over-cooking it. The fried onions are an optional topping, but they work so well that it would be a shame to leave them out. Remember to slice them thinly and they will become crisp as they cool.

Prep time: 20 minutes. Cooking time: about 30 minutes.
Easy to Make Gluten-Free
Serves 4

Ingredients:
1 x 500g pack dried macaroni (use gluten-free if needed)

For the Cheese Sauce:
45g vegan margarine
3 tbsp gram flour
750ml plant milk (I used almond)
1 veg stock cube (make sure it's gluten-free, if needed)
3 tbsp nutritional yeast
1 tsp Dijon mustard
½ tsp sriracha sauce (optional)
75g vegan cheese (I used smoked)
Salt and pepper to taste.

For the Veggies:
3 tbsp olive oil
300g fresh asparagus (about 30 spears), the woody bottom stem removed, and the rest cut in halve
4 medium vine-ripened tomatoes, cut into 6 wedges each.

For the Fried Onions: (optional, but worth the effort)
1-2 whole onions, peeled and sliced into very thin rings
Enough vegetable oil to fill about 2cm deep in a small saucepan.

Method:
First cook the pasta. Bring a large saucepan of water to the boil, pour in the packet of macaroni and simmer for 10-12 minutes, until al-dente. Strain into a colander and run under cold water to cool and stop the cooking process. Set aside.

Now make the cheese sauce. Melt the margarine in your empty pasta saucepan and add the gram flour. Take off the heat and stir with a whisk until a thick doughy roux is formed. Add a little of the milk and whisk in to thin it out a little. Add a bit more and whisk into a smooth paste. Put the pan back on the heat and continue to add the milk, a bit at a time, whisking any lumps out as you go. Bring the sauce up to the boil and turn the heat down to a gentle simmer. Add the rest of the ingredients and whisk thoroughly. Simmer very gently for about 4 minutes, until you have a thick and yellow cheese sauce. Take off the heat, cover with cling film or a plate and set aside.

To cook the vegetables, heat the olive oil in a non-stick frying pan or wok. Sauté the asparagus for 8-10 minutes, stirring often to prevent burning. Add the tomato wedges and cook for another 4-5 minutes, until they have softened.

While you are doing this, you can heat the vegetable oil in a small saucepan to fry the onions. You'll want the oil hot enough so that it begins to bubble when you drop in an onion slice. Fry the onions, in 2-3 batches, until quite browned but not black. This will only take a minute or so, so don't stray too far. When they are ready, remove the onions with a pair of cooking tongs and leave to drain and cool on some kitchen paper.

Heat the cheese sauce back up and add the vegetables, then add the pasta and mix it all together. Leave it for a minute or so to heat the pasta back up, and then serve into four bowls. Top with some of the cooled crispy onions and serve immediately.

Mac N Cheese with Asparagus and Tomato

Quinoa with Broccoli and Cashew Nuts

Prep time: 10 minutes. Cooking time: 30 minutes.

Gluten Free
Serves 2-3

Ingredients:
150g quinoa
2 tbsp olive oil
1 head of broccoli, cut into small florets
I pack pre-cut, ready to eat tofu
65g cashew nuts
3 cloves garlic, chopped
2 medium tomatoes, cut into wedges
1 tbsp paprika
Juice of 2 oranges
Salt and pepper to taste
1 medium carrot, grated

Method:
First wash the quinoa thoroughly to remove the bitterness. Put the grains into a saucepan and add double the amount of water. Bring to the boil and gently simmer, with a lid on, for 18-20 minutes. Drain any excess water and set aside.

In a large frying pan or wok, heat the olive oil and fry the broccoli and tofu together for 5-7 minutes, stirring often.

Add the cashew nuts and cook for 2-3 more minutes, then put in the chopped garlic and give it a minute more. Put in the tomato wedges and cook for 3 more minutes, stirring often, then add the paprika and orange juice. Once the orange juice has simmered for a minute or two, mix in the quinoa and season to taste with the salt and pepper. Heat the whole dish through and mix in the grated carrot. Serve immediately.

*****

Brown, Red and Wild Rice with Courgettes, Peppers and Tomatoes

This dish is made using one of those mixed packs of rice and is a very colourful and enticing way of serving rice as a centrepiece. It works as a meal on its own, but you can also add various side dishes if you're entertaining or want to turn it into an occasion.

Prep time: 20 minutes. Cooking time: about 1 hour 10 minutes
Gluten-Free
Serves 4

Ingredients:
For the Rice:
2 tbsp olive oil
1 medium onion, diced
2 cloves garlic, chopped
250g mixed brown, red and wild rice, washed in a few changes of water and drained

600ml veg stock (make sure it's gluten-free)

For the Vegetables:
3 tbsp olive oil
2 courgettes, diced
2 red or orange peppers, diced
1 red onion, large diced
2 cloves garlic, chopped
3 large tomatoes, cut into wedges
Salt and pepper to taste
A few sprigs fresh dill, chopped

Method:
Heat the oil in a large saucepan that has a lid and fry the onion for 4-5 minutes, until soft and starting to brown. Now add the garlic and fry for 2 minutes more. Stir in the rice for about a minute, until the grains are completely covered with the oil.

Now pour in the veg stock and bring to the boil. Cover with a tea towel and then put the saucepan lid on top to create a tight-fitting lid (keep the towel away from any flames). Turn the heat down to its lowest and cook for 40-45 minutes. Do not stir or remove the lid. Once the time is up, turn off the heat and leave to rest for 10 minutes.

While the rice is resting, cook the courgettes, peppers and onion in the olive oil for about 10 minutes, until beginning to brown. Add the garlic and cook for a minute and then put in the tomatoes and give it about 5 more minutes or so. Season with the salt and pepper and throw in the dill. Stir the vegetables in with the cooked rice and serve immediately.

*****

Brown, Red and Wild Rice with Sugar Snap Peas and Woodland Mushrooms

This is another recipe that will help you use up the pack of mixed rice, if you made the previous one. You can use any pack of wild or woodland mushrooms, or if your local grocer has them loose, just pick the ones you prefer. Oyster and shitake are always a favourite of mine because of their firm texture. The cooking techniques in this are more or less identical to its twin recipe, the only real difference is the vegetable ingredients.

Prep time: 20 minutes. Cooking time: About 1 hour.
Gluten Free
Serves 4:

Ingredients:
For the Rice:
3 tbsp olive oil
250g wild or woodland mushrooms, very roughly chopped
250g brown, red and wild rice
600ml vegetable stock (make sure it's gluten-free)

For the Vegetables:
2 tbsp olive oil
1 clove garlic, chopped
150g sugar snap peas
200g cherry tomatoes, halved
Large handful parsley leaves, roughly chopped
A squeeze of lemon juice
Salt and pepper to taste

Method:
Start with the rice by cooking the mushrooms in the olive oil, using a large saucepan that has a lid. Cook for 5 minutes, until they begin to brown, then stir in the rice. Pour on the veg stock and bring to the boil. As with the previous rice dish, cover with a tea towel and a lid and turn the heat down to its lowest. Cook this way for 40-45 minutes, then leave the lid on and rest for 10 minutes.

To cook the vegetables, sauté the garlic in the oil for 2 minutes, then add the sugar snap peas and cook for a couple of minutes more. Chuck in the tomatoes and cook for another 3-4 minutes, until they have softened, then stir in the parsley leaves and the lemon juice. Season to taste, and then stir the vegetables in with the cooked mushroom rice. Serve immediately.

*****

Creamy Kale Polenta with Roasted Tomatoes

I am deeply in love with polenta. When I have it I think to myself *'why am I not having this all the time?'*

It's true that it can be hard work to cook, and it does make a mess of the pan, but don't let any of that put you off. Polenta is awesome, it's as simple as that. You can buy it in the supermarkets ready-made, but I haven't tried it so can't give it a recommendation. In my experience, however, nothing is as good as when you make it yourself.

This is the course grain cornmeal, which you can buy in the world food section of any supermarket. All you do is whisk it into boiling water to make the polenta. Sounds easy enough, but you do need to get a good whirlpool going and pour the grains in gently to minimise the lumps you might get. I've made that especially difficult in this recipe by adding chopped kale into the mix, which makes whisking it a less than smooth operation. Don't expect to get all the lumps out with this one, but you will get most out if you work at it. When it comes to cooling and setting the cooked polenta, the longer you leave it to set in the dish, the more firm it will become. It is much better when completely cooled, and you'll be able to slice it easily.

The good news it that you can just put the tomatoes in the oven and leave them to it while you're pan-frying the polenta. The only looking-after they need is a quick shake halfway through cooking to make sure they don't stick to the baking tray. To break up the workload you can always make the polenta the night before and keep it in the fridge until you are ready to fry it

My last helpful tip would be to soak the polenta pan as soon as you have finished using it. I then use my whisk to remove any that has stuck to the pan during cooking after it has been soaking for a little while. If you haven't cooked polenta before, then please give it a go. It really is a wonderful staple that deserves much more of a centre stage in our cuisine.

Prep time: 20 minutes. Cooking time: About 35 minutes, plus cooling and setting time.
Gluten Free
Serves 4

Ingredients:
For the Polenta:
2 tbsp olive oil, plus a little extra for greasing
3-4 large kale leaves, stalks removed, roughly chopped then washed and drained
3 cloves garlic, finely chopped
A handful of coriander leaves, chopped
1.2 litres light veg stock (use 1 stock cube), make sure it's gluten-free if needed
200g course cornmeal (polenta)
150ml vegan cream
Salt and pepper to season.

For the Roasted Tomatoes:
7-8 vine tomatoes, cut in half
2-3 tbsp olive oil

Pinch of sea salt
Pinch of dried oregano
More olive oil for frying
Vegan parmesan to top

Method:
To make the polenta, heat the oil in a large saucepan and fry the kale for about 3 minutes, or until it has wilted. Add the garlic and cook for another minute, then add the chopped coriander and give it a minute more.

Pour in the vegetable stock and bring to the boil, then whisk the water to create a whirlpool. While the whirlpool is going, slowly add the polenta, keeping the whisk going at the same time to get rid of as many lumps as possible. You'll still have some but keep coming back to it with the whisk and most will disappear by the time it's cooked. Simmer the polenta for 10 minutes.

Add the vegan cream and season with salt and pepper if desired. Cook for 3-4 more minutes.

Use a little olive oil to grease a deep baking dish and then pour the polenta into it. It will begin to set immediately so flatten it out as best you can. Leave to set until cool, which should take about 90 minutes. When it is cool, tip it out onto a chopping board and cut into 6 even squares. Cut those squares in half again so that each square becomes 2 triangles. You will have 12 triangles of polenta at the end.

Preheat the oven to gas 7/220C/425F.

Put the tomatoes on a baking sheet and drizzle with the olive oil. Season with the salt and oregano and then place at the top of the oven. Cook the tomatoes for 20 minutes, giving them a shake halfway through to make sure none are sticking.

During this time, heat a couple of tablespoons of olive oil in a frying pan, until quite hot. Fry 4 of the polenta triangles at a time, for about 4 minutes each side, until they are crisp and golden. Put the fried polenta in the bottom of the oven to keep warm while you are cooking the rest.

When they are all done. Serve 3 slices of polenta on a plate, top with a few roasted tomatoes and grate on the vegan parmesan.

Creamy Kale Polenta with Roasted Tomatoes

Beetroot Risotto

Prep time: 10 minutes. Cooking time: 30 minutes.
Gluten-Free
Serves 2

Ingredients:
2 tbsp olive oil, more during cooking if needed
2 sticks celery, thinly sliced
1 onion, finely diced
2 whole beetroot, peeled and diced
2 cloves garlic, chopped
½ pack (250g) Arborio risotto rice
1 litre veg stock (make sure it's gluten-free)
A dash of black pepper
A knob of vegan butter
A dollop of vegan cream cheese, plus extra to serve
A handful of coriander leaves, roughly chopped

Method:
Heat the olive oil in a large frying pan or wok and gently cook the celery and onion for about 4 minutes. Stir them often and make sure they don't colour or burn.

Add the beetroot and cook for 4 more minutes, then put in the chopped garlic and give it 2 minutes more.

Now stir in the dry rice for 2-3 minutes, until completely covered with the oil. Pour in the veg stock, about 100ml (1 ladleful) at a time, waiting for the rice to absorb each amount before you add more. This whole process will take about 20 minutes. If you run out of water before the rice is cooked just finish it off with regular water. Don't allow the last ladleful to be completely absorbed, as the dish should be quite wet after cooking and resting.

Stir in the dash of black pepper and then add the knob of butter and the cream cheese. Cover and leave to rest for 5 minutes. Stir in the coriander leaves and then serve the risotto with a dollop more of cream cheese.

*****

Roasted Red Pepper and Aubergine Pasta Sauce

Pasta sauces are great for those nights when you just want to throw something together with the minimum fuss possible. I came up with this one when I suddenly found myself with a load of people to feed and not much time (or many ingredients) with which to do something creative. This dish was literally thrown together with the stuff I had in at the time. Plus, I had my coeliac daughter watching my every move to make sure it was gluten-free! The main flavour came from a jar of roasted red peppers that were in my cupboard, which most supermarkets should have in stock. Just make sure you drain them thoroughly before using them. The result is a rich, tomato pasta sauce with plenty of vegetables to keep you going.

Prep time: 15 minutes. Cooking time: 45 minutes.
Gluten-Free
Serves 4-6.

Ingredients:
2 tbsp olive oil
1 aubergine, diced
2 small courgettes, diced
200g mushrooms, diced
3 cloves garlic, finely chopped
1 x 480g jar of roasted red peppers (or nearest equivalent), drained and diced
3 tbsp tomato puree
1 tbsp dried oregano
2 vegan and gluten-free stock cubes
2 cans chopped tomatoes
½ can cold water
2 tbsp vegan and gluten-free Worcester sauce

Method:
Heat the oil in a medium to large saucepan and fry the aubergine, courgettes and mushrooms together for about 10 minutes, stirring often. Add the garlic and cook for another 3 minutes, then add the roasted peppers. Cook all of this for a further 5 minutes, then add the tomato puree, oregano and stock cubes. Pour over the tomatoes and the water, add the Worcester sauce and then bring the whole lot to the boil. Reduce the heat and simmer for 30 minutes, until you have a thick and rich pasta sauce. Serve with your favourite spaghetti.

*****

Baked Spaghetti with Tomatoes and Parmesan

This is a simple pasta dish with only a few ingredients, all of which are easy to obtain. It makes a perfect mid-week meal, when you don't want any fuss. Garlic, onions and tomatoes are the only vegetables here, but you can always add more if you want to fill it out a little. Mushrooms, peppers and aubergines would work very well. If you want to make this gluten-free, just change the pasta.

Prep time: 10-15 minutes. Cooking time: 1 hour.
Easy to make Gluten-Free.
Serves 4

Ingredients:
500g dried, wholewheat spaghetti
50ml olive oil
3 large cloves garlic, chopped
1 red onion, sliced
150g cherry tomatoes, halved
1 ½ tsp dried oregano
3 tbsp tomato puree
75g vegan parmesan, grated
Salt and pepper to taste
2 tbsp coarse cornmeal

Method:
Bring a large pan of water to the boil and put in the dried spaghetti. Boil for 10-12 minutes, until *al-dente*, then rinse, drain and set aside.

Preheat the oven to gas 7/220C/425F.

Slowly heat the olive oil in a large frying pan or wok and fry the chopped garlic for 3 minutes, moving often. You want to fry them very gently, on a low heat, so that the garlic flavour infuses with the oil. You don't really want the garlic to brown too much during this step, and you definitely don't want it to burn.

When the three minutes are up, add the sliced onion, turn up the heat a little, and cook for another 2 minutes, stirring frequently. Now add the cherry tomatoes and cook for another 3-4 minutes.

Stir in 1 tsp of the dried oregano, all of the tomato puree and cook for a further 2 minutes. Now turn off the heat.

Mix in the drained pasta and two-thirds of the grated vegan parmesan (you might find it easier to use a larger pot to do this). Season generously with the salt and transfer to an oiled baking dish.

In a small bowl, add the remaining grated parmesan, the final ½ tsp of dried oregano and the coarse cornmeal. Mix together briefly and sprinkle over the top of the pasta. Bake in the middle of the oven for 30-35 minutes, until crisp and browned on top.

*****

Quinoa, Beetroot and Date Burgers

Despite the presence of chilli, this is by no means a spicy burger. What the chilli does here is balance the sweetness of the dates and the bulk of the quinoa. If your pallet is sensitive then you might notice it, otherwise you will not. This is a very earthy burger that is also vibrant in colour, due to the beetroot, which is grated raw into the mix. The sweetness comes from dates and coconut nectar (which you can replace with maple syrup if that's easier to get hold of).

The final mix is quite soft, so I would recommend putting the patties in the freezer for at least a couple of hours before cooking them, to help them retain their shape. I froze mine overnight and they held their shape perfectly.

I've kept the recipe entirely gluten-free, but if you have no such issues then you can use any bread you like for both the mixture and final bread rolls. A word of warning here: not all gluten-free bread is vegan, even though it may say dairy-free. Some contain eggs, so make sure you read the packaging.

For the burger salad I've chosen pan-fried thin strips of courgette, to which I added a little sea salt and dried sage. I also used pea shoots instead of lettuce. The dressing is a very simple vegan mayo with a teaspoon of Dijon mustard, but if ketchup is your thing, then go for that.

Prep time: 20 minutes (plus freezing time). Cooking time: 20 minutes.
Gluten-Free
Makes 8-10 patties.

Ingredients:
For the Burgers:
150g raw quinoa, washed and cooked according to packet instructions
200g Mejool dates, pitted
1 large, mild, red chilli, deseeded and roughly chopped
2 tsp dried sage
1 tbsp smoky chipotle sauce (or your favourite sweet chilli sauce).
4 tbsp tamari (gluten-free soy sauce)
1 tbsp coconut nectar (or maple syrup)
2 raw beetroot bulbs, peeled and grated
100g gram (chickpea) flour
150g gluten-free (and vegan) bread, blended into crumbs (or your preferred bread)
1 tsp salt
Sprinkle of black pepper
Olive oil for frying
8 gluten-free (and vegan) bread rolls (or your favourite bread rolls)

For the Salad:
2 tbsp olive oil
1 courgette, thinly sliced lengthways
½ tsp dried sage
Pinch sea salt
Enough pea shoots (or other lettuce) for 8 burgers
4 tbsp vegan mayonnaise

1 tsp Dijon mustard

Method:
Once your quinoa is cooked, set aside and leave to cool.

Put the dates, chilli, dried sage, chipotle sauce, tamari and coconut nectar into a blender. Add a couple of tablespoons of cold water to help facilitate blending, and then blitz until fairly smooth.

In a large mixing bowl, put the grated beetroot and cooled quinoa. Add the blended dates and then mix together. Add the gram flour, breadcrumbs, salt and pepper, and mix thoroughly.

Shape into 8-10 burger shapes and place onto greaseproof paper. Freeze for at least two hours or preferably overnight.

When they are ready to cook preheat the oven to gas 6/200C/400F.

Heat a tablespoon or two of olive oil in a frying pan and fry the burgers, 2-3 at a time, for about 4 minutes on each side, until browned. Place the fried burgers on a baking tray and cook in the oven for about 10 minutes to finish off.

Once your frying pan is empty, heat two more tablespoons of olive oil and fry the courgette slices for a couple of minutes on each side. You may need to do this in batches, and you want them soft but not too coloured. Season with salt and a little dried sage while cooking.

To make the dressing mix the mayonnaise and mustard together in a small bowl.
Serve the burgers on the buns with the pea shoots, courgettes and mustard mayo.

Quinoa, Beetroot and Date Burgers

Brown Rice Salad with Edamame Beans and Toasted Cashews

Quick, easy, healthy and filling. With great flavour to boot, this salad makes a perfect meal or side dish for any time of the week.

Prep time: 15 minutes. Cooking time: 20 minutes, including rice cooking time.
Gluten-Free
Serves 3-4

Ingredients:
For the Salad:
200g frozen edamame beans
1 mug brown rice, cooked to packet instructions (takes about 20 minutes) and cooled
100g cashew nuts
200g baby plum tomatoes, halved
1 red pepper, diced
Sea salt to taste

For the Dressing:
4 tbsp tamari (gluten-free soy sauce)
2 tbsp olive oil

Method:
Bring a small saucepan of water to the boil and cook the edamame beans for 3-4 minutes. Drain and allow to cool (you can rinse in cold water to speed this up). Put the beans in a large mixing bowl with the cooled rice.

Heat a dry frying pan and toast the cashew nuts for 2-3 minutes, until they begin to brown and you get that toasted nut aroma. Be careful not to burn them. Add the nuts to the rice and beans, then throw in the tomatoes and the red pepper.

Pour over the dressing ingredients and stir with a spoon until fully mixed. Keep in the fridge until ready to serve.

*****

Fettuccine with Mushrooms, Vegan Haloumi, Sundried Tomatoes and Pesto

For this recipe I've used an edamame fettuccine, which is gluten-free, in addition to being high in protein and fibre. It's also firmer and more substantial than wheat-based pastas, so you need to eat less of it. Bean or lentil-based pastas are a good alternative for those looking to cut back on their carbs, or who want to increase their plant-based protein intake. That said, you can use any fettuccine you like for this recipe, or use tagliatelle if you prefer.

Prep time: 10 minutes. Cooking time: 25 minutes.
Gluten-Free, if using gluten-free pasta
Serves 3-4

Ingredients:
200g fettuccine, cooked and drained
3 tbsp olive oil
100g vegan haloumi, diced
300g mushrooms, sliced
100g sundried tomatoes (from a jar), sliced
½ batch parsley pesto (see page114)
250ml vegan cream
Salt and pepper to taste

Method:
Heat half the olive oil in a large frying pan or wok and fry the diced halloumi for 6-8 minutes, turning it over halfway through cooking to brown on both sides. Remove the browned haloumi and set aside.

Heat the rest of the olive oil and fry the mushrooms for another 6-8 minutes, until nicely browned. Add the sundried tomatoes, along with a little of the oil from the jar. And cook on a high heat for another 3-4 minutes. Season with a little salt and pepper at this point.

Put the haloumi back in the pan and add the pesto and the vegan cream. Simmer for 2 minutes and then stir in the pasta. Season to taste and serve.

*****

Red Lentil Pasta with Purple Sprouting Broccoli and Garlic Dressing

Purple sprouting broccoli is one of the many great delights of spring: beautifully coloured heads on top of thin and tender stalks. This colourful veggie is one of the first signs that an abundance of great food is on the way. Though it is available all year round in supermarkets, its season runs from January to May, so late winter to spring is the best time to enjoy it. I like to have mine as simple as possible, cooked so that the broccoli is tender but there is still plenty of bite. I prefer to serve it with subtle flavours so as not to mask its clean, nutty taste.

This dish is one that allows the broccoli to be the centre piece. There are no other vegetables served with it because, in my opinion, it doesn't need any. The broccoli is steamed for just a couple of minutes prior to cooking (you can do this either in the microwave or in a steamer), so that it stays firm and retains its vibrant colour. It is far better to steam rather than boil purple sprouting broccoli. Boiling them directly in the water will cause them to not only discolour but also lose their nutrients. It's also extremely easy to overcook them this way. I know some people prefer mushy veg, but the truth is that all the goodness and flavour drains away when you overcook them. With this dish you are also going to pan fry them a little with the pasta, so keeping them under done is essential.

I've used red lentil pasta for this, which you can find in any supermarket. Not only is it gluten-free, but it's also quite a firm pasta that's high in protein. Even if, like me, you have no problem with gluten, it's still worth trying this pasta just as a nutritious alternative to your usual brand.

Prep time: 10 minutes. Cooking time: 15-20 minutes
Gluten-Free
Serves 2-3

Ingredients:
250g (1 pack) dried red lentil pasta (gluten-free)
150g purple sprouting broccoli
3-4 cloves garlic, peeled (or 2-3 tsp garlic mince)
¼ tsp salt (if using fresh garlic)

3 tbsp olive oil
½ tsp Dijon mustard
Juice of 1 lemon
Salt and pepper to taste
Handful of vegan parmesan shavings (shaved with a veg peeler)

Method:

First cook your pasta. Bring a large pot of water to the boil and pour in the pasta. Simmer for 8-10 minutes, until tender. You will need to skim the water a little when the pasta first boils to remove the foam. Drain when it is cooked and plunge straight into cold water to stop the cooking process. Drain again when cooled.

While the pasta is cooking you can steam your broccoli. First cut the bottom of the stem off each head of broccoli, then you can steam one of two ways:

1. Put the broccoli into a microwavable container with about 1 centimetre of cold water at the bottom. Attach a loose-fitting lid, making sure you allow steam to escape, and microwave on full power for 3 minutes.
2. Or you can put an inch or two of water in a saucepan fitted with a steamer and lid. Bring the water to the boil, put the broccoli in the steamer and put on the lid. Steam for 3-4 minutes.

Once the broccoli is cooked plunge it straight into cold water to stop it cooking any further. Drain when cooled.

If you are using fresh garlic, pound the cloves with the salt in a pestle and mortar until you have a paste.

Heat the oil gently in a wok, or large non-stick pan, add the garlic and fry for a couple of minutes on a low heat. You want the garlic to infuse with the oil, so don't cook it too rapidly here. Add the mustard and the lemon juice and turn up the heat a little. Stir to incorporate, then put in the broccoli and pasta.

Cook for 5 minutes or so, stirring often, until the pasta and broccoli have thoroughly heated through. Season with salt and pepper to taste and then serve with thin shavings of the vegan parmesan cheese.

Red Lentil Pasta with Purple Sprouting Broccoli and Garlic Dressing

Root Vegetables

Asparagus with Celeriac Mash, Mushrooms and Garlic Butter

Sweet Potato and Carrot Soup

Lemon and Garlic Roasted New Potatoes

Garlic Braised Swede with Button Mushrooms, Rosemary and Tomatoes

Sautéed Potatoes with Rosemary

Pan-Fried Fennel with Olives, Garlic and Lemon Juice

Dad's Potato Fritters

Onion Bhajis with Cucumber Raita

Baked Rhubarb with Sweet Potato, Swede and Crushed Hazelnuts.

Cumin Spiced Potatoes with Green Beans

Sausage Pittas with Sweet Potato and Beetroot Yoghurt

Roast Parsnip Soup with Cavolo Nero Dumplings and Toasted Cumin Seeds

Roasted Oca Root with Artichoke Hearts and Parsley Pesto

Asparagus with Celeriac Mash, Mushrooms and Garlic Butter

This recipe uses garlic butter through every aspect of it, from the mash to the mushrooms and the asparagus, giving it all a deeply rich, garlic flavour. You can make the garlic butter any time in advance, as it will keep for about 5 days, and have it stored in your fridge ready for use. Mushrooms cooked in garlic butter is such a wonderful combination, and it also makes a great sauce for the asparagus, so you need to add nothing to this dish once you've finished.

Prep time: 20 minutes. Cooking time: 35 minutes.
Gluten-Free
Serves 2-3

Ingredients:
4 cloves garlic, minced or grated on a micro plane
75g vegan butter, softened
2 tbsp lemon juice
A dash of black pepper
3 medium potatoes, peeled and quartered
½ celeriac, peeled and diced
3 tbsp olive oil
200g closed cup or chestnut mushrooms, sliced
200g fresh asparagus, the woody end cut off
50ml vegan cream
Salt and pepper to taste

Method:
First make the garlic butter by combining the garlic, butter, lemon juice and pepper into a small dish or bowl. Mix well and then cover and store in the fridge until ready to use.

Put the potatoes and celeriac into a medium to large saucepan. Fill the pan with water to about an inch over the top of the veg, then bring to the boil. Simmer with a lid on for 15-18 minutes, until tender, then drain and set aside.

While the potatoes are cooking, fry the mushrooms in 2 tbsp of the olive oil for about 5 minutes on a high heat, stirring often. Add a tablespoon of the garlic butter and cook for another 3 minutes on a slightly lower heat. Season with salt and pepper to taste. Set aside and keep warm.

Now heat the remaining olive oil and fry the asparagus for 5 minutes, until browned and *al dente*. Add 2 tbsp of the garlic butter and cook for another 3-4 minutes on a lower heat.
Drain the potatoes and celeriac, add the vegan cream, 1-2 tbsp of the garlic butter and mash in the pan. Season with salt and pepper to taste.

Spoon some mash onto a plate, top with the mushrooms and then the asparagus. Drizzle any remaining garlic butter from the pan on top.

*****

Sweet Potato and Carrot Soup

A simple and warming soup that has a real sense of autumn to it. It has a slightly sweet taste, a wonderful aroma and is thick enough to be a meal unto itself. Just make sure you've got a loaf of your favourite bread to serve it with.

Prep time: 15-20 minutes. Cooking time: about 45 minutes
Gluten-Free
Serves 4

Ingredients:
3 tbsp olive oil
2 medium sweet potatoes, peeled and diced quite small
2-3 carrots, peeled and diced
1 red onion, diced
2 tsp garlic puree
1 heaped tbsp miso paste
3 tbsp tomato puree
2 litres vegan vegetable stock (make sure it's gluten-free)
100ml vegan cream
Salt and pepper to taste

Method:
Heat the olive oil in a saucepan and sweat the potatoes and carrots for 8-10 minutes, moving them frequently, until they are soft and slightly browned. Add the diced onion and cook for another 4-5 minutes. Put in the garlic and give it another minute or so.

Now put in the miso paste, tomato puree and vegetable stock, bring to the boil and simmer gently for about 30 minutes, until all the veg has cooked and the flavours fully infused.

Take of the heat and blend with a hand-blender (if using a jug blender, allow it to cool a bit first to prevent a steam build-up). Put the blended soup back on the stove and stir in the vegan cream. Gently simmer for just a minute or two, season with salt and pepper to taste, and serve.

*****

Lemon and Garlic Roasted New Potatoes

This is a fantastic accompaniment to a variety of dishes that's so easy to make it feels like you're doing nothing at all. The flavour, however, is outstanding. But I'm not going to babble on about it here, all I'm going to say is that you must try them.

Prep time: 5 minutes. Cooking time: 40 minutes.
Gluten-Free
Serves 3-4

Ingredients:
3 tbsp coconut oil
750g – 1kg baby new potatoes, washed and dried
1 whole bulb of garlic, cut in half through the middle of the cloves
Salt and pepper
Juice and zest of 1 lemon
A few sprigs of fresh thyme

Method:
Preheat the oven to gas 7/220C/425F.

Put the coconut oil in a roasting tray and heat in the oven until quite hot. Meanwhile, even out the sizes of the new potatoes by cutting the larger ones in half.

When the oil is hot enough to sizzle the potatoes, drop them into the roasting tray, along with the two halves of the garlic bulb, then season with the salt and pepper and stir to coat everything in the oil. Place in the oven and roast for 30 minutes, moving them around half way through cooking.

After 30 minutes, pull the potatoes out and sprinkle on the lemon zest and squeeze on the juice. Mix the potatoes around again to evenly coat them and then place them back in the oven for another 10 minutes or so, until crisp and browned. When done, sprinkle on the fresh thyme and serve with your main dish.

Lemon and Garlic Roasted New Potatoes

Garlic Braised Swede with Button Mushrooms, Rosemary and Tomatoes

Swede is a hearty winter root that is all too often overlooked in cookbooks. Like many people, I grew up with a dollop of mashed swede piled next to my roast potatoes on a Sunday afternoon, or as the base of some stew. But that was as far as my encounters with the vegetable went. For that reason, I've included a few more creative things to do with it in this book.

This is a one-pot dish that you can serve with potatoes or rice. You need to make sure that the swede is cooked through and tender in the first step, or it will remain firm by the end of cooking. You can test it by piercing it with a small, sharp knife.

Prep time: 10 minutes. Cooking time: about 30 minutes.
Gluten Free
Serves 3-4

Ingredients:
2 tbsp coconut oil
1 swede, about 700g in weight, peeled and diced
200g button mushrooms
1 knob vegan margarine
3 tomatoes, quartered
1 tbsp fresh rosemary, chopped
¼ tsp ground nutmeg
1 ½ tsp wholegrain mustard
150ml vegan cream
Salt and pepper to taste

Method:
Melt the coconut oil in a medium-large saucepan that has a lid and add the diced swede. Cook, with the lid on, for 10-15 minutes, stirring every few minutes, until the swede is tender.

Add the button mushrooms and cook, without the lid this time, for 5-7 minutes, stirring often. When the time is up, put in the knob of margarine and wait for it to melt, then add the tomatoes and rosemary and cook for 5 minutes on a high heat.

Now add the rest of the ingredients and bring to a gentle simmer. Cook for 3-4 more minutes, until you have a thick, rich sauce, and then serve with rice or mash.

*****

Sautéed Potatoes with Rosemary

Prep time: 10 minutes. Cooking time: 35 minutes.
Gluten-Free
Serves 3-4

Ingredients:
4-5 good sized potatoes, peeled and cut into 8-12 pieces each
2 tbsp coconut oil
A generous pinch of salt
2 cloves garlic, chopped

2 sprigs of rosemary leaves, chopped
Juice of half a lemon

Method:
Put the potatoes in a pan of cold water and bring them to the boil. Simmer for 5-6 minutes, until just cooked on the outside but not all the way through, then drain thoroughly.

When the potatoes are completely drained, heat the coconut oil in a large frying pan or wok, until quite hot, and sauté on a medium-high heat for about 20 minutes, stirring often, until they are golden all around.

Season generously with the salt and then turn down the heat a little. Now add the garlic and rosemary and cook for another 4-5 minutes, then squeeze on the lemon juice and give them a minute more. Serve immediately.

*****

Pan-Fried Fennel with Olives, Garlic and Lemon Juice

I put this together having been inspired by Middle-Eastern cooking. The combination of fennel, garlic and lemon juice are incredibly harmonious. Add to that the saltiness of the green olives and the earthiness of the parsley and you've got a stunning lunch or supper to have with fresh bread and some dips (try this with my Baba Ghanoush – page 223). Fennel can take a while to cook all the way through, so make sure the heat is on low enough that the outside doesn't burn before they are tender.

Prep time: 15 minutes. Cooking time: about 40 minutes.
Gluten-Free
Serves 2-3

Ingredients:
3 tbsp olive oil
2 fennel bulbs, sliced to about 5mm (1/4 inch) through the width of the bulb. Keep the root intact to hold it together but cut the tops of the woody stems off.
2-3 cloves garlic, peeled and sliced
100g pitted green olives, halved
Juice of 1 lemon
A good pinch of sea salt
A small handful of flat-leaf parsley, roughly chopped

Method:
Heat the olive oil in a frying pan, or large saucepan, that has a lid. Add the sliced fennel and gently cook for about 20 minutes, stirring from time to time to brown them all over. Start with the lid off then, after 10 minutes of cooking, place the lid on to allow some steam to build up. If you find the fennel getting dry, just add a few tablespoons of water to keep it moist.

Once the fennel is tender, take the lid off the pan and add the sliced garlic. Cook for 3-4 minutes, then put in the olives and cook for 5 minutes more, stirring often.
Squeeze over the lemon juice and give it a good pinch of salt, then put the lid back on the pan and finish cooking for another 5 minutes or so. Serve with bread and dips.

Pan-Fried Fennel with Olives, Garlic and Lemon Juice

Dad's Potato Fritters

These aren't strictly my father's potato fritters, as he puts milk and eggs in the batter and uses regular flour. So, in truth, these are an *adaptation*. A vegan and gluten-free homage to something that would have me running around in glee as a child, knowing they would be for dinner that night. These are, very simply, sliced potatoes that are dipped in batter and deep fried. Most of us deep fry very little at home these days (I only do it myself a few times a year), and air-fryers have become a mainstream kitchen appliance in an attempt to reduce our fat intake. There is, in my opinion, still room for the deep fryer, but only on occasions where it is a necessity to produce a certain type of food.

This, again in my opinion, is one such food.

As a child, when the nation was still in its early transitional period from deep-frying to more healthy options, my family and I would have these fritters every couple of months when my father got the urge to make them. He would dip sliced potatoes in a regular, dairy-based batter, and fry them to a very deep brown. We would have piles of them, served usually with fried eggs, baked beans and lakes of tomato ketchup. Their crisp outer layer, covering soft potato is a fond memory of mine. I asked him about them while writing this, and it turned out that he doesn't dip the potatoes in flour first, just straight into the batter. I have elected for the more traditional flour coating first for better adhesion. I've used a mixture of two flours in the batter: a general-purpose gluten-free flour and gram flour, which I use in this recipe mostly for colour. This is very much a Japanese-style tempura batter, made simply with some seasoning and cold water, also some ice cubes to chill the batter right down. If you have no gluten issues, then just use regular plain flour.

This is glorious chip shop food done in your own kitchen, all you need to do is add lashings of ketchup!

Prep time: 15 minutes. Cooking time: About 12 minutes per batch.
Gluten-Free
Serves 4.

Ingredients:
Enough vegetable oil for deep frying
1 kg potatoes, peeled and cut into slices about 1cm thick, then stored in a bowl of water
About 200g gram (chickpea) flour for dusting

For the Batter:
250g gluten-free flour
100g gram flour
1 ½ tsp salt
A generous sprinkle of black pepper
1 tsp wholegrain mustard
350ml cold water
4 ice cubes

Method:
Fill a saucepan half full with the vegetable oil and, on a medium heat, bring up to frying temperature. DO NOT fill the pan more than half full.

Set the cut potatoes to one side and place the gram flour into a medium sized bowl. Next, whisk all the batter ingredients together in another bowl and line it up next to the gram flour. You should have the three bowls next to each other: potatoes on the left, gram flour in the middle, and batter on the right.

Take about 8 slices of potato from the water and place them in the gram flour. Shake them in the bowl until they are fully coated and then lift them, one at a time, from the flour. Shake off any excess flour and then drop the potatoes, again one at a time, into the batter. Carry the batter over to the pan of hot oil, then test that it is hot enough by dropping a small amount of batter into it. It will sizzle and float if it is hot enough.

Gently lift each potato from the batter and place it into the oil until all 8 are submerged. After they have been cooking for about 30 seconds, gently stir them with a slotted spoon to separate any that have stuck together. Be very careful when doing this to not splash any of the oil onto yourself.

Cook the batch for about 12-15 minutes, until they are golden brown, then lift them out of the oil and onto a plate containing kitchen paper or a tea towel. Allow them to drain for a few minutes while you prepare the next batch. Transfer the cooked potatoes onto a baking tray and keep warm in a low oven while you continue cooking the others. Do this until all the potatoes are gone.

Dad's Potato Fritters

Onion Bhajis with Cucumber Raita

Prep time: 20 minutes. Cooking time: 8-10 minutes per batch, plus 10 minutes in the oven
Easy to Make Gluten-Free
Serves 4

Ingredients:
For the Onion Bhajis:
200g chickpea flour
1 ½ tsp salt
2 tsp mild chilli powder
2 tsp ground turmeric
2 tsp mild curry powder
2 tsp baking powder
300ml cold water
500g (4-5 medium) onions, peeled and thinly sliced
150g plain (or gluten-free) flour
Enough sunflower oil for deep frying

For the Raita:
200g dairy-free yoghurt
1 clove garlic, minced on a micro plane
¼ cucumber, grated
Small handful coriander leaves, chopped
Salt and pepper to taste
Coriander leaves and sliced red chillies to garnish

Method:
Put the chickpea flour, salt, spices and baking powder into a large mixing bowl, then gradually whisk in the water, until you get a smooth, thick batter. Add the onions and flour to the batter and mix until fully incorporated. Leave to rest for 10 minutes.

Fill a saucepan no more than half full with the sunflower oil and bring up to deep-frying temperature.

Take a large spoonful of the batter and use your hands to mould it into a round shape (this is a messy job). Put 3-4 of these balls into the oil and deep fry for 8-10 minutes, until crisp and browned. Drain them onto kitchen paper and repeat until all the batter had been used up.

Preheat the oven to gas 5.

Place the drained onion bhajis onto a baking tray and finish off in the oven for 10 minutes.
To make the raita, put all the ingredients, apart from the garnish, into a bowl and mix together. Cover and chill in the fridge to allow the flavours to infuse, then garnish with the coriander and chilli before serving.

Onion Bhajis with Cucumber Raita

Baked Rhubarb with Sweet Potato, Swede and Crushed Hazelnuts.

Rhubarb lends itself well to savoury dishes if given the right sweetness during cooking. It is also an extremely delicate plant to cook with and as such must be dealt with carefully if you want to keep it intact. For this recipe the rhubarb is baked in a syrup for about 15 minutes, without touching it, until it is soft but not mushy. It is then used as a base for the rest of the meal. If you have not considered using rhubarb in a savoury dish before, I urge you to give this a try. You'll be pleasantly surprised with the results.

Prep time: 10-15 minutes. Cooking time: about 25 minutes.
Serves 2
Gluten Free

Ingredients:
For the Rhubarb:
2 tbsp olive oil
300g fresh rhubarb, cut into 1-inch pieces
2 cloves fresh garlic, hit with the flat of a knife to break it up
1-inch piece fresh ginger, very finely sliced
160g unrefined sugar
3 tbsp water

For the Sweet Potato and Swede Mix:
2 tbsp olive oil
1 small swede, peeled and diced into 1 $\frac{1}{2}$ cm pieces
1 sweet potato, peeled and diced the same
Generous pinch sea salt
2-3 spring onions, finely sliced. Set some aside to garnish at the end.
30g whole hazelnuts

Method:
Preheat the oven to gas 6/200C/400F

To cook the rhubarb, pour the olive oil into a small baking tray that is wide enough to hold all the rhubarb flat. Put the rhubarb onto the tray and toss around in the oil. Add the garlic and the ginger slices, then pour over the sugar and sprinkle on the water. Cook in the middle of the oven for about 15 minutes. You can check it's done by prodding a piece with the back of a spoon. It will give easily. Set aside and allow the rhubarb to sit in the garlic syrup until you are ready to serve it.

Meanwhile make the sweet potato mix. Heat the olive oil in a saucepan that has a lid and fry the sweet potato and swede for 2 minutes, stirring often. Season with the sea salt, then put the lid on the pan and turn the heat down. Cook for about 20-25 minutes, stirring often, until the swede is tender. The potato will have mushed by this time, but that is fine. 5 minutes before the end of cooking, remove the garlic from the rhubarb syrup, chop it up a bit and add it to the swede mix, along with the spring onions.

When this is done, break up the hazelnuts with the bottom of a heavy saucepan, then chop them up just a little.

If the rhubarb has gone cold by this point, just pop it in the oven for a minute or two to heat back up, then divide it between two plates, setting the syrup aside for the moment.
Serve the swede mix on top of the rhubarb, then top with half the crushed hazelnuts and sprinkle on some spring onion to garnish. Pour a couple of spoonfuls of the syrup over the top and serve immediately.

Baked Rhubarb with Sweet Potato, Swede and Crushed Hazelnuts

*****

Cumin Spiced Potatoes with Green Beans

This is a fragrant little Asian side dish that will go with almost any curry you care to put together. It's spicy without being too hot and is a great accompaniment if you're making either a family meal, or have some other guests around that make it worth putting several dishes on the table. The potatoes take a long time to cook, so it's important to make sure they stay hydrated while they are simmering. If your heat is too high you will find that you have no sauce left but the potatoes are still not cooked through, so keep the simmer going gently and add more water if you need to. The desired result is a small amount of thick and intensely-flavoured sauce before you add the cream, but the potatoes need to be quite cooked at this point as the cream will split if cooked for too long.

Prep time: 15 minutes. Cooking time: 1 hour
Gluten-Free
Serves 4 as a side.

Ingredients:
1 heaped tbsp coconut oil
1 cinnamon stick
4 dried red chillies
1 tbsp cumin seeds
1 large onion, sliced
2-3 medium potatoes, skin on and sliced to about 1 cm thick
3 cloves garlic, roughly chopped
1 tbsp ground turmeric
2 tsp ground coriander
2 tsp garam masala
1 tbsp gram (chickpea) flour
500ml veg stock (using 2 stock cubes)

Large handful of frozen whole green beans
100-150ml vegan cream
Salt and pepper to taste

Method:
Heat the oil in a large saucepan or wok and add the cinnamon stick and dried chillies. Cook gently for 2-3 minutes, making sure you don't burn them, then add the cumin seeds and fry for another 40 seconds or so.

Add the sliced onions and the potatoes and then cook for 15-20 minutes on a medium heat, stirring reasonably often but being careful not to break up the potatoes too much.
Add the garlic and cook for another 3 minutes, then stir in the three spices and the gram flour.

Pour in the vegetable stock and bring to the boil, then simmer for 25-35 minutes, until the potatoes are tender, and the sauce thickened and reduced by quite a lot (you can add more water if it runs too dry).
Stir in the green beans and add the vegan cream, then cook for a few more minutes, until the beans are cooked and the potatoes fully tender. Season with salt and pepper to taste and serve immediately.

※※※※

Sausage Pittas with Sweet Potato and Beetroot Yoghurt

This is a nice and quick mid-week thing to do that doesn't take too much effort, which means that you can get to cosying up in front of the TV in no time at all. Use any vegan sausages you like, though firmer varieties will cut better than the softer ones. I cook mine in a little oil in a frying pan, but grill or bake them in the oven if you prefer.

Prep time: 10 minutes. Cooking time: up to 30 minutes.
Serves 2-3

Ingredients:
For the Beetroot Yoghurt:
180g dairy-free yoghurt
4 tbsp olive oil
2 cloves garlic
2 small (or 1 medium) fresh beetroot
Salt and pepper to taste

For the Pittas:
A little oil if frying
6-8 vegan sausages
2 sweet potatoes, peeled cut into small cubes
Green salad leaves such as rocket or baby spinach
Salt and pepper to taste
4-6 pitta breads

Method:
First make the beetroot yoghurt, so that the flavours have a little time to infuse before the rest of the dish is ready. Put the yoghurt into a small dish or bowl and stir in the olive oil. Use the fine side of a grater or a micro plane to very finely grate the garlic into the yoghurt. Now peel the beetroot and do the same with that, grating with the fine side of the grater, to allow it to fully infuse with the yoghurt. Mix thoroughly and then season to taste. Store in the fridge until ready to use.

Cook the sausages, either according to the packet instructions, or by gently frying them in the oil for 15 minutes or so.

While they are cooking you can also cook the sweet potatoes, either by steaming them in a pan for about 8-10 minutes, until they are tender, or by putting them in a microwavable bowl, with a little water and a lid, and cooking them for around 6 minutes or so, until you can easily pierce them with a sharp knife. Drain the cooked potatoes fully.

Now sauté the sweet potatoes in a little more oil, on a good high heat, for about 10 minutes. You'll want to stir them quite often to brown as much of them as possible. Season to taste and set aside.

Once the sausages are cooked, cut them into diagonal slices and set aside.

Toast the pittas and then cut them open from the top (the steam should allow them to open easily). Put a few of the sausage slices in the pitta and then top with some sweet potato. Spoon in a little of the beetroot yoghurt and then top with the salad leaves.

*****

Roast Parsnip Soup with Cavolo Nero Dumplings and Toasted Cumin Seeds

Parsnip soup is always better if you roast the parsnips first, and roast parsnips are always better if you add a little sweetness and some garlic during the roasting. I've used coconut nectar for the sweetness here, but you can substitute that for maple syrup if you prefer. The root is left on the onion to keep it together during roasting. This prevents small onion pieces from burning before the parsnips have had time to roast properly.

The use of finely-chopped kale adds an extra touch to the dumplings and turns them into something a bit more than just flour and suet, plus there's the bonus nutritional value on top. Vegetable suet is not always vegan, so make sure you check the ingredients.

The topping of cumin seeds is entirely optional and depends on your taste. I think it lends an incredible contrasting taste to the soup that works extremely well, but the choice is entirely yours.

Prep time: 30 minutes. Cooking time: 1 hour 40 minutes.
Serves 4

Ingredients:
For the Soup:
3 medium parsnips, peeled and cut into chunks
1 onion, peeled and quartered (leave the root on so that the onion holds together for roasting)
2 cloves garlic, peeled
4 tbsp flavourless oil
Generous pinch salt
1 tbsp coconut nectar (or maple syrup)
2 tbsp vegan butter
1 ½ litres veg stock (made with 2 stock cubes)
2 tsp Dijon mustard

For the Dumplings:
60g vegetable suet (make sure it's vegan)
120g self-raising flour
Salt and pepper
2 leaves of Cavolo Nero kale, washed, stalks removed, and the leaves finely chopped
50ml plant milk

To Top:
2 tbsp coconut oil
½ tbsp cumin seeds

Method:
The first thing you want to do is roast the parsnips. Preheat the oven to gas 6/200C/400F, then put the parsnips, onion, garlic, oil, salt and coconut nectar into a bowl and mix thoroughly with your hands. Lay the mixture out onto a baking tray and place in the middle of the oven for 45 minutes to 1 hour, until the veg is tender and slightly browned.

Now make the dumplings by putting all of the dumpling ingredients into a mixing bowl and bringing together with your hands to form a dough. Knead a little until the dough is fully mixed, then cover and set aside.

Once the parsnips have roasted, you can now begin to make your soup. To do this, melt the butter in a large saucepan, trim the roots off the roasted onions and fry them, with the garlic, for 3-4 minutes, stirring often. Add the roasted parsnips and cook for 4 minutes more.
Now add the veg stock and the mustard and bring to the boil. Simmer for 15 minutes, then take off the heat and blend until completely smooth.

Roll the dumpling dough into small balls (about the size of large marbles), then put the soup back on the heat and add the dumplings. Simmer the soup for a further 15-20 minutes, until the dumplings are swollen and cooked through. Adjust seasoning to taste.

For the topping, heat the oil in a frying pan and gently toast the cumin seeds for 40 seconds, until they are slightly browned and fragrant.

Serve the soup onto bowls, along with some of the dumplings and drizzle the cumin seeds and oil over the top.

*****

Roasted Oca Root with Artichoke Hearts and Parsley Pesto

Oca is an interesting potato substitute native to South America. They are small tubers, often with pink skins that have a tangy, almost lemony taste. They are not overly easy to find, but some supermarkets stock them and your local greengrocer might be able to help you source some. However, if you really can't find them, or are not inclined to go hunting for them, simply substitute them for new potatoes in this recipe. The artichoke hearts I've used are from a can, which saves a lot of fiddling about and filling up your food waste bin with artichoke leaves. Just make sure to rinse them off first to get rid of any briny taste from the liquid they are stored in.

The dish goes well with a parsley pesto, which you can make a couple of days in advance and keep in the fridge for a whole number of uses. The recipe for the pesto makes more than is needed for this dish, so you'll have plenty left over for something else.

Prep time: 20 minutes. Cooking time: 35 minutes.
Gluten-Free
Serves 2

Ingredients:
For the Oca Root:
250g fresh oca roots, thoroughly scrubbed (a toothbrush is ideal for this). Cut any larger ones in half to make the sizes even
A splash of olive oil
A pinch of sea salt

For the Parsley Pesto:
65g cashew nuts
1 large bunch of fresh, flat-leaf parsley, washed
2 cloves garlic, peeled
Juice of 1 lemon
100ml olive oil
100ml sunflower oil
1 tsp Dijon mustard
20g grated vegan parmesan
Salt and pepper to taste

For the Artichoke Hearts:
2 tbsp olive oil

1 can artichoke hearts, washed, drained and cut in half
2 cloves garlic, sliced
Salt and pepper to taste

Method:
Preheat the oven to gas 6/200C/400F.

Put the scrubbed oca roots into a roasting dish. Drizzle on the olive oil and sprinkle on the sea salt. Shake the roots so that they are coated and then put them in the middle of the oven for 25-30 minutes, until crisp, browned and cooked all the way through.

While they are cooking you can make the parsley pesto. Put all of the pesto ingredients, apart from the salt and pepper, into a blender and blend until smooth. Season with the salt and pepper to taste, then cover and put in the fridge until ready to use.

10 minutes before the potatoes finish cooking start working on the artichokes. Heat the olive oil in a frying pan and fry the artichoke hearts for 8-10 minutes, until slightly browned. Add the sliced garlic and cook for another 3 minutes, stirring often, then season with the salt and pepper.

To serve, divide the potatoes between 2 plates. Spoon on the artichokes, plus any garlic and olive oil in the pan, then drizzle on the parsley pesto.

Roasted Oca Root with Artichoke Hearts and Parsley Pesto

Squashes

Pumpkin and Rice Cakes with Lemon Sauce

Pumpkin Chilli Tacos

Halloween Spiced Pumpkin Muffins

Oven-Roasted Courgettes with Salsa Verde

Butternut Squash and Carrot Burger

Winter Squash Stew

Courgettes in Garlic Sauce

Butternut Squash and Celeriac Cakes

Courgette Fritters with Basil and Dill Dressing

Solstice Pie

Roasted Butternut Squash Stuffed with Aubergine Curry

Pumpkin and Lemon Drizzle Cake

Pumpkin and Lentil Stew

Pumpkin and Rice Cakes with Lemon Sauce

When October time comes and pumpkins start appearing in the shops, food writers go crazy developing pumpkin dishes. It's suddenly in every recipe out there, from soups to drinks and anything in between. I'm no exception to this and you'll find a few pumpkin-based delights in this chapter, as well as other parts of the book.

I know why we do it, why these enormous squashes fill our every waking thought during October: it's because we're starved of it through the rest of the year, and because it really is versatile enough to go in so many different things. Brussel sprouts only come out for a short time of the year as well, but I've yet to make a sweet pie out of them. The pumpkin is also big and orange which, in my view, is a real selling point.

So, while you're working your way through the myriad pumpkin recipes out there, and tripping over the ever-increasing number of giant squashes lying around your kitchen, you might want to add this one to the repertoire. This is very similar to a potato cake. The pumpkin is grated, and the excess moisture is squeezed out in a tea towel prior to cooking. It's then mixed with cooked rice and sweet potato (which needs no squeezing), as well as other things, pressed into a patty and shallow fried. If you haven't tried making potato cakes before, they can be a little daunting. It's one of those things that doesn't seem like it's going to work when you put it in the pan, and you can imagine them falling apart the moment you try to turn them. This, of course, can happen, but it's easily avoidable if you turn them gently and with confidence. Also, as the cakes cook, the grated vegetables soften and stick together better, so they are not as fragile as when you first put them in to fry.

Prep time: 15 minutes. Cooking time: 8 minutes per batch, plus 10-15 minutes in the oven.
Gluten Free.
Makes about 16 cakes.

Ingredients:
For the Pumpkin Cakes:
500g pumpkin flesh, grated, the excess moisture squeezed out in a tea towel
1 medium sweet potato, peeled and grated
250g cooked rice (I used a pre-cooked packet)
1 red pepper, finely diced
1 tsp dark, mild chilli powder
2 tbsp nutritional yeast
6 tbsp gram flour
Generous pinch black pepper
150g frozen peas
50ml tamari (gluten-free soy sauce)
3 tbsp natural vegan yoghurt
Generous pinch salt
Oil for shallow frying

For the Lemon Sauce:
50g vegan margarine
2 tbsp gram flour
250ml plant milk
Juice and zest of 1 lemon
1 ½ tbsp maple syrup
½ tsp salt
Pinch white pepper

Avocado slices to serve

Method:
Preheat the oven to gas 6/200C/400F.

Put all the pumpkin cake ingredients, up to and including the frozen peas, into a large bowl and mix together. Now add the rest of the ingredients, apart from the oil, and use either a spoon or your hands to fully combine.

Heat a little oil in a frying pan, until quite hot, and mould about 1 ½ tablespoons of the mixture in your hands to form a round, flat shape. Gently put it into the pan and repeat until you have 4 patties frying. Cook for 4 minutes each side on a medium heat, pressing down occasionally with your spatula to help them brown and hold their shape.

Once the four cakes are browned on each side, transfer them to a baking sheet, then continue shaping and frying the others. Do this until all the mixture is gone, or your baking tray is full, then put the tray in the middle of the oven and cook for 10-15 minutes to finish off.

While the cakes are in the oven, you can make the sauce. Melt the margarine in a saucepan and whisk in the gram flour to make a roux. Add the plant milk, a little at a time, whisking continuously to prevent lumps from forming. As the sauce gets hotter it will thicken. Bring to a gentle simmer and then add the lemon zest and juice, plus the salt, pepper and maple syrup. Simmer gently for about 3 minutes, whisking often.

To serve, put some avocado slices on a plate, stack the pumpkin cakes three high on top of the avocado, then pour over a little of the lemon sauce.

*****

Pumpkin Chilli Tacos

These are a nice little change to regular tacos, plus a great way of getting some extra veg into everybody. Change the pumpkin for any squash if it's not in season.

Prep time: 20 minutes. Cooking time: about 1 hour 15 minutes
Gluten Free
Serves 4

Ingredients:
3 tbsp olive oil
½ pumpkin flesh (about 500g), diced
2 onions, diced
3 cloves garlic, chopped
150g baby plum tomatoes, halved
2 tbsp mild chilli powder
1 tbsp dried oregano
2 veg stock cubes (make sure they're gluten-free)
1 ½ tsp chipotle chilli flakes
2 tsp hot sauce (see my recipe, page 225, or use any hot sauce)
300ml espresso coffee
2 tsp yeast extract
3 tbsp tomato puree
2 cans chopped tomatoes
1 can water
2 tbsp cacao nibs
300g cooked kidney beans
75ml maple syrup
100g dried vegan and gluten-free mince (regular vegan mince is fine if you have no issues with gluten, but use a small pack of the frozen kind)

8=10 taco shells

Method:
Heat the olive oil in a large pan and cook the diced pumpkin for about 15 minutes, until tender. Add the onion and cook for 3-4 minutes more, then add the garlic and give it another 2 minutes, stirring often. Now put in the baby tomatoes and cook, on a high heat, for about 3 minutes or so, until they have softened.

Stir in the chilli powder, oregano, veg stock and chipotle chilli flakes and cook for 3 minutes to release their flavour. Now put in the rest of the ingredients, apart for the vegan mince, bring to the boil and then gently simmer, with a lid on, for 30-35 minutes, stirring from time to time to prevent sticking.

Now add the vegan mince and cook for another 10 minutes with the lid on. Take off the lid and give it 5 more minutes on a higher heat to evaporate as much water as possible. Season to taste if needed.

Allow the chilli to cool a little and then spoon into the taco shells. Top with lettuce, grated vegan cheese and vegan sour cream.

*****

Halloween Spiced Pumpkin Muffins

We love Halloween in our house, and we go all out every year with the decorations and the food. We dress up and take our son out to trick-or-treat in the early evening and we have party food waiting for us at home, even if we're not having anyone around. For me, of course, the food is very important, and it shouldn't just be for the kids. I've created some more grown-up muffins that aren't as sweet as others and that are topped with vegan cream cheese.

With their delicate hints of cinnamon, ginger and nutmeg they are certainly aimed more at the adult pallet, but that doesn't mean the little ones can't enjoy them as well. They also use the buckwheat flour to keep them gluten-free. Give them a try this year, or at any time over the autumn, just remember to keep them refrigerated.

Prep time: 20 minutes. Cooking time: 35 minutes.
Gluten Free.
Make 12-14 muffins.

Ingredients:
350-400g diced pumpkin flesh (half a small pumpkin)
1 tbsp flaxseeds (I used ground)
4 tbsp cold water

Dry Ingredients:
300g buckwheat flour
1 tsp baking powder
1 tsp bicarbonate of soda
½ tsp salt
250g unrefined light brown sugar
2 tsp ground cinnamon
1 tsp ground ginger
½ tsp mixed spice
½ tsp ground nutmeg

Wet Ingredients:
1 tsp vanilla extract
60g vegan margarine, softened
300ml almond milk
2 tbsp golden syrup

30g pumpkin seeds, plus extra to decorate
1 tub vegan cream cheese.
You will also need a 12-hole muffin tin and spooky Halloween muffin cases.

Method:
Preheat the oven to gas 6/200C/400F.

Cook the pumpkin flesh by either steaming it or putting it in the microwave with a little water and a loose lid. Microwave on 80% power for 6 minutes. Steam for 8-10 minutes until the flesh is soft. Drain and set aside to cool.

Mix the flaxseeds with the water and leave for 10 minutes to form a gloopy mixture. Put all the dry ingredients into a large bowl and combine, then add the wet ingredients, including the flaxseed mixture and the drained pumpkin and blend together with a whisk until you have a smooth batter. Stir in the pumpkin seeds at the end.

Line your muffin tin with the cases and spoon the mixture into each one until about half a centimetre below the top.

Cook at the bottom of the oven for 25 minutes, until a toothpick comes out clean when inserted. Allow to cool and then either pipe or spoon the cream cheese on top. Decorate with some more pumpkin seeds.

Halloween Spiced Pumpkin Muffins

Oven-Roasted Courgettes with Salsa Verde

This is a nice little side or accompanying dish to go with a whole range of other foods. The courgettes are cut in half lengthways, tossed in olive oil and seasoning, then roasted until soft and browned. That really is the only cooking involved. That doesn't mean you won't get a bit of a workout making this: all the herbs for the Salsa Verde have to be chopped by hand until quite small, so you'll definitely get some exercise.

You can make the dressing ahead of time. Do bear in mind, however, that the olive oil will solidify in the fridge, so it will have to be taken out a good half hour or so before you are planning to use it. The Salsa Verde can also be made on its own to put with something else if you like.

Prep time: 15 minutes. Cooking time: 30-35 minutes.
Gluten-Free
Serves 2-4

Ingredients:
For the Roasted Courgettes:
4 courgettes, cut in half lengthways
3 tbsp olive oil
Salt and black pepper

For the Salsa Verde:
A small handful of mint leaves
A small handful of parsley leaves
A small handful of basil leaves
4 small (or 2 medium to large) gherkins
2 tbsp capers
2 cloves garlic
125ml olive oil
3 tbsp white wine vinegar
1 tsp Dijon mustard
Salt and pepper to taste.

Method:
Preheat the oven to gas 7/220C/425F

Place the courgettes into a mixing bowl and add the olive oil and salt and pepper. Mix around with your hands until the courgettes are fully coated. Place them onto a baking tray, flesh side up, and pour any remaining oil from the mixing bowl over them. Roast in the middle of the oven for 20 minutes. Turn the courgettes over with cooking tongs, so that they are face down and roast for another 10 minutes. Turn them back the right way up again and cook for a further 5 minutes if necessary.

While the courgettes are cooking, chop all of the herbs with the gherkins and capers, until quite fine. Put them into a mixing bowl and then chop the garlic as fine as you can. Put the garlic in the bowl, then pour in the olive oil. Add the white wine vinegar and mustard and mix the whole lot until fully incorporated. Season with salt and pepper to taste.

Serve the courgettes while hot, 2 or 4 to a plate, and drizzle over the Salsa Verde.

Oven-Roasted Courgettes with Salsa Verde

Butternut Squash and Carrot Burger

This burger is not only full of flavour but also very light, so that you don't feel like you've eaten a load of stodge once you've finished. The main ingredients in this are butternut squash and carrots, both of which are grated raw into the mix. The binding comes from ground flaxseeds mixed with orange juice, which also serves to give you a good boost of fibre. You can make the mix the day before if you would prefer, but it can also be done right before cooking. The recipe makes about 8 thick patties, which are totally good for freezing. My advice is to shape all the burgers and then wrap up those you are not going to use. Just make sure to put a square of greaseproof paper between each patty before you freeze them, so that you can separate them out again later.

Prep time: 20 minutes. Cooking time: 10 minutes, plus 15 minutes in the oven.
Make 8-10

Ingredients:
3 tbsp ground flaxseeds
Juice of 1 orange
½ small butternut squash (about 300g), peeled and grated
2 medium carrots, peeled and grated
1 red pepper, deseeded and finely diced
1 red chilli, deseeded and finely sliced
200g bread, about 1 day old
1 can haricot beans, drained
1 ½ tsp flaked sea salt
A dash of black pepper
50g coarse cornmeal
3 tbsp sweet chilli sauce

To Cook:
2 tbsp groundnut oil per batch for frying.

Method:
Preheat the oven to gas 6/200C/400F.

First mix the flaxseeds with the orange juice in a small bowl and leave to set while you put together the rest of the ingredients.

In a large mixing bowl, add all the ingredients up to, but not including, the bread. Put the bread into a food processor and blitz until you get fine breadcrumbs. Pour those in with the other ingredients, then add everything else on the list, including the flaxseeds. Give it a good mix with a large spoon and then use your hands to bring it all together so that it binds.

Place a sheet of greaseproof paper down on a flat surface, which you will use to place your shaped burgers. You can use a moulding ring, a pastry cutter, or just your hands if that's what you have. If you're using a ring or cutter, place it on the greaseproof paper and fill it with some of the mixture. Press it in tightly and then remove the ring. You can then press it down slightly with the palm of your hand to make it a little flatter and wider. Do this until all the mixture is gone.

Heat 2 tbsp of oil in a non-stick frying pan and fry 2-4 of the burgers, depending on the size of your pan, for 4-5 minutes on each side, until golden brown. Repeat this with all the burgers you are using, then put them on a baking tray. Cook them in the middle of the oven for 10-15 minutes, until they are cooked through.

Butternut Squash and Carrot Burger

Winter Squash Stew

A winter stew can take the chill out of a cold night and fill you with warming goodness, all from a single bowl. It's like a magic pot of slow-cooked heaven. There's barely a one of us who cannot recall digging into a bowl of nourishing stew in their early years. Its ease of cooking (all done in one pot) and its capacity to not only feed an entire family with minimum effort, but also its uncanny ability to vacuum up any and all leftover vegetables out of the fridge, make it a solid choice for all sensible cooks.

Some peoples' stews will remain the same year after year (my grandmother was a prime example of this), while others will vary each and every time. I belong to the latter group because, to me, you make a stew out of what's lying around. If you have squash, swede and carrots, as is the case with this recipe, that's what you make a stew out of. If you happen to have courgettes, spring onions and flat leaf parsley, then there's no reason not to use those and make something different. That's the beauty of them. This recipe uses winter veg with the addition of some more contrasting ingredients like tomatoes and tamari, which add real depth to it. A sprig of rosemary thrown in early will gently infuse through the whole thing by the time cooking is done, and never underestimate the depth of flavour that can be achieved by adding a teaspoon or two of yeast extract.

Prep time: 20-30 minutes. Cooking time: 1 hour 45 minutes.
Gluten-Free
Serves 4

Ingredients:
2-3 tbsp olive oil
1 small winter squash, peeled, deseeded and diced
2 carrots, peeled and sliced
1 red onion, peeled and diced
½ swede, peeled and diced
2 cloves garlic, chopped
3 medium tomatoes, cut into wedges
1.2 litres veg stock (using 2 stock cubes – make sure they're vegan and gluten-free)
50ml tamari
A generous dash of vegan Worcester sauce (also gluten free)
2 tsp wholegrain mustard
1 tsp yeast extract
A generous dash of black pepper
2 medium potatoes, peeled and diced
1 small sprig of rosemary

Method:
Heat the oil in a large saucepan. Add the squash, carrots, onion and swede and sweat on a low-medium heat for 10-15 minutes, until they have softened slightly. Put in the garlic and the tomatoes and cook for 5 minutes more, stirring often.

Pour in the veg stock and add the rest of the ingredients. Bring the stew to the boil, turn down the heat and gently simmer for about 90 minutes, stirring from time to time to prevent sticking. About 20 minutes before the end of the cooking time, mash the veg up a little using a potato masher. This will also help thicken the stew.

Serve with your favourite bread.

*****

Courgettes in Garlic Sauce

This is a quick and easy pasta dish using fresh courgettes and a good amount of garlic. You want to cut the courgettes as thinly as you can, so that they fold nicely into the pasta at the end. A mandolin or a vegetable peeler is ideal for this task. You can save any leftover courgette and use it to make a soup at a later date. Grated or pureed garlic is better for this recipe, as it will dissolve in the sauce, rather than remaining in lumps if you were to simply chop it. Cook pasta ahead of time, or use this dish to make use of any leftover pasta already in the fridge.

Prep time: 10 minutes. Cooking time: 15 minutes.
Easy to make Gluten-Free.
Serves 2-3

Ingredients:
3 tbsp olive oil
2 courgettes, cut into thin lengthways strips using either a veg peeler or a mandolin
3 cloves garlic, grated on a micro plane (or use 2 tsp garlic puree)
200ml vegan cream
1 tsp all-purpose flour (use gluten-free if desired)
1 tsp dried oregano
Juice of ½ lemon
100ml cold water
Salt and pepper to taste

2-3 servings of cooked pasta
Vegan parmesan to top

Method:
Heat 2 tbsp of the olive oil and gently fry the courgette slices for 6-8 minutes, turning from time to time to ensure even cooking (be careful not to break them while doing this). Once they are cooked, empty them out onto a plate and set aside.

Wipe the pan clean and heat the remaining tablespoon of olive oil. Gently fry the minced garlic for 2 minutes, stirring often and being careful not to burn it. Pour in a little drop (about 2 tbsp) of the vegan cream and stir in with the garlic. Add the flour and mix well, to form a roux, then gradually pour in the rest of the cream, stirring constantly.

Now add the oregano, the lemon juice and the water and bring to the boil. Simmer for 2-3 minutes, until you have a sauce consistency, then season with the salt and pepper to taste. Put the courgettes back into the sauce, then stir in the cooked pasta and warm until it is heated through. Serve into bowls and top with the vegan parmesan.

*****

Butternut Squash and Celeriac Cakes

Prep time: 15-20 minutes. Cooking time: 8 minutes per batch, plus 15 minutes in the oven.
Makes about 15.
Gluten-Free

Ingredients:
½ celeriac (about 500g), peeled grated and mixed with a little lemon juice
600g butternut squash, peeled and grated
A small bunch of coriander, chopped
1 tsp salt
A generous dash of black pepper
2 tbsp ground paprika
1 tbsp sriracha sauce (or other mild chilli sauce)
3 tbsp buckwheat flour
150ml orange juice
2 tbsp olive oil
3 cloves garlic, chopped

Enough flavourless oil, such as sunflower oil, for shallow frying

Method:
Put all of the ingredients, apart from the olive oil and garlic, into a large bowl and mix together.

Heat the olive oil in a frying pan, but make sure it is not too hot. Add the chopped garlic and gently fry for 2 minutes, stirring continuously, until the garlic has infused into the oil. Make sure the garlic does not burn as this will create a bitter flavour. Now pour the garlic and the olive oil into the cake mix and stir until fully combined.

Take about 2 tablespoons of the mixture into your hands and press together into a ball, then flatten it slightly with your palm and set aside on a plate. Repeat this until all of the mixture has been used up. This should make about 15 patties.

Preheat the oven to gas 6/200C/400F.

Wipe clean the frying pan and heat enough flavourless oil to allow for shallow frying. Fry the cakes in batches of three or four for about 4 minutes each side, until golden brown and crisp, then turn them out onto a baking tray. Once all of the cakes have been cooked, put the baking tray in the middle of the oven and cook for a further 10-15 minutes to finish off.

*****

Courgette Fritters with Basil and Dill Dressing

Vegetable fritters are an ingeniously tasty way of getting vegetables in you. They're basically a pancake batter that's crammed with whichever vegetables you happen to have lying around. I've chosen courgettes and spring onions because of their fresh taste and the fact that courgettes grate really well (though you do have to squeeze the moisture out before cooking them).

These are ready to start frying in about 10 minutes and are also gluten-free, so everybody can enjoy them. They are great to have with rice, or even some bread and humous. I had mine this way with the addition of some stuffed vine leaves. Pan-fried tomatoes give these a real Mediterranean feel, so it's worth considering this in your choice of accompaniments.

Prep time: 10 minutes. Cooking time: 6 minutes per batch, plus about 8 minutes for the tomatoes.
Gluten-Free
Serves 4.

Ingredients:
For the Batter:
200g chickpea flour
3 tbsp nutritional yeast
1 tsp salt
Pinch black pepper
1 tsp Dijon mustard
2 tsp garlic puree
300ml cold water

For the Veggies:
2 courgettes, washed
2-3 spring onions, thinly sliced
A few sprigs fresh dill, chopped
2 tbsp flavourless oil per batch for frying

For the Basil and Dill Dressing:
30g fresh basil leaves
30g fresh dill
2 tsp garlic puree
10g vegan parmesan, grated
30g chopped hazelnuts
¼ tsp salt
200ml olive oil

Juice of ½ lemon

To Serve:
3-4 Large tomatoes, cut into quarters
1 tsp dried oregano
Pinch salt
A few sprigs of fresh dill.

Method:
First make the batter by putting all the batter ingredients, apart from the water, into a mixing bowl. Add the water gradually, whisking the whole time to prevent lumps from forming.

Grate the two courgettes with a standard grater, then put the gratings onto a clean tea towel and squeeze them out over the sink to get rid of as much moisture as possible. Add them to the batter, then put in the spring onions and dill and stir until combined. Set aside until ready to cook.

Now make the basil and dill dressing by putting all of the dressing ingredients into a blending jug and blending until completely smooth. Pour the dressing into a container and chill until ready to use.

Heat two tablespoons of oil in a frying pan, until quite hot, then spoon 2 heaped tablespoons of the courgette batter into the pan to make one fritter. Do this three or four times, leaving room between each fritter so that you can easily turn them over (I comfortably got four in my pan).

Cook the fritters for 3-4 minutes each side over a medium high heat, until they have browned nicely, then transfer each batch to a low oven to keep warm. Repeat this until all of the batter is gone.

To cook the tomatoes, heat a little more oil in the pan and fry the tomatoes for 6-8 minutes, until they start to char (they will spit quite a bit during this, so you might want to use a splatter guard to protect your cooker top). Add the dried oregano and salt to the tomatoes about 1 minute before the end of cooking.

To serve, put 4 of the fritters onto a plate and drizzle over the dressing, serve some of the tomatoes on the side and add a sprig of dill.

Courgette Fritters with Basil and Dill Dressing

Solstice Pie

My wife, Samantha, thought of the name. This pie is made using seasonal produce from the autumn and the winter and was created around the winter solstice. It is essentially a pumpkin pie with cranberries, and comes out looking very much like a giant jam tart. It is incredibly delicious and is perfect to make around that crossover point in the seasons. It is worth buying a few extra pumpkins in the autumn and hanging onto them until you start seeing fresh cranberries in the stores. Pumpkins keep very well in a cool part of your house and will last into the winter. This pie is best served chilled.

Prep time: 30-40 minutes. Cooking time: 1 hour 15 minutes, plus cooling time.
Makes 1 large pie

Ingredients:
For the Pastry:
½ batch sweet apple pie pastry (see page 75)
Vegan margarine for greasing

For the Pumpkin Filling:
½ medium sized pumpkin, peeled, diced and cooked until tender
280ml vegan cream
100g golden caster sugar
100g brown sugar
2 tbsp apricot jam
1 tsp vanilla extract
1 tsp agar agar
½ tsp mixed spice
¼ tsp ground nutmeg

For the Cranberry Filling:
300g fresh cranberries
250g golden caster sugar
1 tsp vanilla extract
50ml water

Method:
Grease a 9 ½ inch (24cm) loose-bottomed tart tin with vegan margarine and preheat the oven to gas 4/180C/350F.

Put all of the pumpkin filling ingredients into a saucepan and bring to the boil. Simmer for 5 minutes, allow to cool slightly and then blend until completely smooth.

Now put all of the cranberry filling ingredients into a saucepan and simmer for 15 minutes, until you have a jam-like consistency. Allow to cool a little again.

Pour the two fillings separately into the pastry case and give them a little swirl with a spoon to marble them slightly.

Now place the tart tin on a baking tray and bake in the lower-middle part of the oven for about 1 hour 15 minutes. Allow the tart to cool in the oven with the door ajar before transferring it to the fridge to completely chill. Serve with vegan ice cream or vegan cream.

*****

Roasted Butternut Squash Stuffed with Aubergine Curry

Prep time: 25 minutes. Cooking time: about 1 hour 45 minutes
Gluten-Free
Serves 4

Ingredients:
For the Roasted Butternut Squash:
2 small butternut squashes
2-3 tbsp olive oil
½ tsp ground cinnamon
Generous pinch sea salt

For the Aubergine Curry:
2 tbsp coconut oil
1 onion, diced
½ aubergine, diced
1 red pepper, sliced
2 large cloves garlic, chopped
3 medium tomatoes, cut into wedges
1 red chilli, sliced
1 tsp turmeric
1 tbsp ground coriander
2 tbsp tandoor masala curry powder (or similar curry powder blend)
1 tbsp paprika
1 tsp salt
3 tbsp tomato puree
4-5 tbsp plain dairy-free yoghurt
Handful fresh coriander leaves, chopped
250ml cold water

To Garnish:
1 red chilli, thinly sliced
A few coriander leaves
Small amount of sunflower seeds

Method:
First roast the butternut squash. Preheat the oven to gas 5. Cut each squash in half lengthways and then scoop out the seeds on both sides. Rub the olive oil all around the squashes and then sprinkle the cinnamon and salt over the flesh. Place the squashes onto a baking tray and bake in the middle of the oven for about 1 hour 15 minutes, or until they are browned and feel tender when pierced with a sharp knife.

Once the squashes are cooked you can make the curry, just turn the oven down low to keep them warm. Heat the coconut oil in a large wok or saucepan and fry the onions, aubergines and peppers for 5 minutes, until softened. Add the garlic and cook for 2 more minutes, then add the tomatoes and sliced chilli and cook for 5 minutes more.

Add all of the spices, the salt, tomato puree, yoghurt and coriander and stir in. Cook for 2 minutes, then add the cold water. At this point scoop out a little of the centres of the squash, to make a place for the curry to sit, and then add the flesh to the curry. Bring the water to the boil and simmer for 10 minutes, stirring often.

Load the squashes with the curry and then top with the sliced chilli, coriander and sunflower seeds. Serve with rice.

Roasted Butternut Squash Stuffed with Aubergine Curry

✶✶✶✶✶

Pumpkin and Lemon Drizzle Cake

If you don't have any pumpkin, then butternut squash will make a good substitute in this recipe. The squash won't be quite as moist as the pumpkin, so you may need to add a little more yoghurt into the cake mix if you're taking that option.

This is quite a moist cake mix, and as such you need to cook it for longer. To prevent the top from burning, place a sheet of greaseproof paper over the batter and then foil on top of that. This will prevent the cake from browning, so you'll be taking it off for the last 20 or 30 minutes of cooking. If you have no gluten issues, just use regular self-raising flour and leave out the xanthan gum.

Prep time: 30 minutes. Cooking time: 1 hour 40 minutes, plus cooling time.
Gluten Free
Serves 12

Ingredients:
400g vegan margarine, plus extra for greasing
400g unrefined sugar
5 tbsp vegan natural yoghurt
2 tsp vanilla extract
800g pumpkin flesh, diced, steamed for 15 minutes, and well drained (make sure to squeeze moisture out of the cooked pumpkin)
Juice and zest of 2 lemons
400g gluten-free self-raising flour (or regular self-raising if you prefer)
50g gram (chickpea) flour
2 tsp baking powder
2 tsp xanthan gum (leave out if not using gluten-free flour)

For the Syrup:
250g unrefined sugar
75ml lemon juice
3 tbsp golden syrup

Method:
Preheat the oven to gas 4/180C/350F.

Put the margarine and sugar into a large mixing bowl and beat with an electric whisk, until you get a light and fluffy mixture. Now add the yoghurt, vanilla, pumpkin and lemon juice and zest and beat again until it is fully incorporated.

Add the two flours, the baking powder and the xanthan gum and gently mix with a wooden spoon until you have a smooth cake batter.

Grease a large, square cake tin (use a large round if that's what you have) and line the bottom with greaseproof paper. Pour in the cake batter and gently shake the tin a little to even it out. Cover the top with another sheet of greaseproof paper and then place a sheet of tin foil loosely on top of that. Bake in the lower part of the oven for 1 hour and 10 minutes, then remove the top foil and greaseproof paper and bake for another 20-30 minutes, until the top is golden and risen and a toothpick inserted comes out clean.

Let the cake cool in the tin for 10 minutes and then turn it out, upside down, onto a wire rack. Remove the bottom sheet of greaseproof paper, which will now be on top, but do not discard it. Instead, place it back in the tin, in its original position. Allow the cake to completely cool.

Once the cake has cooled, slide it off the rack and onto a chopping board, then cut it with a sharp knife into 12 equal pieces, making sure to keep it all together in its original shape. Once it is cut, place the cake tin back over it, with the greaseproof paper in place. Press the cake tin and the chopping board together and gently turn the whole thing over, so that the chopping board is now on top. Remove the chopping board to reveal the cake back inside its tin, with the greaseproof paper once again at the bottom.

Now make the syrup. Put all of the syrup ingredients into a small saucepan and bring to a gentle simmer. Simmer for 2-3 minutes, until the syrup is clear and golden, then take off the heat. Leave it to cool slightly for about 10 minutes, then gently pour it all over the cut cake. Allow the cake and syrup to cool completely and then cover and refrigerate for a few hours or overnight.

Pumpkin and Lemon Drizzle Cake

Pumpkin and Lentil Stew

Prep time: 20 minutes. Cooking time: about 90 minutes
Gluten Free
Serves 4

Ingredients:
2 tbsp coconut oil (or other oil)
600g pumpkin flesh, peeled and diced
1 red pepper, diced
2 small apples, diced
3 tbsp tomato puree
1.2 litres veg stock (make sure it's gluten-free)
¼ tsp mild chilli powder
2 tsp Dijon mustard
1 tsp ginger paste
2 tbsp ground paprika
3 tbsp tamari (gluten-free soy sauce)
1 can cooked lentils, drained
1 carton coconut cream (250ml)
Salt and pepper to taste

Method:
Heat the oil in a large saucepan and cook the pumpkin flesh for about 15 minutes, until it is tender and a little browned. Add the diced pepper and apples and cook for 5-7 minutes more. Now put in the tomato puree, veg stock, the spices and the tamari. Bring it all to the boil and simmer for 20 minutes.

After this time, add the cooked lentils and simmer for another 40 minutes or so. About 15 minutes before the end, use a potato masher to mash up the veg in the stew a little bit, this will help create a thicker stew consistency.

Once the cooking time is up, stir in the carton of coconut cream and give it another 10 minutes. Season with salt and pepper to taste, then serve with your favourite bread.

More 'Meaty' Things

Very 'Meaty' Vegan Mozzarella Burgers

Moroccan Style Vegan Sausages

Spinach and Vegan Mince Koftas

Vegan Sausages with Kale and Beans

Vegan Chicken-Style Nuggets

Apple and Red Onion No-Meatballs

Vegan Tenders with Kale and Apple Slaw and Homemade Fries

Vegan Cheese, Ham and Sundried Tomato Slices

Very 'Meaty' Vegan Mozzarella Burgers

I refer to the term 'meaty' quite loosely here. It's intended meaning being something of substance, something that you can chew on. Once you've been vegan for a while you lose any taste you once had for meat (at least that has been my experience), but it still is nice to get something with some real texture, especially when it comes to burgers. To achieve this, I've turned to vital wheat gluten, which provides an incredible amount of texture to any patties, or sausages that you might be making. You can buy vital wheat gluten online, or at health food stores. In my house I have to be careful with it, as my daughter is coeliac. She thinks I'm a whole new breed of evil for buying the very thing she's allergic to in concentrated form, but I keep it in a sealed container and am ginger with its application.

This recipe uses soya mince, as well as vegan mozzarella, which is mixed in with the patty to allow it to melt while cooking. It is very much a vegan replica of the traditional way of making burgers and, as a result, produces a deeply satisfying meal.

Prep time: 15 minutes. Cooking time: 25 minutes.
Makes 4-6 Patties

Ingredients:
150g dried or fresh vegan soya mince (if using dried, rehydrate in hot water for 10 minutes then drain well)
1 small onion, finely diced
6 tbsp dark soy sauce
½ cup (75g) vital wheat gluten
3 slices granary bread, blended into crumbs
50ml tamari
1 tbsp dried oregano
2 ½ tsp English mustard
Pinch black pepper
1 tsp harissa paste
50g grated vegan mozzarella style cheese
Oil for frying

Method:
Put all the ingredients, apart from the oil, into a large mixing bowl and mix thoroughly with your hands. Leave to stand for 10-15 minutes.

Shape the mixture into burger patties of your desired size (I use a mould for this) and set aside on greaseproof paper.

Preheat the oven to gas 6/200C/400F.

Heat some oil in a frying pan and fry the burger patties, in batches, for about 4 minutes each side, until they are nicely browned and sealed. Place the sealed burgers on a baking sheet in the oven and cook for a further 10 minutes or so to finish off. Serve in burger buns with your favourite dressings.

Very 'Meaty' Vegan Mozzarella Burgers

Moroccan Style Vegan Sausages

I'm crazy about vegan sausages, so I'm always finding new and interesting ways to create an evening meal with them. You can use any vegan sausage you have lying around the fridge or in your freezer for this recipe. The firmer types will hold up better when cooking in the sauce, so choose these if you can.

Prep time: 10-15 minutes. Cooking time: 30 minutes.
Serves 2-3.

Ingredients:
2 tbsp olive oil
2 medium carrots, peeled and cut into batons
200g fresh green beans, stalks removed (you can also use frozen)
1 medium onion, sliced
1 apple, diced
2 cloves garlic, chopped
4 vegan sausages, sliced widthways to about 1cm thick
2 tbsp ground paprika
1 tbsp mild curry powder
2 tsp ginger paste
½ tsp ground cinnamon
1 veg stock cube
Zest of half an orange
Juice of whole orange
1 can chopped tomatoes
½ can water
A small handful of coriander leaves, roughly chopped
2 tbsp coconut nectar (or maple syrup)

Method:
Heat the olive oil in a large saucepan or wok and fry the carrots and green beans together for 4-5 minutes, stirring often. Add the onion and fry for 2 more minutes, then add the apple and give it two minutes more. Put in the chopped garlic and the sliced sausage and cook for a couple more minutes, then add the spices, the veg stock, the orange juice and zest, the canned tomatoes and the water. Bring to the boil and simmer for 20 minutes, until you have a thick sauce. Stir in the chopped coriander and the coconut nectar and serve with rice.

*****

Spinach and Vegan Mince Koftas

Koftas are traditionally beef or lamb, but thankfully we can make them perfectly using frozen vegan mince from the supermarket. I haven't as yet found the same kind of mince that is also gluten-free, which means that this dish wouldn't be so easy to make a gluten-free version of. Hopefully that will change in the future. That being said, you might be aware of a product that I am not, so it's worth further investigation.

Koftas are great to have with rice and salad, or on flatbreads, with a good dollop of dairy-free yoghurt and humous. A little squeeze of your favourite hot sauce does wonders too. You can also try mixing the above yoghurt with about 1 tsp of mint sauce to add a refreshing minty taste to this dish. They'll keep for a few days and can easily be reheated either in the microwave or in the oven, so you can make them in advance. They will, of course, always be better straight out of the pan the moment you make them.

Prep time: 20 minutes. Cooking time: up to 40 minutes.
Serves 3-4

Ingredients:
2 tbsp olive oil
1 onion, diced
3 cloves garlic, chopped

1 bag of frozen vegan mince (about 500g)
50ml tamari
1 tsp ground cumin
2 tsp ground coriander
1 tbsp fresh thyme leaves, chopped
2-3 handfuls of ready-to-eat baby spinach leaves
4-5 tbsp plain dairy-free yoghurt
6 tbsp general purpose flour

Oil for shallow frying

Method:
Heat the olive oil in a frying pan and gently cook the onion for 5 minutes, until soft and translucent. Add the garlic and cook for 2-3 minutes more, stirring often to prevent burning.
Pour the bag of vegan mince into the pan and cook, on a slightly higher heat, for about 6-8 minutes, until it is cooked through. Keep it moving while cooking to stop it from sticking to the bottom of the pan.

Now add the rest of the ingredients apart from the flour and the oil and cook, stirring continuously, for another 3-4 minutes.

Take off the heat and transfer to a mixing bowl. Stir in the flour and then leave until cool enough to shape.

Once the mixture has cooled, preheat the oven to gas 6/200C/400F. Shape the mix into small, round patties and fry in hot oil for 6-8 minutes, turning frequently. You will probably have to do this in batches. Transfer the cooked patties to the oven for 10 minutes to finish off.

*****

Vegan Sausages with Kale and Beans

Frozen vegan sausages don't always have to be cooked in the oven and then served with chips. Sometimes you might want to do something a little more adventurous with them. There's also nothing wrong with using pre-made, frozen sausages in a whole variety of healthy vegan meals. Just remember, if you were eating meat, you wouldn't make your own pork sausages for a casserole, would you?

You can use whichever are your favourite. It's important to shallow fry them before cutting them up. This will not only make them taste better, but also firm the outside up so that they hold together better. The beans I've used for this are cannellini, but you can use any that you have lying around. Because of my choice of sausages, this recipe is not gluten-free, so make sure to change those if you have a problem with gluten.

Prep time: 10 minutes. Cooking time: 15-20 minutes.
Easy to make gluten-free.
Serves 1-2

Ingredients:
2 tbsp olive oil
3 vegan sausages
1 red onion, peeled, cut in half, and then cut into thick wedges
2 handfuls ready-cut kale (or cut up 3-4 leaves)
50ml cold water
5 cherry tomatoes, halved
1 small, or half a full size can of cannellini beans, drained
2-3 tbsp tamari
Pinch of black pepper
Pinch of salt (if required)

Method:
Heat the oil in a large frying pan or wok and fry the sausages for 4-5 minutes on a medium heat, moving them often to cook all around. Add the onion wedges and cook for another 4 minutes. Once the onions are soft and

slightly browned, remove the sausages and cut them into chunks when they are cool enough to handle (I use tongs for this).

Put the kale in with the onions and fry for 2 more minutes, then pour in the water. It should bubble and steam immediately. Cook this down for 4 more minutes, then add the cherry tomatoes, the cannellini beans, the tamari and the pepper. Cook for 3-4 minutes, until you have a small amount of sauce and everything is cooked through, then put the cut sausages back into the pan. Gently stir the sausages in and add salt only if necessary (I did not), bring everything back up to temperature, then serve straight away.

Vegan Sausages with Kale and Beans

Vegan Chicken-Style Nuggets

This is a little something for kids and grown-ups alike. Sure, you can buy these already frozen in the supermarket, but nothing beats making them yourself. For one thing, you know exactly what's going into them. It's surprisingly easy to make a chicken substitute, and once again we're using the vital wheat gluten, which binds this recipe together and gives it it's firm 'meaty' texture. It is also the key ingredient in this and lots of other meat substitute recipes.

This batch of basic vegan 'chicken' breast can be used in most recipes where you want a chicken substitute, including shaping it into a fillet and pan-frying it. You can use it as soon as you make it, but it does bind and shape much better if you make it the day before, or at least give it a few hours to chill in the fridge, giving the gluten time to do its magic.

You'll need a food-processor, *not* a blender. A food processor runs more slowly and chops and mixes the food together, which is what you want here. You blitz it until it comes together into a large doughball, and that really is about as complicated as making this stuff gets. All you do then is chill it in an airtight container. There's also nothing to stop you making a few batches and freezing some for later use. You could either freeze it as one block, or shape it into what you want first and then freeze it. If it's properly wrapped it'll last a couple of months in the freezer.

Prep time: 10 minutes, plus chilling and setting time. Cooking time for the nuggets: about 8 minutes per batch. Makes about 28 nuggets.

Ingredients:
For the 'Chicken':
1 x 400g block firm tofu, drained
1 cup (140g) vital wheat gluten
Juice of 1 lemon
½ small onion, diced
1 clove garlic, finely chopped or grated with a fine grater
A dash of black pepper
½ tsp salt
1 tbsp tamari
2 tbsp water, if the mixture seems too dry.

For the Batter:
150g plain flour
2 tbsp gram flour
1 tsp baking powder
1 tsp salt
1 tsp garlic granules
½ tsp Cajun seasoning
½ tsp ground ginger
1 tsp Dijon mustard
350ml plant-based milk

You Will Also Need:
150ml plant milk, to dip the nuggets in
100g gram (chickpea) flour for dusting the nuggets
Enough vegetable or sunflower oil for deep frying.

Method:
To make the 'chicken' substitute, put all the ingredients, apart from the water, into a food processor and blitz until it forms a doughball. This takes about 90 seconds. Check to see if it feels a little dry and, if it does, add the 2 tablespoons of water and blitz again. If you are unsure, just add the water anyway.

Take the blade out for safety and then remove the doughball from the food processor. Pack the dough into an airtight container and place in the fridge, preferably overnight but at least for a few hours.

When the dough is ready, remove it from the container and tear off small pieces about the size of a large marble. Roll each one into a ball and then place it in the circle made by touching the index finger and thumb of one hand. Use the fingers of the other hand to press the dough into a nugget shape. This will give you perfect nugget size every time. Do this until all the dough is used up.

Now make the batter by putting all the batter ingredients, apart from the milk, into a mixing bowl and then gradually whisking in the milk, until you have a reasonably lump-free mixture.

Now take two more bowls and pour the 150ml of milk into one and the 100g gram flour into the other. Line the containers up so that you have milk on the left, flour in the middle and batter on the right.

Fill a saucepan half full with the vegetable oil and heat, on a medium heat, to frying temperature. DO NOT fill the pan more than half full.

Take about 8 nuggets and place them in the milk for just a moment, then take them out and put them in the gram flour. Shake them in the bowl until they are fully coated and then lift them, one at a time, from the flour. Pat off any excess flour in your hands and then drop the nuggets, again one at a time, into the batter. Carry the batter over to the pan of hot oil, then test that it is hot enough by dropping a small amount of batter into it. It will sizzle and float if it is hot enough.

Gently lift each nugget from the batter and place it into the oil until all 8 are submerged. After they have been cooking for about 30 seconds, gently stir them with a slotted spoon to separate any that have stuck together. Be very careful when doing this to not splash any of the oil onto yourself.

Cook the batch for about 8-10 minutes, until they are golden brown then lift them out of the oil with the slotted spoon and onto a plate containing kitchen paper or a tea towel. Allow them to drain for a few minutes while you prepare the next batch. Transfer the cooked nuggets onto a baking tray and keep warm in a low oven while you continue cooking the others. Do this until all the nuggets are gone, then keep them warming in the oven until you are ready to serve them.

Vegan Chicken-Style Nuggets

Apple and Red Onion No-Meatballs

Prep time: 25 minutes. Cooking time: 30-35 minutes.
Makes about 14.

Ingredients:
1 red onion, roughly diced
1 yellow pepper, roughly diced
1 red apple, cored and roughly diced
2 tbsp olive oil
A drop of cold water
1 tbsp cider vinegar
150g day-old bread, blended into breadcrumbs
1 tsp dried sage
½ tsp mild chilli powder
50ml tamari or soy sauce
Juice of 1 lemon
½ tsp salt
A generous dash black pepper
100g vital wheat gluten
200ml cold water
Flour for dusting
Enough Oil for shallow frying

Method:
Put the onion, yellow pepper and apple into a food processor and blitz for a few seconds, until they are chopped into small pieces.

Heat the olive oil in a pan and fry the mixture for about 10 minutes, adding the drop of water and cider vinegar at the end to prevent burning. Turn off the heat and allow the vegetables to cool.

Transfer them to a mixing bowl and add the rest of the ingredients, apart from the dusting flour and frying oil. Mix, first with a spoon or knife and then with your hands, until fully incorporated, then leave to rest for 15 minutes.

Use your hands to mould the mixture into balls approximately golf ball size, using the dusting flour to help you, and place the balls on a plate, ready for cooking.

Heat the frying oil in a large frying pan and cook the no-meatballs, in batches, for 8-10 minutes, turning often, until they are golden and crisp all around and cooked through.
Keep warm in a low oven until they are ready to use.

Serve with a tomato sauce, such as the pizza sauce in this book (page 209), and spaghetti.

*****

Vegan Tenders with Kale and Apple Slaw and Homemade Fries

To make the Vegan Tenders:
Ingredients:
For the Tenders:
½ 400g block (200g) firm tofu, drained
100g (3/4 cup) vital wheat gluten
Juice of 1 lemon
½ small onion, finely diced

1 clove garlic, micro planed or chopped
Dash black pepper
1 tsp salt
1 ½ tbsp nutritional yeast
2 tsp BBQ seasoning
1 tbsp tamari
75g plain flour
50ml cold water

For the Batter:
275g plain flour
1 tbsp mild chilli powder
2 tsp Cajun seasoning
1 tbsp oregano
2 tbsp nutritional yeast
2 tsp salt
1 tsp wholegrain mustard
1 tsp harissa paste
1 tsp garlic puree
3 tbsp tomato puree
450ml cold water

150g plain flour for dusting
1 tsp salt.
Enough sunflower oil for deep frying

Method:
To make the tenders, put all the tender ingredients, up to and including the tamari, into a food-processor and blitz until everything is chopped up fine and brought together into a dough ball. Put the contents of the food-processor into a mixing bowl and add the flour and the water. Stir with a table knife and then knead with your hands for approximately 10 minutes, until you have an elastic dough consistency.

Bring a saucepan of water to the boil. While it is coming to the boil, divide the dough into 12 equal parts, then roll those into sausage shapes, about 4 inches in length. Use the palm of your hand to flatten out the sausage shapes.

When the water is boiling, put in the tenders and simmer, with a lid on, for 20 minutes. Drain and allow to cool.

To make the batter, put all the batter ingredients, apart from the water, into a mixing bowl and then add the water, a little at a time, whisking constantly to prevent lumps from forming.

Once the tenders have cooled, put them in a bowl of cold water to soak, then take a third bowl and put in the 150g plain flour and the salt.

Fill a saucepan NO MORE THAN HALF FULL with the sunflower oil, and bring up to frying temperature. While the oil is coming up to temperature, line up your three bowls so that you have the vegan tenders on the left, the seasoned flour in the middle and the batter on the right.

Preheat the oven to gas 4/180C/350F.

Take 4 of the tenders from the water and put them in the flour. Give the flour a gentle shake to completely coat the tenders, then transfer them over to the batter, making sure to shake off any excess flour first. Cover the tenders fully in the batter, then take the batter bowl over to the hot oil. Check that the oil is at the right temperature by dropping a little of the batter into it. It will bubble and rise to the surface straight away.

Now gently add your four tenders, one at a time, to the oil and deep fry for 6-8 minutes. After they have been cooking for about a minute, use a slotted spoon to gently move them around a bit, so that they don't stick to each other. When they are golden brown, remove them with the slotted spoon and drain them off on a piece of kitchen paper. Repeat this process until all the tenders are cooked, then put them onto a baking sheet and place in the middle of the oven to keep warm.

To make the Kale and Apple Slaw:
Ingredients:
3-4 black kale leaves, washed, stalks removed and finely sliced
50g walnuts, roughly chopped
2 celery stalks, finely sliced
40g raisins

For the Dressing:
100g vegan mayonnaise
1 tsp wholegrain mustard
Juice of ½ lemon
Salt and pepper to taste
Splash of white wine vinegar
3 tbsp maple syrup (or coconut nectar)
1 red apple, very finely sliced

Method:
Put the first 4 ingredients into a mixing bowl. Put all the dressing ingredients into a separate bowl and mix together with a whisk or fork, until fully combined. Pour the dressing over the ingredients in the mixing bowl, then add the sliced apple. Mix thoroughly, making sure the apple is completely covered with the dressing to keep it from going brown. Store in the fridge until ready to use.

For the Homemade Fries:
2-3 medium potatoes (sweet potatoes are also great for this)
Oil for deep frying

Method:
Wash the potatoes, leaving their skins on, and cut them into slices just under 1 cm in thickness. Cut those slices again into strips, so that the potatoes are cut into fry shapes.
Deep fry, in batches if necessary, until the fries are crisp and golden. Drain on some kitchen paper and serve immediately with a little sea salt.

To assemble the meal:
Lay a wrap on a chopping board. Take two vegan tenders and cut into slices, then place them along the middle of the wrap. Spoon on some of the kale and apple slaw, then drizzle on your favourite hot sauce. Roll the wrap closed and cut in half, then serve with a portion of the homemade fries.

Vegan Tenders with Kale and Apple Slaw and Homemade Fries

Vegan Cheese, Ham and Sundried Tomato Slices

These are basically vegan pasties, which is kind of like the Holy Grail of vegan junk food. At the time of writing there aren't many of these around (though there has been a recent surge of vegan sausage rolls appearing in stores). So, until the day comes when we can stroll into our local bakery and pick from a range of plant-based pastries, get to making this one, and when you've got that down, start experimenting with your own fillings.

This slice uses ready-rolled puff pastry, so do check that the brand you are using is vegan. Most of them are, so you should be fine. There is also a gluten-free version made by Jus Roll, so use that pastry if you want to make these coeliac-friendly (you will also need to find a coeliac-friendly vegan ham).

Prep time: 20 minutes. Cooking time: 35 minutes, plus cooling time.
Easy to make gluten-free
Makes 4 large slices

Ingredients:
2 tbsp vegan margarine
1 medium onion, thinly sliced
150g sundried tomatoes from a jar, sliced, plus a little of the oil
1 tsp garlic puree
100g vegan ham or bacon, chopped (find gluten-free, if needed)
½ tsp Dijon mustard
2 tbsp gram flour
350ml plant milk, plus extra for brushing
200g vegan cheese, cut into small cubes
2 tbsp nutritional yeast
½ tsp salt
Pinch black pepper
2 rolls of ready-rolled vegan puff pastry
Pinch of sea salt to top

Method:
Melt the margarine in a saucepan and cook the onions for about 4 minutes, stirring often, until soft and translucent. Add the sundried tomatoes, along with some of the oil, and cook for another 2 minutes, then put in the garlic puree and give it a minute more. Now add the ham pieces and the mustard and cook for 2 more minutes, then stir in the gram flour. Gradually pour in the plant milk, stirring continuously to prevent lumps from forming, then add the cheese, nutritional yeast and salt and pepper. Bring to the boil and simmer for 2 minutes, stirring all the time, until the cheese has melted, and you have a very thick sauce. Allow to cool.

Preheat the oven to gas6/200C/400F.

Lay out 1 sheet of the ready-rolled pastry on top of greaseproof paper. Gently cut the sheet widthways into three equal rectangular pieces then spoon about one sixth of the mixture (you may have a little left over at the end) onto the bottom half of each piece. Don't over fill them or it will all come out the sides. Brush all around the edges of the pastry with the plant milk and then fold the empty top half of the pastry over the filling. Gently press around the edges with a fork to seal them.

Repeat this with the three pastry rectangles, then set them onto a baking sheet lined with greaseproof paper. Repeat the process again with the second roll of pastry, until you have six of the vegan slices.

I managed to fit all six of mine onto one baking sheet, but if you can't do this then cook them in two batches.

Once the slices are on the baking sheet, pierce the tops a little with a sharp knife to let steam escape and then gently score the tops of the slices into diamond shapes, being careful not to go right through the pastry.

Brush all of the slices with plant milk and then sprinkle with sea salt.

Bake in the middle of the oven for 20-25 minutes, until they are golden and risen. Allow to cool a little before serving.

Vegan Cheese, Ham and Sundried Tomato Slices

Nuts

Cranberry and Raisin Granola Protein Bars

Roasted Aubergine and Walnut Pesto

Vegan Christmas Stuffing Balls

Salad of Vegan Halloumi and Tomatoes with Cashews and Potato Bread

Vegan Aubergine, Blue Cheese and Walnut Spring Rolls

Christmas Fruit and Nut Roast Stuffed with Pears Mushrooms and Tomatoes

Sweet and Spicy Almonds

Vegan Lemon Tart

Coffee, Banana and Walnut Pie

No Bake Blueberry Tart

Cranberry and Raisin Granola Protein Bars

Sometimes we're all in a hurry and need something quick to eat and being vegan can, on occasion, really limit you when you're on the go (I can't tell you how many times I've had to have a packet of crisps or peanut brittle for my lunch while out at work, simple because there was nothing else to choose from). Though things are getting better out there, it's always good to have something in your bag for when you need a quick energy boost. I've created this recipe with that in mind. It's a cereal bar with added pea protein. You can make them in the evening after work, or at the weekend if you prefer, then take them into work with you. The recipe makes 20 bars, so there's plenty to last you for the whole working week. It is better to toast the oats first, so that the bars don't come out too soft. I also heat the dates up with the syrup mixture, which softens them and helps them blend better. Use gluten-free oats if you need to.

Prep time: 20 minutes. Cooking time: 20-25 minutes. Chilling time: 2 hours.
Easy to make gluten-free
Makes 20 bars

Ingredients:
200g porridge oats
50ml groundnut, or other flavourless oil
Pinch sea salt
100g pitted dates
3 tbsp coconut oil
4 tbsp coconut nectar
75ml maple syrup
50g pea protein
50g toasted almond flakes
50g dried cranberries
50g raisins
You will also need a deep-sided baking tray approximately 30cm long and about 20cm wide.

Method:
Preheat the oven to gas 4/180C/350F.

First toast the porridge oats by putting them into a mixing bowl with the oil and the salt. Mix thoroughly, then pour out onto your baking tray. Cook in the middle of the oven for 20 minutes, then give them a bit of a stir and cook them for another 5 minutes. Set aside to cool.

While they are cooking, heat the dates, coconut oil, coconut nectar and maple syrup in a saucepan, until bubbling slightly and the dates have softened (about 3 minutes). Let it cool a little, then pour the mixture into a blender and blend until smooth.

Pour the oats back into your mixing bowl and add the pea protein, almonds, cranberries and raisins and mix together. Scrape in the blended date mixture and stir until completely combined.

Line the baking tray with greaseproof paper, making sure it covers the sides, then spoon the oat mixture into the tray. Press down firmly with your hands until it is tight into the corners and flat. It should be just under 1cm thick all around. Put it in the fridge to chill for 2 hours.
To serve, turn the tray upside down onto a chopping board and cut into 20 bars.

Cranberry and Raisin Granola Protein Bars

Roasted Aubergine and Walnut Pesto

The unfortunate thing about pesto is that it comes in teeny tiny little jars. Also, there are only a couple around that are vegan and gluten-free. It is so easy to make your own, however, and so much better tasting than the shop bought variety. Most pesto recipes you can just shove into a food processor and blitz until it is ready. This recipe does require the extra step of roasting the aubergine and garlic together first, rather than simply blending everything. Trust me, it's worth it. When you try it, you'll see why you went to the trouble.

Prep time: 15 minutes. Cooking time: 40 minutes, plus cooling time.
Makes about 500g.

Ingredients:
1 aubergine
1 bulb of garlic
3 tbsp olive oil
Salt and pepper
60g walnuts, either halves or pieces
30g fresh basil leaves
8 sundried tomato pieces from a jar
2 tbsp tomato puree
75ml olive oil
75ml rapeseed oil
½ tsp salt
Generous dash black pepper

Method:
Preheat the oven to gas 6/200C/400F.

Remove the stalk from the aubergine and cut it in half lengthways. Cut each half in half again so that you have 4 pieces. Now take the garlic bulb and cut it straight through the middle of the cloves, so that each clove is cut in half. The top half of the bulb will probably come apart while doing this. Put the aubergine and garlic into a mixing bowl and add the 3tbsp of olive oil and a little salt and pepper. Mix around until everything is coated and then transfer to a baking tray. Cook in the middle of the oven for 40 minutes, turning the aubergine and garlic half after 25 minutes to avoid them getting too dry. The aubergine is ready when you can easily slip a sharp knife into the flesh. Set aside to cool.

Once the aubergine and garlic have cooled, remove the aubergine flesh with a spoon and put it into a food processor. Pop out all the roasted garlic flesh from the bottom half of the garlic bulb and put those in the food processor also. Refrigerate the remaining garlic from the top half for another dish.

Put the walnuts, basil, sundried tomatoes and tomato puree into the food processor and then pour in the two oils. Pulse on full speed for a second or two at a time until you have a fully amalgamated mixture, then add the salt and pepper and pulse again.

Transfer the pesto to an airtight container and keep in the fridge for up to a week.

Vegan Christmas Stuffing Balls

This recipe uses ready-made stuffing mix as a base. I used sage and onion (and, of course, made sure it was vegan) but you can use whichever is your favourite. You can do your own breadcrumbs and flavourings if you want to. I personally think there's enough to do on Christmas day already, so I try to cut a few corners where I can. There is a lot in this recipe that isn't gluten-free. You can leave them all out, but they will probably not have that firm sausage-like texture that this recipe gives you. I've rolled the mixture into balls and pan-fried them, but you can coat them in a little oil if you like and put them in the oven. I tend to put mine in the oven to keep warm after I've fried them anyway, unless I'm jostling for space with everything else that's got to go in there.

Prep time: 15-20 minutes. Cooking time: 25 minutes, plus 30 minutes rest time.
Makes about 22

Ingredients:
2 tbsp oil
1 large onion, finely diced
1 can braised tofu, chopped
75g dried apples (about 6 slices), chopped
60g dried cranberries
1 tsp garlic puree
1 tsp wholegrain mustard
1 heaped tsp yeast extract
800ml hot, light veg stock (made with 1 stock cube)
340g (2 packs) sage and onion stuffing mix (make sure it's vegan)
50g vital wheat gluten
Salt and pepper to taste
Oil for shallow frying

Method:
Heat the oil in a frying pan and fry the onion and braised tofu together for 6-8 minutes. Add the dried apples and cranberries and cook for 4-5 minutes more. Put in the garlic puree and give it another two minutes.

Now add the rest of the ingredients, apart from the frying oil, and mix them all together until fully combined. Cover and leave to rest for about 30-40 minutes, until all the water has been absorbed and the mixture is cool enough to easily handle.

Roll into balls roughly the size of golf balls and set aside on a plate, then heat enough oil to shallow fry in your frying pan. When the oil is quite hot, put in about 8 stuffing balls (depending on the size of your pan. You want to give them room to move about) and fry on all sides for 8-10 minutes, until crisp and brown all over. Place in the oven to keep warm while you fry the next batch, or set aside to reheat later.

Vegan Christmas Stuffing Balls

Salad of Vegan Halloumi and Tomatoes with Cashews and Potato Bread

This is one of those 'what have I got in the fridge?' recipes. My wife, Samantha, had bought some potato bread that she wanted me to do something with, and we had some leftover Vegan haloumi in the fridge that needed eating. These, and a few other miscellaneous ingredients, and you've got yourself a good meal. I chose to make a warm salad using tomatoes, cashews and coriander, in addition to some orange slices placed on top. The only dressing I used for this was balsamic vinegar. Trust me, it's all you need.

Prep time: 15 minutes. Cooking time: 15 minutes.
Serves 2

Ingredients:
2 tbsp olive oil
2 wedges (1 pack) vegan haloumi cheese, each cut into 4 strips
4 slices (1 pack) potato bread, make sure it's vegan
50g cashew nuts
1 clove of garlic, very thinly sliced
200g baby plum tomatoes (cherry tomatoes are also fine) cut in half
2 tbsp balsamic vinegar
Pinch sea salt
One medium orange, peeled with a knife
A small handful of fresh coriander leaves, torn with your hands

Method:
Heat the oil in a frying pan and fry the haloumi strips, on a high heat, for about 4 minutes on each side. They should be slightly browned when done, but not burned. Set aside on a plate and cover to keep warm.

Put the potato bread slices in the hot pan, without adding any more oil, and fry for about 1 minute on each side, until just a little browned. When done, serve two each onto two plates.

Now add a drop more oil to the frying pan and cook the cashews and garlic on a medium heat for 2 minutes, moving them often to make sure they don't burn. Add the tomatoes and cook for another 2 minutes, to soften them just a little. Pour in the balsamic vinegar and add the pinch of salt, then cook until some of the vinegar has evaporated. Turn off the heat.

Serve the haloumi evenly on top of the potato slices and then top with the tomato and cashew mixture. Take your orange and cut into slices. Place them on the top of the dish and then sprinkle over the torn coriander leaves. Serve immediately.

Salad of Vegan Halloumi and Tomatoes with Cashews and Potato Bread

Vegan Aubergine, Blue Cheese and Walnut Spring Rolls

I first put vegan blue cheese in a spring roll some months back at a party for which I was catering. Those spring rolls went almost before the gathering had even begun. Something about that sharpness of the blue cheese with the crisp bite of the spring roll pastry was astounding, so much so that those who ate them, myself included, didn't want to stop, and there were people at the party who didn't even get a chance to try them.

These are a little different to those spring rolls, in that the rest of the filling has changed, but that same moreish taste remains. The wrappers for these are easily bought at any Chinese supermarket, and usually come in a couple of different sizes or amounts in the pack. If you're not making many then get the smallest pack you can, as the whole thing has to be defrosted to be able to pull any lose. There's room to be a little more generous with the filling in these than there are with dumplings, which are much smaller. You still don't want to over-stuff them, however, or they'll leak during cooking.

Prep time: about 30 minutes. Cooking time: about 35 minutes
Makes 15-18

Ingredients:
3 tbsp olive oil
½ aubergine, very finely diced
1 red pepper, very finely diced
1 ½ tsp fresh thyme leaves, chopped
50g walnuts, chopped small
1 ½ tsp garlic paste
1 tsp Dijon mustard
100g vegan blue cheese, finely chopped
A generous pinch of salt
2 tbsp natural dairy-free yoghurt
Oil for brushing
About 18-20 spring roll wrappers, defrosted

Method:

Heat the olive oil in a large frying pan and fry the aubergine and peppers for 4-5 minutes, moving them around often to prevent burning. Now add the thyme leaves and cook for another 2 minutes. Add the garlic, mustard and blue cheese together and cook for a couple more minutes, until the cheese has melted. Season with the salt and spoon in the yoghurt. Stir it all in thoroughly, keeping the heat going for a couple of minutes more, then transfer the mix to a bowl and allow to cool.

Once the filling has cooled down, preheat the oven to gas 6/200C/400F and line a baking tray with greaseproof paper. Lay out a spring roll wrapper so that one of the four corners are pointing towards you. Place about 2 tsp of the mixture towards the end of the wrapper and roll the end over to form a spring roll shape. Roll the wrapper tightly, tucking in the sides, until you have a small triangle left at the end. Wet this with water and stick down to seal. Repeat this until all the filling is used, then place the spring rolls on the baking tray and brush with oil. Cook in the oven for 20-25 minutes, until golden brown.

Vegan Aubergine, Blue Cheese and Walnut Spring Rolls

Christmas Fruit and Nut Roast Stuffed with Pears Mushrooms and Tomatoes

This is a very hearty, gluten-free main course that has so much of a taste of Christmas that my family and I got the full sense of the festive season while we were eating it. The recipe calls for fresh, unshelled chestnuts, but you can go ahead and use pre-cooked ones if you prefer. Make sure, when you serve it, that each guest gets some of the orange topping. The flavour is incredible.

Prep time: Up to 1 hour. Cooking time: about 3 ½ hours
Gluten-Free
Serves 6-8

Ingredients:
For the Fruit and Nut Roast:
850g chestnuts (weight while still in their shell)
2 tbsp oil, plus extra for greasing
100g vegetable suet (make sure it's vegan)
150g pecan nuts
140g chopped, dried apricots
75g dried cranberries
3-4 cloves fresh garlic, peeled and bashed with the flat of a knife
1 red onion, peeled and roughly chopped
150g buckwheat flour
100g gram (chickpea) flour
50ml tamari
¼ tsp ground nutmeg
100ml cold water
½ tsp salt
Large pinch black pepper

For the Filling:
2 medium pears, peeled and sliced
3-4 chestnut mushrooms, sliced
8 cherry tomatoes, halved
30g dried cranberries
Handful of whole pecans
75g redcurrant jelly
50g marmalade
Salt and pepper to taste

For the Topping:
2 tbsp oil
1 large orange, cut into thin slices
2 tbsp brown sugar
50ml cold water
1 heaped tbsp marmalade

Method:
First you need to cook the chestnuts. Preheat the oven to gas 6/200C/400F and, using a small serrated knife, cut a cross into the top of each chestnut. Be careful here as it is so easy to slip and cut yourself.

When all the chestnuts are crossed, put them onto a baking tray and pour over the two tablespoons of oil. Mix the chestnuts so that the oil covers all of them, then roast in the oven for 35-45 minutes, until the shells are crisp and the nut inside is tender. Remove from the oven and allow the chestnuts to cool enough to be able to handle them easily.
If the nuts peel easily then remove the shell from each one and put the flesh into a bowl. If they do not come off easily (mine didn't) then break the shell apart and scoop the flesh out with a teaspoon (don't worry, you are going to process it anyway).

Turn the oven down to gas 5/190C/375F.

Once all the flesh is free from the shells, discard the shells and put the flesh into a food processor. Put in the vegetable suet, pecans, apricots, cranberries, garlic and onion, and process until quite smooth. This is a large amount, so do it in batches if you need to.

Pour the processed mixture into a large mixing bowl and add both the flours. Stir it all together to fully combine, and then add the rest of the nut roast ingredients. Mix well and bring together with your hands to form a dough.

Grease a lipped baking tray with a little oil and then line it with greaseproof paper, making sure it goes up over the sides of the tray. Place the dough in the middle of the tray and roll out so that it is even and fills out all sides (I used a plastic beaker for this instead of a rolling pin).

Once it is rolled out, line the middle of the dough with the pears, mushrooms, tomatoes, cranberries and pecans. They should form a line that stops about 3cm from the edge of the dough (see picture). Put the redcurrant jelly and marmalade together in a microwavable bowl and microwave them for about 30 seconds, until they are almost liquid. Mix them together and pour them over the top of the filling, then season with the salt and pepper. Now the hard bit: bring up the left and right edges of the chestnut dough, so that they are easier to seal when you roll the whole thing. Grab the sides of the greaseproof paper closest to you and furthest away from you, and draw them together, so that the dough rolls up around the filling. Press together any parts of the dough where the filling might leak out, and then wrap the rest of the paper around it. Take another sheet of greaseproof paper and place that on top of the rolled dough. Wrap that around as well, so that the dough is now covered with two sheets of greaseproof paper. Tuck any loose bits of paper in so that it is nice and tight.

Now do the same with two sheets of tin foil, wrapping the top and bottom to completely cover the roast. Get some kitchen string and tie the rolled log shape together (you might want a second person to help you with this). You should now have a tightly-wrapped, large sausage-shaped roast, tied together with string (see picture).

Take the same baking tray you rolled the dough into and fill it about one third full with cold water. Place the wrapped roast into the centre of the water and then bake in the oven for 2 hours. You might need to add a little more water towards the end to stop it from drying out.

Once the two hours are up, remove the tray and drain off the water.

Turn the oven back up to gas 6/200C/400F.

Now cut the string and carefully unwrap the roast, leaving just the bottom sheet of greaseproof paper for the roast to sit on. If the roast has split open at all (mine did just a crack), make sure this side is up during the next steps, so that the filling doesn't leak out. Cut the excess paper off around the roast, so that it all fits in the tray, then pop it back in the oven and roast, uncovered, for another 25-30 minutes, until it has browned, but not burned.

While it is roasting, it's time to make the topping. Heat the oil in a frying pan and fry the orange slices on a medium heat for about 5 minutes, until they are just starting to brown. Add the sugar, the water and the marmalade and cook for a few more minutes, until you have a nice glaze. Allow to cool a little.

Remove the roast from the oven and arrange the orange slices on top, covering up any cracks that might have formed, then spoon over the rest of the glaze. Put it back in the oven for an additional 15 minutes or so, until you have a nice caramelised top. Allow to rest for 10-15 minutes before cutting into slices and serving.

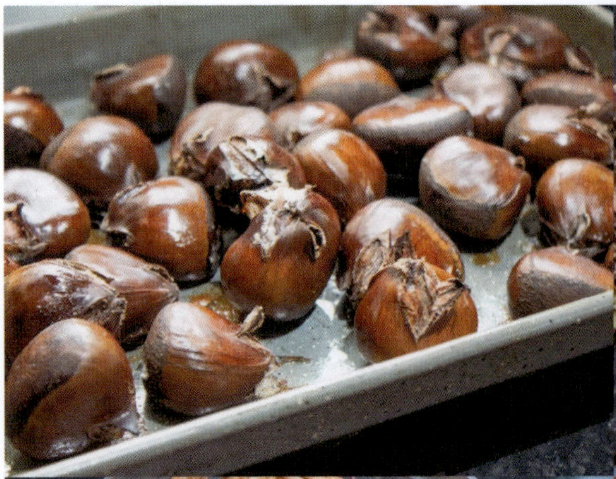
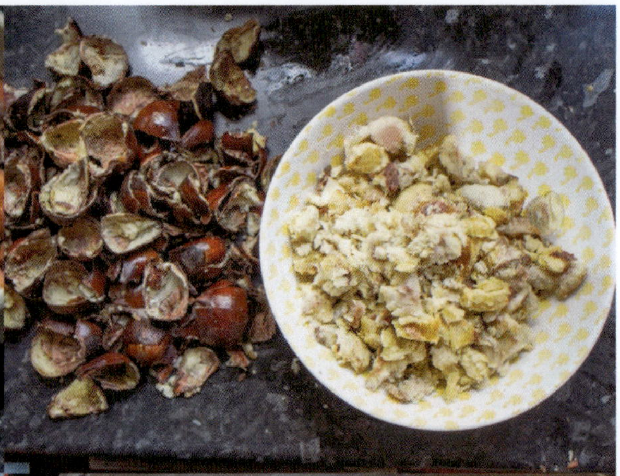
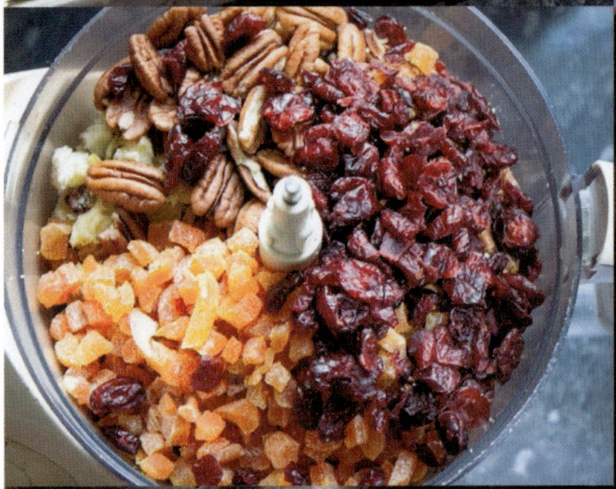
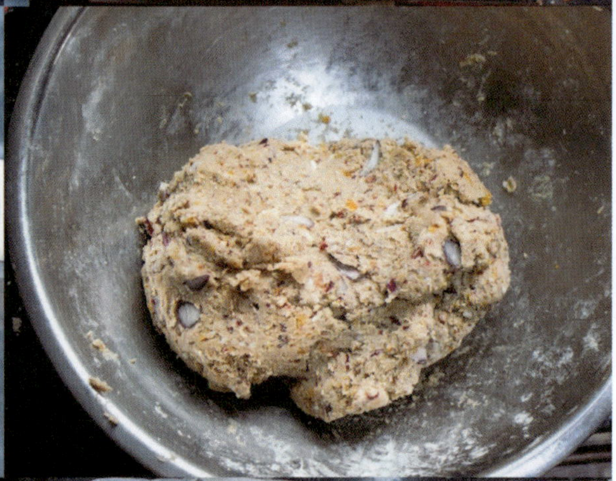
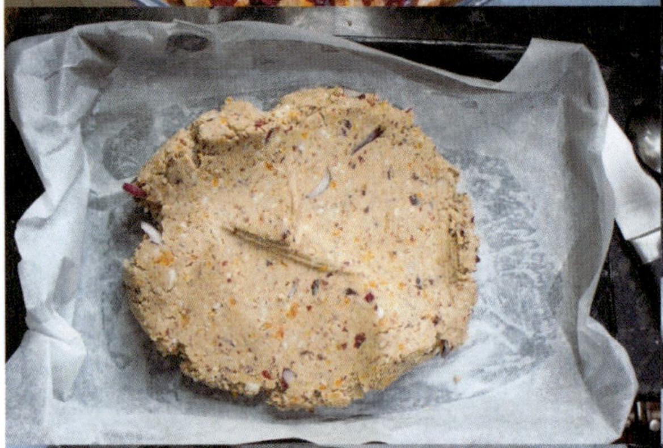
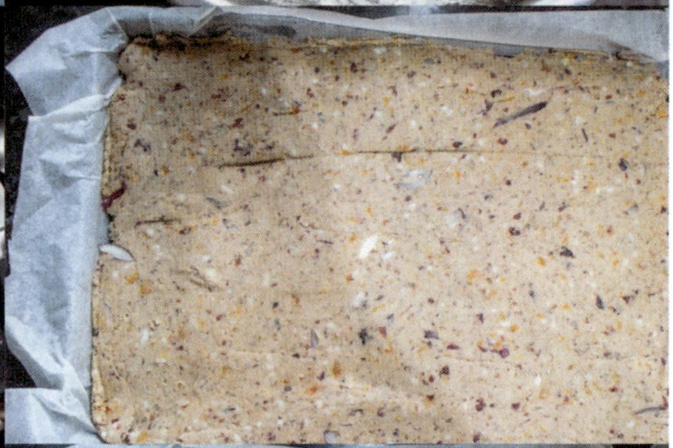
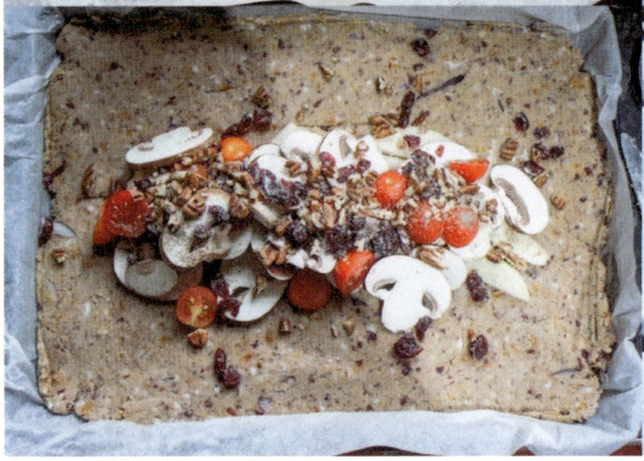
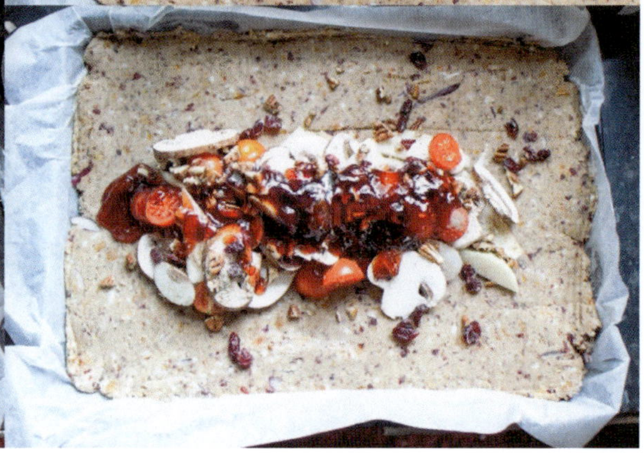

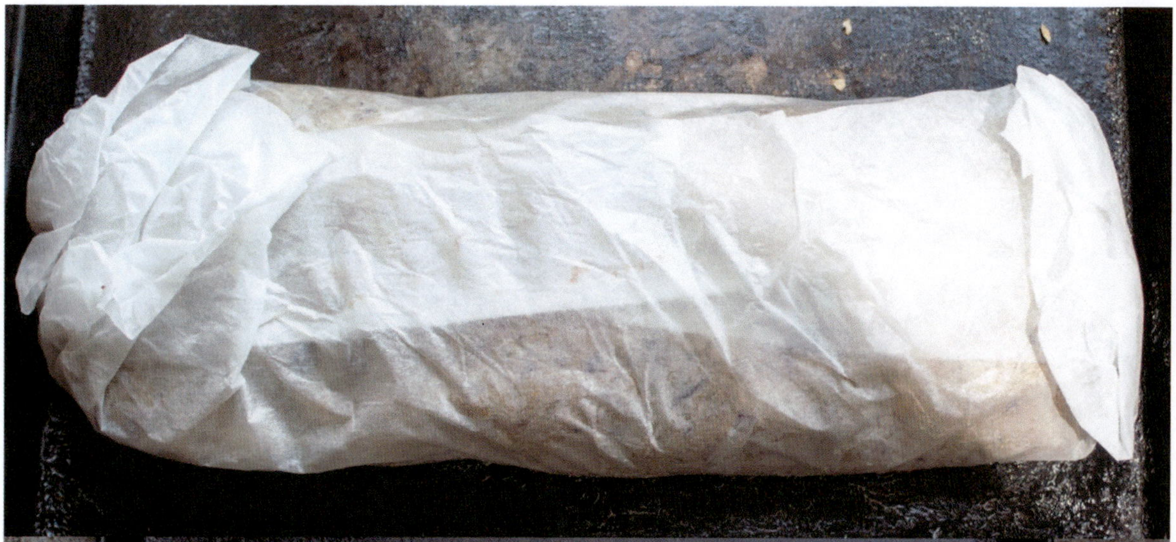

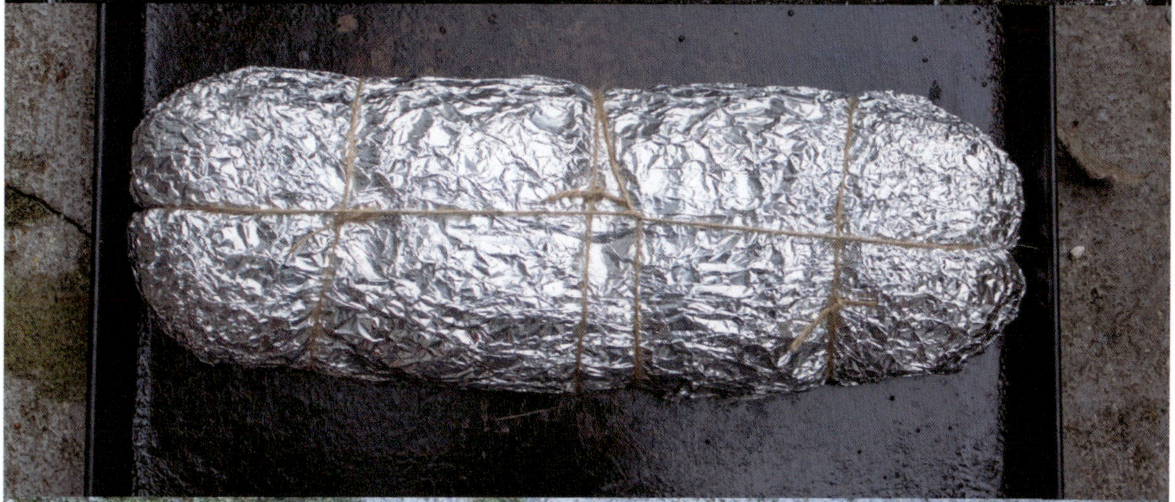

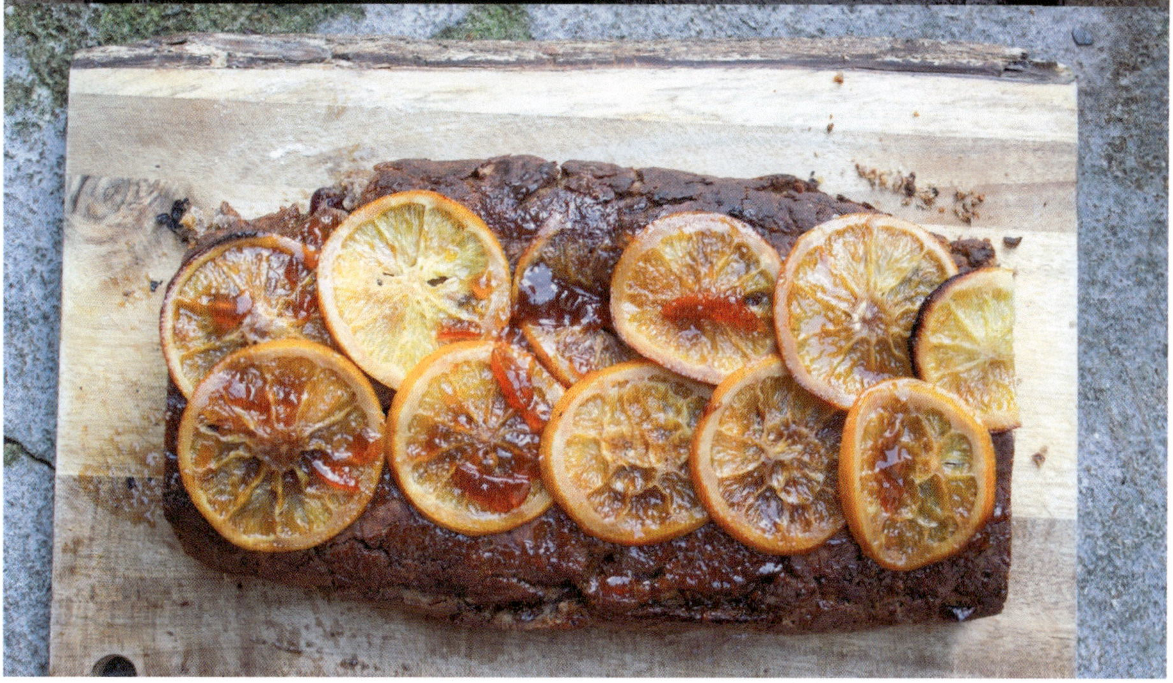

Christmas Fruit and Nut Roast Stuffed with Pears Mushrooms and Tomatoes

Sweet and Spicy Almonds

These are a super quick little snack that will stop you opening a packet of dry-roasted peanuts when you're feeling peckish. These almonds are sweet, with just a subtle hint of lemon and spice that makes them incredibly moreish. They cook in just a few minutes and will easily last a week in a sealed container. They do stick together quite easily, so you will find yourself having to break them up a little before eating them. No great chore, considering how delicious they are.

Prep time: 5 minutes. Cooking time: 10 minutes.
Gluten-Free
Serves 4-6

Ingredients:
2 tbsp sesame oil
340g raw almonds
1 tsp paprika
½ tsp ground cumin
½ tsp mild chilli powder
A good pinch of sea salt
4 tbsp brown sugar
4 tbsp coconut nectar (or maple syrup)
Juice of ½ a lemon

Method:
Heat the oil in a frying pan and fry the almonds for 3-5 minutes, stirring often. Add the spices and the salt and cook for 2 minutes more, then put in the sugar, coconut nectar and lemon juice. Cook the nuts for another 2-3 minutes, stirring almost constantly and being careful not to burn them, then turn off the heat and transfer them to a container to cool. Can be eaten warm or at room temperature.

*****

Vegan Lemon Tart

I'd missed lemon tarts since becoming vegan and I've been meaning to get around to making one for some time now. So, finally, here it is. The only thing not gluten-free in this is the pastry, which you can easily switch by changing the flour. Just add a teaspoon of xanthan gum to help bind it.

I've added an extra touch to this by sprinkling sugar on at the end of baking and burning it with a chef's blow torch. If you don't have one of these then dusting with icing sugar will do just fine.

Prep time: 25 minutes. Cooking time: about 1 hour 40 minutes, plus cooling time.
Easy to make Gluten Free
Makes 1x9 inch tart.

Ingredients:
For the Pastry:
250g plain flour
1 tsp baking powder
½ tsp salt
75g unrefined sugar
50g gram (chickpea) flour
100g vegan margarine, plus extra for greasing
75ml plant milk

For the Filling:
200g macadamia nuts, soaked in hot water for 20 minutes, and then drained
1 x 400g block firm tofu, drained
300ml plant milk
¼ tsp ground nutmeg
Juice and zest of 2 lemons
100ml vegan cream
300g unrefined sugar
½ tsp ground turmeric

Method:
First make the pastry by putting all the pastry ingredients, apart from the milk, into a mixing bowl and rubbing together between your fingers, until the mixture resembles fine breadcrumbs.

Add the plant milk and bring the mixture together with your hands. Knead for a couple of minutes to form a dough and then cover and chill in the fridge for 1 hour.

To make the filling, put all of the filling ingredients into a blender and blend until completely smooth.

Preheat the oven to gas 6/200C/400F and grease a 9-inch, loose-bottomed tart tin with margarine.

Roll out the chilled pastry large enough to fill the tart tin all the way up to the sides. Line the tin with the pastry and then line that with greaseproof paper. Fill with dried rice or baking beans and blind bake in the oven for 15 minutes.

Once the pastry is done, remove the rice and paper and then place the tart tin on a baking tray. Pour in the lemon filling until it almost touches the top.

Turn the oven down to gas 4/180C/350F and place the tart, on the baking tray, into the lower middle of the oven. Cook for about 1 hour and 20 minutes, until the filling has risen, browned slightly and wobbles when you gently move it.

Allow the tart to cool by turning off the oven and leaving the tart in there with the door ajar.
When the tart is cool, either dust the top with icing sugar, or sprinkle a couple of spoons of caster sugar on top and heat with a chef's blow torch, until the sugar melts and turns golden brown.

Chill for at least 2 hours before serving.

Vegan Lemon Tart

Coffee, Banana and Walnut Pie

This is a wonderful chilled, sweet pie that uses tofu as its base. Tofu is great for taking on the properties of eggs when baking tarts and pies as it sets firmly, like an egg-based pie would. The dessert is gluten-free, but you can use a standard vegan pastry base if you have no issues with wheat or gluten.

I've used instant coffee here, which I think gives it the right type of coffee flavour, even though I don't actually drink instant. It also allows you to use a very small amount of water for a more concentrated taste.

There are some lengthy chilling times, because you need the filling to be fully set before you pour on the topping. I would recommend making the base and filling the night before you want to eat it, and then putting the topping on a couple of hours before you want to serve it.

Prep time: 30 minutes. Chilling time: overnight, plus 2 hours. Cooking time: 2 hours.
Gluten Free
Make 1 x 9-inch pie

Ingredients:
For the Base:
250g gluten-free self-raising flour
150g coconut flour
1 tsp baking powder
1 tsp xanthan gum
200g vegan margarine, plus extra for greasing
100g unrefined sugar
½ tsp salt
150ml plant milk

For the Filling:
1 x 400g block firm tofu, drained
2 ripe bananas
15g instant coffee, mixed with 50ml hot water
30g walnuts
250ml vegan cream
150ml plant milk
300g light brown soft sugar
2 tsp vanilla extract
¼ tsp ground nutmeg

For the Topping:
150g dark brown soft sugar
50g vegan margarine
100ml vegan cream
2 tsp instant coffee
A handful of roughly chopped walnuts to garnish.

Method:
First make the pastry. Combine the flours, baking powder, xanthan gum and margarine in a mixing bowl and rub between your fingers until you get a fine breadcrumb texture (about 5 minutes). Stir in the sugar and salt and then pour in the plant milk. Bring the pastry together with your hands, knead for just a couple of seconds to fully combine, then cover and chill in the fridge for about 30 minutes.

Grease a 9-inch, loose-bottomed tart tin with margarine and preheat the oven to gas 6/200C/400F.

Once the pastry has chilled, roll it out to just beyond the size of the tart tin. Gluten-free pastry doesn't bind as well as regular pastry, so I find it helpful to roll it out onto greaseproof paper, then tip it upside down into the tart tin. It will probably still break up a little doing this, so you might have to do some patching in the tin itself. Press the pastry down and into the edges and sides of the tin, then trim any excess pastry that overlaps.
Now line the pastry with greaseproof paper, up and over the edges, and fill that with dried rice or baking beans. Put the tart tin on a baking tray and bake in the middle of the oven for 15 minutes, until the pastry is cooked but not really browned. Remove from the oven, then remove the baking beans and paper and set aside.

Turn the oven down to gas 4/180C/350F.

Now make the filling by putting all of the filling ingredients into a blender and blending until you have a completely smooth mixture. You might need to stop and scrape down the sides of the blender with a spatula in between blends.

Pour the mixture into the cooked pastry case, to about ½ cm below the rim and then gently put it back in the middle of the oven, keeping it on the baking tray in case of spillage. Bake for 90 minutes, or until the filling is risen and set. Now turn off the oven and leave the door ajar. Cool the pie in the oven until it is ready to be transferred to the fridge, then cover and chill overnight.

Once the pie has completely chilled and set, you can make the topping. Put all of the topping ingredients into a saucepan and bring to a simmer. Simmer for 2-3 minutes, until you have a thick caramel sauce, stirring almost constantly, then turn off the heat and allow to become quite cool. Stir every five minutes or so while it is cooling to keep it smooth.

Once it is cool enough but still pourable, pour the topping over the tart filling and then rotate the tart from side to side to evenly spread it. Sprinkle the chopped walnuts on top and set, uncovered, in the fridge for about 2 hours. Serve chilled.

Coffee, Banana and Walnut Pie

No Bake Blueberry Tart

This tart is much more in the style of a cheesecake, with its biscuit base and deep-filled centre. The reason I have refrained from calling it a cheesecake is because I have not used anything resembling a soft cheese flavour. If you want to experiment, then I see no reason why not to use some vegan soft cheese in this recipe. Do try it as it is first. It has a clean and fruity flavour and holds up beautifully thanks to the agar powder. There is no baking involved at all here, and the only cooking you will need to do is simmer the filling for 5 minutes to allow the agar to work. It still takes a while because of chilling times, but don't let that put you off. This dessert really is worth the effort.

The recipe here is not gluten-free because of the biscuit base, but you can easily substitute that for a packet of gluten-free ones. Have in mind that you may then need to add some sugar to the base if you're using a less-sweet biscuit to the ginger ones I've used here. I've put food colouring in the filling recipe because blueberries can lose their colour when cooked. It has no other purpose, so you don't need to use it if you don't want to.

You will definitely need a good blender for this recipe. You will also need a 9-inch wide spring-formed cake tin that has a good depth.

Prep time: 30 minutes. Cooking time: 5 minutes. Chill time: A few hours to overnight.
Easy to make gluten-free
Makes 8-10 slices.

Ingredients:
For the Base:
250g (1 pack) ginger biscuits (make sure they're vegan)
60g chopped hazelnuts
50g melted vegan butter, plus extra for greasing

For the Filling:
150g cashew nuts, soaked in hot water for 20 minutes, then drained
300g frozen and fresh blueberries (use half and half)
1 can coconut milk
350ml oat milk
½ tsp ground nutmeg
300g unrefined sugar
4 tbsp coconut nectar (maple syrup is also fine)
1 x 400g block firm tofu, drained
2 ½ tsp agar agar powder
½ - 1 tsp violet food colouring paste (optional)

For the Topping:
300g frozen blueberries
150g unrefined sugar
3 tbsp lemon juice
About 150-200g fresh blueberries to top.

Method:
First grease your cake tin with vegan butter.

To make the base, put the biscuits in a blender or food processor and whizz until they are just crumbs. Add the hazelnuts and whizz again to break the nuts up a bit but not completely. Put the biscuit crumbs into a bowl and add the melted butter. Stir until completely combined, then line the base of your cake tin with the biscuit mix, pressing down with the back of a spoon to make sure it is tightly packed. Store in the fridge or freezer to chill completely while you make the rest.

To make the filling, put all the filling ingredients into a blender and blend until completely smooth. Pour the mix into a saucepan and bring to the boil. Simmer gently for 5 minutes, then turn off the heat. You can stir in your food colouring here if you are using it. Allow the mix to cool down to just above room temperature. You will need to whisk it often as it cools to stop a skin from forming on the top. About every 10-15 minutes should do it.

When the mix is cool enough, pour it onto the biscuit base and chill for at least 2 hours, or until fully set. It will wobble but won't move too much when it is ready.

To make your topping. Put all the topping ingredients, apart from the fresh blueberries, into a pan and bring to the boil. Simmer for about 15 minutes, stirring often, until the sauce easily coats the back of a spoon. Give it 10 minutes to cool and then blend it until completely smooth. When it is cool enough to touch, spoon it over the top of your chilled tart and then evenly place the fresh blueberries on top. Chill again until firm, or even leave it overnight to serve the next day. You can also freeze it at this point, just take it out about 90 minutes before you are ready to serve it.

No Bake Blueberry Tart

Breads, Pastries and Batters

Rosemary Flatbreads

Classic Vegan 'Egg' Bread

Vegan Scones and Homemade Strawberry Jam

Five Ways with Pizza

Oven-Roasted Tomato, Asparagus and Basil Pizza

Potato, Onion and Rosemary Pizza

Aubergine, Red Pepper and Rocket Pizza

Wholewheat Pizza Dough

Vegan Sausage and Mushroom Pizza

Calzone Style Vegan Margarita Pizza

Garlic Croutons

Sundried Tomato and Black Olive Bread

Sweet Gluten-Free Shortcrust Pastry

Vegan and Gluten Free Yorkshire Puddings

Vegan Toad in the Hole

Tofu, Sweetcorn and Pineapple Quesadilla

Buckwheat Raspberry Pancakes

Spooky Halloween Gingerbread Biscuits

Curry-Spiced French Toast

Plaited Wholelmeal Bread

Sweet French Toast with Forest Fruits and Banana

Rosemary Flatbreads

If you have the time, these are gorgeous little breads to make. You can either use them as a side to something, or just have them on their own with dips (they're so good that I was happy to eat mine just by themselves). Once they have cooled after baking, cover them until you are ready to eat them, and they are best eaten the same day you make them.

Prep time: 20 minutes. Proving time: about 1 hour. Cooking time: 15-20 minutes per batch
Makes 6 flatbreads

Ingredients:
250g strong white bread flour, plus extra for dusting
100g strong wholewheat flour
1 ½ tsp salt
2 tsp dried yeast
2-4 sprigs fresh rosemary, (only 2 finely chopped for now, 2 kept aside for topping the bread)
225-250ml lukewarm water
Olive oil for brushing and greasing
A couple of pinches of sea salt

Method:
Put the flours, salt, dried yeast and the 2 chopped sprigs of rosemary into a large mixing bowl. Make a well in the centre and pour in the water, then mix fully with a table knife until a dough begins to form. Bring it all together with your hands and knead for about 5 minutes, until you have a good, stretchy dough.

Put the dough back in the bowl and rub a little olive oil over the surface, then cover the bowl with a towel and leave in a warm place to rise for about an hour.

Preheat the oven to gas 6/200C/400F and grease a large baking sheet with a little olive oil.
Once it has doubled in size, bring the dough back to your worktop and push all the air out of it. Knead briefly again and then separate it into 6 equal balls.

Roll out 2 or 3 of the doughballs, depending on what you can fit on your baking sheet, to approximately the size of large saucers. Use a dusting of flour to help you.

Now lay the flatbreads out onto your tray, brush the tops of them with oil, roughly chop the remaining rosemary and sprinkle some of it on top of the bread (remember you need to leave enough to cover 6). Finally, sprinkle a little sea salt on top of the bread and bake near the top of the oven for 15-20 minutes, until slightly golden brown. Repeat the whole process with the remaining balls of dough.

*****

Classic Vegan 'Egg' Bread

I grew up with egg bread as a staple in our household, and I was relieved to discover that switching to a plant-based diet didn't mean that had to change. It is, after all, bread that is dipped in a batter and then fried. I have found that gram flour and nutritional yeast-based batter is the perfect substitute. I also use a dairy-free cheese sauce mix, also gluten-free, which you can find in the free from section of most large supermarkets. This is not an essential ingredient if you cannot find it, I just think it adds a little something special. Give my version here a go and see if you're converted. The batter itself is gluten-free, so you just need to pick an appropriate bread if you are intolerant.

Prep time: 5 minutes. Cooking time: about 4 minutes per side of bread.

Makes enough batter for 6-8 slices.
Easy to Make Gluten Free.

Ingredients:
100g gram (chickpea) flour
3 tbsp nutritional yeast
1 tsp salt
A dash of black pepper
1 ½ tsp Dijon mustard
1 tsp garlic puree
3 tsp dairy-free cheese sauce mix (make sure it's gluten-free)
300ml almond milk

Oil for shallow frying
6-8 slices of bread

Method:
Put all of the ingredients, apart from the almond milk, bread and oil, into a mixing bowl. Gradually pour in the almond milk, whisking constantly, until you have a smooth batter. Leave to stand for 5 minutes.

Heat a couple of tablespoons of oil in a frying pan until quite hot. Dip a slice of bread into the batter, until it is completely covered, but don't leave it in there as it will start to fall apart. Take the bowl over to the frying pan to avoid getting drips everywhere and gently place the bread into the pan. Repeat with a second slice straight away if you have room in your pan and fry both slices for about 4 minutes each side, until the batter is cooked and they are golden brown.

Keep warm in a low oven while you fry the rest of the bread. Serve immediately.

*****

Vegan Scones and Homemade Strawberry Jam

Before making these, I can't remember the last time I had a scone. I didn't even miss them until I was sitting down eating one, then I remembered how good they were. Sweet and crumbly, they taste of outdoor adventures in warmer weather. Paired with strawberry jam (and cream if you like), scones are a memory as much as they are a flavour. They are tea shops on a weekend afternoon. They are trips to the countryside with your parents, and the smell of spring grass underfoot. Scones are as quintessentially British as red telephone boxes and are worth your time if you choose to make them.

These, of course, are adapted to be vegan and lose nothing of the original flavour. The recipe makes 8-10, more than enough for afternoon tea with a couple of friends. The jam I made on a whim out of strawberries that needed using up. You can just use shop-bought jam, but I really can't recommend enough that you make it yourself. If you haven't done it before, it's a lot easier than you might think.

Strawberry Jam.

Prep time: 15 minutes. Cooking time: about 2 ½ hours
Makes 1 jar.
Ingredients:
800g ripe strawberries, stalked and quartered
300g sugar
1 apple, peeled, cored and diced
150ml cold water

Method:
Put all the ingredients into a large saucepan and bring to the boil. Put a lid half on (that is, leave a gap for steam to escape) and gently simmer for 1 hour.

Remove the lid and simmer for another 90 minutes or so, stirring occasionally, until you have a thick, jam-like consistency. Allow to cool a little and then either pour into a clean jam jar or can properly in canning jars. It will keep in the fridge for about a month in a jam jar.

Vegan Scones.

Prep time: 15-20 minutes. Cooking time: 15-20 minutes.
Makes 8-10

Ingredients:
400g self-raising flour
½ tsp salt
2 tsp baking powder
1 tsp bicarbonate of soda
100g vegan margarine
100g unrefined caster sugar
100g raisins
175ml plant milk
1 tsp vanilla extract

Method:
Preheat the oven to Gas 7/220C/425F and line a baking tray with greaseproof paper.
Put the flour, salt, baking powder, bicarb of soda and margarine into a bowl and rub together with your fingers until it resembles fine breadcrumbs (takes about 5 minutes).

Add the rest of the ingredients and bring together with your hands. Knead on a lightly-floured surface until fully combined, and then roll out to about 3cm thick. Use a medium-sized pastry cutter to cut out your scone shapes and then load them onto the baking tray, leaving a little space in between them. Re-roll the pastry to use as much as possible.
When you are done, put the baking tray in the middle of the oven and cook for 15-20 minutes, until the scones are risen and golden. Allow to cool before serving.

Vegan Scones and Homemade Strawberry Jam

Five Ways with Pizza

I was thirteen years old when I first learned to make pizza. I was visiting family in Leicester when, on a visit to a book store, I came across Antonio Carluccio's *An Invitation to Italian Cooking*. I bought the book, published the year before, after a brief flick-through of its glossy pages, and set to reading it when I got back. The book contained many recipes too exotic in taste of my virginal teenage fumblings with cookery, but I was instantly attracted to the pizza recipe. It seemed familiar and exciting. It seemed *doable*.

When I got back from my holiday, I set to gathering the ingredients and making the pizza. It was the first time I'd made my own bread and seen it rise during the proving process. It was akin to watching a magic trick. The dough swelled to beyond the capacity of the bowl I had put it in. It lifted the towel I had used to cover it into a dome-like structure and threatened to spill over the edge. When I kneaded it a second time it was soft and light; so different from when I had first put it together. And then finally, rolling it out, shaping it into its characteristic large disc, spooning the sauce over the dough before sprinkling on the toppings.

I was hooked.

I made pizza again and again, the way you obsessively repeat a new thing you have learned that fascinates you. I went on to make countless dishes after, to learn (and keep on learning) the essence of cooking, but I always remember my first experiments with this Italian classic.

Now, thirty years on, I only make pizza from time to time. When I do, however, the passion I felt as a teenager is instantly rekindled. Pizza is, to a great extent, my first love.

The Pizza Dough

Your pizza base should be light and airy. It should crunch just slightly when you bite into it and tear apart with ease. It should be soft to chew and work in perfect harmony with the other flavours in your mouth. People notice a pizza base without actually noticing it. When it is perfect it blends in seamlessly with the whole experience. A perfect pizza base is not an exception, but a prerequisite to a satisfying meal. It doesn't matter how good your toppings are if your pizza base is dense, unrisen and chewy.

This recipe will give you the light and crispy pizza base you are looking for. As with all bread, it takes a little time to make, but most of it is proving the dough, during which time you'll be able to get on with something else.

Prep time: 20 minutes. Proving time: about 2 hours 10 minutes.
Makes 6 medium-sized pizzas

Ingredients:
1 kg strong white bread flour
250g semolina flour
1 tbsp salt
750ml tepid water
3 tsp (2 sachets) dried yeast
1 tsp sugar
2 tbsp olive oil

Method:
Place the 2 flours and the salt into a large mixing bowl and combine. Pour 50ml of the tepid water into a mug and mix in the dried yeast and sugar until you have a reasonably good blend (the yeast has a way of clumping on the spoon, so you won't get it perfect). Leave this mixture to rest for 15 minutes, until you end up with about half a cup of foam (if this doesn't happen, the yeast is probably dead and shouldn't be used, as the bread won't rise). Now make a well in the centre of your flour and pour in the yeast mix. Stir it in a little and then add the rest of the tepid water (you can hold some water back if you are concerned about it being too wet, but you should be able to use all of it without problems).

Mix the dough with a table knife, until it all starts to clump together, then turn it out onto a floured surface and knead fully for about 10 minutes, until you have a soft and elastic dough.

Clean out the mixing bowl and put the finished dough back in. Rub the olive oil over the surface, then cover the bowl with a tea towel and leave in a warm place to prove for about 90 minutes (airing cupboards and next to radiators work well), until it has doubled in size.

Once this is achieved, take the dough back to your work top and knock all of the air back out of it. This process is called knocking back. Knead it again for a minute or so, and now you are ready to begin rolling it out into your pizza bases.

You are better off cooking no more than two pizzas at a time (and I usually cook them one at a time), so it is ideal to break off the amount of dough you need – approximately one sixth per pizza – and keep the rest covered until you are ready you use it. The dough will rise again while it is sitting there, but this is totally fine.

On a floured surface, roll out your piece of dough, until you have a flat round approximately 30 cm (12 inches) in diameter and about 0.5 cm (1/4 inch) thick. A good dough will spring back as you roll it, so you will have to keep going to achieve the desired dimensions. Now place your dough onto a large oiled baking sheet or 12-inch pizza tray, and you are ready to put on your toppings.

The Pizza Sauce

This is my recipe for pizza sauce, which you can either use as your standard pizza topping, or as a guide from which to develop your own. It is better to let it cool before putting it on your pizza, so you will ideally begin making it as soon as you start proving your bread, which will give it the time needed. I tend to use pizza sauce sparingly, but there is enough in this batch for you to be quite liberal, if that is your preferred approach. I blend this sauce at the end to help with smooth spreading, but you can skip this part if you prefer it chunky.

Prep time: 10 minutes. Cooking time: 35 minutes, plus cooling time.

Covers 6-8 Pizzas.
Gluten-Free

Ingredients:
3 tbsp olive oil
1 medium onion, finely diced
3 cloves garlic, chopped
2 large tomatoes, diced
4 tbsp tomato puree
1 can chopped tomatoes
1 tsp salt
A pinch of black pepper
50ml water
1 heaped tsp dried oregano
2 tsp balsamic vinegar
2 tsp soft brown sugar (any sugar will do)

Method:
Heat the olive oil in a medium-sized saucepan and gently fry the onions and garlic for 4-5 minutes, stirring often. You want them to soften without browning too much. Add the diced tomatoes and cook for 3-4 more minutes, then put in the rest of the ingredients.

Bring to a gentle simmer and cook, without a lid, for 25-30 minutes, stirring often, until the sauce has reduced by about one third and has become thick and rich. Turn off the heat and leave to cool, then blend using a hand or jug blender if desired.

Pizza Toppings

Now that you've got your base and sauce sorted, it's time to start experimenting with your toppings. You're not going to find any pineapple and sweetcorn here, because I don't think they belong on a pizza. But if they're you're thing – go nuts!

I've started you off with a few ideas on how you can get creative with your toppings while maintaining a balance of flavours that work in harmony with each other. It's tempting to throw everything you can on top of your base, but I urge you to refrain from this practise. Simplicity is often the best way forward.

*****

Oven-Roasted Tomato, Asparagus and Basil Pizza

Prep time: 10 minutes. Cooking time 30-40 minutes.
Makes 2 x 10-12 inch pizzas.

Ingredients:
200-250g cherry tomatoes, halved
100g asparagus, woody end removed
3 cloves garlic, peeled and bashed with the flat of a knife
3 tbsp olive oil
A generous pinch of sea salt
50-75g vegan cheese
A drizzle more of olive oil

2 Portions of pizza base
8-10 tbsp pizza sauce
A handful of fresh basil leaves, torn

Method:
Preheat the oven to gas 7/220C/425F.

Put the cherry tomatoes, asparagus and garlic onto a baking tray and drizzle over the olive oil. Sprinkle over the sea salt and mix together with your hands to make sure the vegetables are fully coated in the oil.

Place in the oven and cook for about 20 minutes. Pull out the asparagus after 10 minutes to stop them from burning and set them aside. Remove the tomatoes once they have started to brown and wilt.

While these are cooking, roll out 2 pizza bases, using the method described above, and lay them on greased baking sheets or pizza trays.

Spoon 4-5 tbsp of the tomato sauce onto each pizza and spread it all over using the back of the spoon. Leave to rest (and prove slightly) for 10 minutes.

Divide the tomatoes, asparagus and garlic between the two pizzas, making sure to distribute evenly, then sprinkle half the vegan cheese on each and drizzle with a little olive oil (which will moisten the cheese and help it melt).

Turn the oven down to gas 6/200C/400F.

Place one or both pizzas in the oven and cook for 15-20 minutes, until risen and browned and the cheese has melted. If you're cooking two pizzas at once, swap them over half-way through cooking to help them cook evenly. Sprinkle on the torn basil leaves after cooking.

Potato, Onion and Rosemary Pizza

Prep time: 15 minutes. Cooking time: 45 minutes.
Makes 2 x 10-12 inch pizzas.

Ingredients:
500g potatoes, peeled and cut into 1-inch pieces
1 tbsp coconut oil
1 red onion, sliced
1 large sprig rosemary, chopped
A generous pinch of sea salt
3 cloves garlic, chopped
50-75g vegan cheese
A drizzle of olive oil

2 Portions of pizza base
8-10 tbsp pizza sauce

Method:
Put the potatoes in a pan of water, so that they are just covered, and bring to the boil. Simmer for 10-12 minutes, until tender but not falling apart, then completely drain.

Heat the coconut oil in a large frying pan or wok, until quite hot, and sauté the potatoes for about 8-10 minutes, stirring often, until they have browned and are slightly crisp. Add the sliced onion and cook for 3-4 more minutes, then add the rosemary and sea salt and cook for 3 minutes. Finally, put in the chopped garlic and give it a minute more.

Preheat the oven to gas 6/200C/400F.

Roll out 2 pizza bases, using the method described above, and lay them on greased baking sheets or pizza trays.

Spoon 4-5 tbsp of the tomato sauce onto each pizza and spread it all over using the back of the spoon. Leave to rest (and prove slightly) for 10 minutes.

Divide the potato mixture between the two pizzas, making sure to distribute evenly, then sprinkle half the vegan cheese on each and drizzle with a little olive oil.

Place one or both pizzas in the oven and cook for 15-20 minutes, until risen and browned, and the cheese has melted. If you're cooking two pizzas at once, swap them over half-way through cooking to help them cook evenly.

*****

Aubergine, Red Pepper and Rocket Pizza

Prep time: 10-15 minutes. Cooking time: 30 minutes.
Makes 2 x 10-12 inch pizzas.

Ingredients:
2 tbsp olive oil
1 aubergine, thinly sliced
1 red pepper, thinly sliced
50-75g vegan cheese
A drizzle of olive oil

2 Portions of pizza base
8-10 tbsp pizza sauce
A large handful of fresh rocket leaves

Method:
Heat the olive oil in a frying pan and fry the aubergine slices for about 5 minutes, turning often, until they are browned and cooked through. Remove from the pan and fry the peppers for about 4 minutes, adding a little more oil if needed.

Preheat the oven to gas 6/200C/400F.

Roll out 2 pizza bases, using the method described above, and lay them on greased baking sheets or pizza trays.

Spoon 4-5 tbsp of the tomato sauce onto each pizza and spread it all over using the back of the spoon. Leave to rest (and prove slightly) for 10 minutes.

Divide the aubergines and the peppers between the two pizzas, making sure to distribute evenly, then sprinkle half the vegan cheese on each and drizzle with a little olive oil.

Place one or both pizzas in the oven and cook for 15-20 minutes, until risen and browned, and the cheese has melted. If you're cooking two pizzas at once, swap them over half-way through cooking to help them cook evenly.

Take the pizzas out of the oven and put on the fresh rocket leaves, then put them back in the oven for a further 2 minutes, until the rocket had wilted slightly.

Oven-Roasted Tomato, Asparagus and Basil Pizza; Aubergine, Red Pepper and Rocket Pizza; Potato, Onion and Rosemary Pizza.

Wholewheat Pizza Dough

Prep time: 20 minutes. Proving time: 90 minutes.
Makes 4 medium pizzas

Ingredients:
400g strong white bread flour
300g strong wholewheat bread flour
2 ½ tsp dried yeast
1 tbsp salt
450ml tepid water
Olive oil to cover

Method:
Put the flours into a large mixing bowl, along with the dried yeast and the salt. Make a well in the centre and pour in the water, then stir with a table knife until it begins to bind. Bring together with you hands to form a dough ball and then knead on a floured surface for about 10 minutes, until you have a smooth, elastic dough.

Place the dough back in the bowl and rub a drizzle of olive oil all around it, then cover with a tea towel and leave in a warm place to prove for 90 minutes, or until it has doubled in size.

Bring the risen dough back to the worktop and knead for another minute or so to knock all of the air out of it. Divide into four balls and roll out into pizza bases as required.

*****

Vegan Sausage and Mushroom Pizza

Prep time: 10 minutes. Cooking time: about 30 minutes.
Make 2 pizzas

Ingredients:
2 tbsp olive oil, plus extra to drizzle after
4-6 vegan sausages, defrosted if frozen and cut diagonally into slices
150-200g Portobello mushrooms, sliced
3 cloves garlic, chopped
75g vegan cheese, grated

2 Portions of pizza base
8-10 tbsp pizza sauce

Method:
Heat the olive oil in a frying pan and fry the sausage slices for 5-6 minutes, until starting to brown. Add the mushrooms and continue cooking, on a high heat, for another 4 minutes or so, then put in the chopped garlic and give it another couple of minutes, stirring often.

Preheat the oven to gas 7/220C/425F.

Allow the sausages and mushrooms to cool while you roll out 2 pizza bases and put them onto baking or pizza trays. Spoon on a couple of tablespoons of tomato sauce and then divide the sausage mix between the two pizzas. Sprinkle half the cheese onto each pizza and then drizzle with olive oil.

Bake in the oven for 15-20 minutes, until risen and browned.

Vegan Sausage and Mushroom Pizza

Calzone Style Vegan Margherita Pizza

This is a pizza cooked in a frying pan and folded in half during cooking to create a crescent-shaped crust. I had something similar in a restaurant in Holland when I was eighteen years old. It was the first time I had ever had pizza in a restaurant, and the fact that you could have a folded pizza grabbed my attention. Eighteen was a long time ago, and this pizza recipe probably bears very little resemblance to the one I actually ate back then, but the memory inspired me to come up with some approximation. Give this a try if you've never cooked a pizza on the stovetop before. I promise you'll be pleasantly surprised.

Prep time: 15 minutes. Cooking time: about 25 minutes per pizza.
Make 2 medium to large pizzas.

Ingredients:
Enough pizza dough for 2 bases
3 tbsp olive oil
2 portions of tomato sauce (8-10 tbsp)
75g vegan cheese, grated

Method:
Roll out one of the pizza bases on a floured surface to a size approximately equalling the base of your largest frying pan. Heat half of the olive oil in your frying pan, until quite hot, and gently place the rolled-out pizza base into the pan. Cook for about 3-4 minutes on the one side, until you see bubbles start to rise on the surface of the uncooked side.

Now gently flip the pizza base over so that you are cooking the other side (use a spatula or a plate to help you with this). As soon as it is flipped over, spoon on your tomato sauce and spread it around the base, then sprinkle half of the grated cheese onto one half of the pizza.

Using your spatula, slowly fold the pizza in half inside the pan, so that it becomes a half-moon shape, with the topping now becoming the filling. Cook on both sides, on a medium heat, for 15-20 minutes, until the pizza is risen, crisp and browned.

You can keep it warm in a very low oven while you make the second one.

Calzone Style Vegan Margherita Pizza

Garlic Croutons

Prep time: 5 minutes. Cooking time: 15 minutes.
Serves 3-4

Ingredients:
½ small loaf of uncut, day old bread, cut into thick slices and then diced
4 tbsp olive oil
A generous pinch of salt
1 tsp dried oregano
½ tsp garlic puree (or 1 clove of minced garlic)

Method:
Preheat the oven to gas 6/200C/400F.

Put all of the ingredients into a mixing bowl and mix thoroughly with your hands until the bread is fully coated. Transfer to a baking tray and then bake in the upper part of the oven for about 15 minutes, until the bread is crisp and browned. Leave to cool before serving.

*****

Sundried Tomato and Black Olive Bread

Breadmaking has been a passion of mine for about 30 years. I was a teenager when I first learned to combine flour and water to make a dough, that adding yeast would make it rise and just enough salt would give it the perfect flavour. I learned that bread didn't happen quickly. It had to be proved, not once but twice, to get the yeast working properly. It takes a couple of hours and a good bit of work to make a loaf of bread. If you do it right, the results are always worth the effort.

This bread is based very much on the focaccia style loaf. I used a large, square tin to bake mine, but you can do this just as well on a flat tray, which will give it a more natural, rounded shape. The important thing is to complete each process thoroughly to get the desired results.

Prep Time: 30 minutes. Total Proving Time: 2 hours 10 minutes, plus cooling time.
Makes 1 large loaf.

Ingredients:
2 ½ tsp dried yeast (2 sachets)
1 tsp sugar
600-650ml lukewarm water
1kg strong white bread flour
1 tbsp salt
100g pitted black olives, chopped
120g sundried tomatoes from a jar, chopped
2 tbsp fresh rosemary, finely chopped
2 tbsp olive oil
A pinch of sea salt

Method:
First put the dried yeast and the sugar into a cup and add a small amount (about 3-4 tablespoons) of the water. Stir until fully mixed and then leave to stand for about 15 minutes. If the yeast is working properly it will activate and become foamy. If this does not happen then the yeast is no good.

Put the flour, salt, olives, sundried tomatoes and rosemary into a large mixing bowl and make a well in the centre. Pour in the yeast mixture and then add the rest of the lukewarm water. Add 2-3 tablespoons of oil from the sundried tomato jar to give the bread a little extra flavour. Use a table knife to bring the mixture together in the bowl, then use your hands to knead a little. Turn the dough out onto a clean surface and knead with both hands for about 10 minutes, until it has a stretchy, elastic texture. This will be very messy at first, but as the dough smooths out it will become easier.

Once the dough is fully kneaded, put the 2 tablespoons of olive oil into a clean bowl that's at least twice the size of the dough. Put the dough in the bowl with the oil and turn the dough over so that it is covered in the oil. Cover the bowl with a clean tea towel and leave in a warm place to prove for 90 minutes, or until it has doubled in size.

Grease a baking tray, or large baking tin and bring the proven dough back to the work surface. Knock all the air out of it and knead gently again for a minute or two. Place the dough on the tray or in the tin and form it into the shape you would like. Brush with more olive oil and season with sea salt, then cover with the tea towel again. Leave to prove for another 40 minutes, until about one and a half times its size.

While the dough is proving a second time, preheat the oven to gas 6/200C/400F.

Gently remove the tea towel, put the dough in the middle of the oven and cook for about 30 minutes. The bread is ready when it is browned, risen and makes a hollow sound when you tap the bottom of it.

Turn the cooked bread out onto a wire rack and allow to cool before serving.

Sundried Tomato and Black Olive Bread

Sweet Gluten-Free Shortcrust Pastry

This is a quick and easy shortcrust pastry for those who are gluten intolerant or coeliac. It holds up nicely for a dessert tart or pie. You can use any brand of plain gluten-free flour you like. Just remember that, without the gluten to bind it, it won't have the same stretchy texture as wheat pastry. As a result, these pastries can easily break up when transferring them to your pie dish or tart tin, so be prepared to have to do a little patch work from time to time. A good trick, especially when it comes to making pie lids, is to roll it out onto greaseproof paper first, then flip the paper over so that the pastry falls, in one piece, onto whatever you want to top.

Prep Time: 15 minutes. Chilling time: 1 hour.
Gluten Free
Makes enough for a 9-inch pie.

Ingredients:
600g plain gluten-free flour
200g vegan margarine
1 ½ tsp salt
5 tbsp sugar
3 tsp xanthan gum
200ml plant milk

Method:
Put the flour and margarine into a mixing bowl together and crumb between your fingers until you have a fine, breadcrumb texture. Add the rest of the ingredients, up to and including the xanthan gum, and mix thoroughly.

Pour in the plant milk and mix with a table knife until large lumps form. Bring together with your hands and knead for a minute or so to form a dough, adding more flour if needed.

Cover and chill for one hour before using.

*****

Vegan and Gluten Free Yorkshire Puddings

I don't mind telling you that this recipe has taken some experimentation to get right, so I'm quite excited to release it now. These are fully vegan, fully gluten-free Yorkshire puddings. Now finally, we can complete our Sunday meals. A 12-hole muffin tin works best for this recipe.

Prep time: 10 minutes. Cooking time: 20 minutes.
Gluten-Free
Makes about 18.

Ingredients:
300g plain gluten-free flour
75g gram (chickpea) flour
1 ½ tsp sea salt
1 tsp xanthan gum
2 tsp baking powder
A dash of ground black pepper
1 ½ tsp Dijon mustard
400ml plain soya milk
300ml cold water
Enough sunflower or rapeseed oil to put a good drop in the bottom of each muffin tin hole.

Method:

Preheat the oven to gas 8/23C/450F.

Put all the ingredients, apart from the oil, into a mixing bowl or blender and either whisk or blend until fully smooth. I used a hand blender, just as I would use for soups. It's important to get a lot of air into the mix to keep it light. Pour the mixture in to a jug for easy pouring. If it seems too thick you can always whisk in a little more water at this point.

Take a 12-hole muffin tin and put a generous drop of the oil into each hole. Place the tray at the top of the oven and heat for 10 minutes, until the oil is smoking hot.

Carefully take the tray out of the oven and place on a heatproof, level surface. Carefully but quickly pour the batter mixture into each hole until they are nearly full. The oil should sizzle as you pour and the edges of the batter should begin to cook. Once all the holes are full, gently place the tray back in the oven as quickly as you can and cook for 20-25 minutes, until risen, crisp and golden. Remove from the oven and serve immediately. If you have more batter left over you will need to heat more oil in the muffin tin and do the same process again to finish it off.

Vegan and Gluten Free Yorkshire Puddings

Vegan Toad in the Hole

The recipe for this batter is almost identical to that of the Yorkshire pudding recipe (which stands to reason, of course), only I've used regular plain flour instead of gluten-free and 50g less. The two are entirely interchangeable, so if you want a gluten-free toad in the hole you can make the necessary adjustments (don't forget to add xanthan gum). Remember that with this pudding batter it is important to get lots of air into the mix. It's equally important to have a very hot oven and smoking hot oil to pour the batter into. The batter must begin to sizzle and cook as soon as it hits the pan. Another important tip is to resist checking it over and over. The more you open the oven door, the more air you're letting in and cooling down the oven, disrupting the cooking process. Try to wait until as close to the end of the allotted time before opening the oven door.

You can use any vegan sausages you like for this, and you more than likely already have your favourites in your fridge or freezer. Make sure they're only just cooked before adding the batter, because they're going to have to cook at a higher temperature for another half an hour or so.

Prep time: 10 minutes. Cooking time: about 45 minutes
Can be made gluten-free
Serves 4

Ingredients:
Enough oil to cover the base of a baking dish to about 5mm (1/4 inch)
8 vegan sausages

For the Batter:
250g plain flour
75g gram (chickpea) flour
2 tsp baking powder
1 ½ tsp sea salt
A generous dash of black pepper
1 ½ tsp Dijon mustard
400ml soya milk
300ml cold water

Method:
Preheat the oven to gas 6/200C/400F.

Pour the oil into your baking dish and place in the oven for a couple of minutes, until it is hot enough to cook the sausages. Put the sausages in and cook for about 15 minutes, turning halfway through cooking.

While they are cooking, put all of the batter ingredients into a blender and blend for a minute or two, until it is completely smooth and has plenty of air in it.
Turn the oven up to gas 8/230C/450F and leave the oven dish in for 3-4 minutes to allow the oil to get really hot.

Now carefully take the dish out of the oven and pour in the batter. It should just about cover the sausages, so that you can still see them, and sizzle as soon as it hits the oil. Gently and quickly return the dish back to the oven and cook for another 30-35 minutes, until the batter is risen, crisp and well browned. Serve immediately.

*****

Tofu, Sweetcorn and Pineapple Quesadilla

The pizza takeaway favourites, sweetcorn and pineapple, sit comfortably sandwiched between two crisp tortillas fried in a large pan. All of the ingredients in this recipe come pre-prepared, either from cans or packets, making this a perfect lazy dinner that you just throw into the pan and let the magic happen. And it's okay. From time to time we can, and should, allow ourselves this luxury.

Quesadillas are a much-loved food that I don't indulge in anywhere near as much as I'd like to, which strikes me as odd, considering how easy they are to put together. I think I do this sometimes with food. There are so many good things to make that getting back to them often can be a challenge.

Like the toppings on a pizza, the filling ingredients suggested here are one of endless possible combinations. As long as you stay within the Tex-Mex theme, you can put whatever you like in, though I suggest giving this one a go to get you stated.

Prep time: 5 minutes. Cooking time: About 35 minutes
Serves 4

Ingredients:
2 tbsp olive oil
1 x 160g pack of pre-cut, marinated tofu
2 medium red onions, large diced
2 cloves garlic, chopped
1 can sweetcorn, drained
1 can diced pineapple, drained
150g cherry tomatoes, halved
1 tbsp mild chilli sauce
2 tbsp tamari (or light soy sauce)
Salt and pepper to taste

Oil for shallow frying
8 large tortillas
200g vegan cheese, grated (I use a vegan jalapeno cheese for mine, to give it an extra bite)

Method:
Heat the olive oil in a large frying pan and fry the tofu for about 2-3 minutes. Add the onion and cook for another 4 minutes, stirring often, then pop in the garlic and give it a minute or two more.

Now turn the heat up and put in the sweetcorn and pineapple. Give them a good 2-3 minutes cooking before adding the tomatoes, and then cook those down for another 5 minutes or so. Stir in the chilli sauce and tamari, season to taste and then transfer to a bowl.
Clean out the pan and heat a tablespoon or 2 of frying oil. Fry a tortilla on one side, while you spoon a quarter of the quesadilla filling onto the side that's facing up. Sprinkle over a quarter of the grated cheese, then lay another tortilla on top. Allow the bottom side to cook for 3-4 minutes in total, then place a dinner plate on top of the quesadilla to help you flip it over (just use a spatula if this is easier for you). Now cook the other side for another 3-4 minutes, until crisp and browned.

Keep the quesadillas warm in a low oven while you cook the rest, then cut into quarters to serve with a dollop of vegan sour cream.

*****

Buckwheat Raspberry Pancakes

Pancakes on a weekend late morning is more than just a breakfast. It's an *occasion*. Making pancakes is not serving up a bowl of cereal and some instant coffee. When you whisk up the batter and cook it in the pan, you are bringing love to the table. Love for yourself and anyone else you're making them for. Pancakes take *effort*, and they are best enjoyed when you've got nowhere else to run off to.

Even if you're not living gluten-free, try the buckwheat flour in these. Their taste has a little more substance to it than with regular flour, and you can get it in any supermarket (usually with the specialty flours like spelt and so on). Your raspberries need to be fresh to the point where they break apart as you're stirring them into the batter. This will create a lovely red marbling throughout the pancake and infuse the flavour. Now put on some fresh coffee and take the morning off with your loved ones. You'll be enjoying these in no time.

Prep time: 10 minutes. Cooking time: 8 minutes per batch.
Gluten Free

Serves 4

Ingredients:
300g buckwheat flour
50g ground almonds
2 tsp baking powder
1 tsp bicarbonate of soda
1 tsp ground cinnamon
75g golden caster sugar
½ tsp salt
450ml plant-based milk
200g ripe raspberries
Coconut oil, or other oil, for frying

Method:
In a large mixing bowl, put all of the dry ingredients, then slowly add the plant milk, whisking continuously, until you have a smooth, thick batter. Stir in the raspberries with a spoon.

Heat a tablespoon of the oil in a non-stick frying pan, until quite hot, then spoon about 2-3 tablespoons of the batter into the hot pan. It should form a thick pancake about 4 inches in diameter. Try to fit 2 or 3 of these into the pan at the same time, but make sure you leave some space between them. Fry on a medium-high heat for about 4 minutes on the one side. They are ready to turn oven when bubbles form on the raw side of the pancakes. Give them another 4 minutes on the other side, or until they are golden brown and risen, then keep them warm in a low oven while you cook the next batch. Repeat until the pancake mixture has gone.

Buckwheat Raspberry Pancakes

Spooky Halloween Gingerbread Biscuits

Gingerbread biscuits are one of those treats that come out at Halloween and Christmas, where they are adorned with as much colourful sugar as gravity will allow and served as a centrepiece at the table. These biscuits are a communal activity that the whole family like to get involved in, even if it's just stealing them off the plate before they're finished. This will keep the kids busy over either holiday. I put my son to work on them and he got totally stuck in. It wasn't long before my wife and daughter were also taking part. My wife, Samantha, made jars to go in the shot and Charlotte, my daughter, rescued me from my pitiful attempts at biscuit decoration with some of her artful designs. Cake decorating – not my thing!

This recipe is vegan and gluten-free, once again making use of the buckwheat flour that I'm so fond of. The dough can be made in about 5 minutes flat, but you *must* chill it for an hour at least if you want to be able to work with it. Sorry, there is no short cut here. The dough makes quite a lot of biscuits, so I would advise rolling out a quarter of it at a time and keeping the rest chilled until you are ready to use it. One quarter of the dough will fill a good-sized baking sheet with biscuits. I rolled my dough out to about 5mm thick, but if you prefer a thicker biscuit then go for it. Just remember that you may need to add a little more time to the cooking.

Prep time: 30 minutes, including cutting. Chill time: 1 hour. Cooking time: 10 minutes per batch.
Gluten-free
Makes about 4 trays.

Ingredients:
Dry:
400g buckwheat flour, plus extra for dusting
1 tsp xanthan gum
1 tsp baking powder
1 tsp bicarbonate of soda
½ tsp salt
1 ½ tsp ground cinnamon
2 ½ tsp ground ginger

Wet:
150g vegan margarine, softened
1 tsp vanilla extract
150g dark brown sugar
50g black treacle
2 tbsp almond milk.

You will also need Halloween-shaped biscuit cutters.

Method:
Put all the dry ingredients into a mixing bowl and combine. In a separate bowl add all the wet ingredients and mix well with a spoon or whisk to fully incorporate. Make a well in the centre of the dry ingredients and pour in the wet then, using a knife or a spoon, mix the whole lot until it starts to clump together. Now is the time to get your hands dirty. Bring the mixture together with both hands to form a dough, then remove from the bowl and knead on a lightly-floured surface for 3-4 minutes, until the dough is smooth. Cover the dough and chill in the fridge for at least an hour.

Preheat the oven to Gas 4/180C/350F.

Line a large baking sheet with greaseproof paper, then take a quarter of the biscuit dough and roll it out on a well-floured surface to about 5mm thick (you can go thicker if you prefer). Use your chosen cutters to make shapes out of the dough and place them on the baking sheet. Leave a little gap between them but you don't need too much as they won't spread – a centimetre will do it. Once you have cut out all you can, roll up the left-over dough again and repeat the process to use up as much as you can. When the baking sheet is full, place in the middle of the oven and cook for 10 minutes, or until golden brown.

Once cooked, leave to cool on a cooling rack while you roll out the next quarter of dough. Repeat the whole process until all the dough is gone. When the biscuits are cooled you can decorate them with coloured icing of your choice.

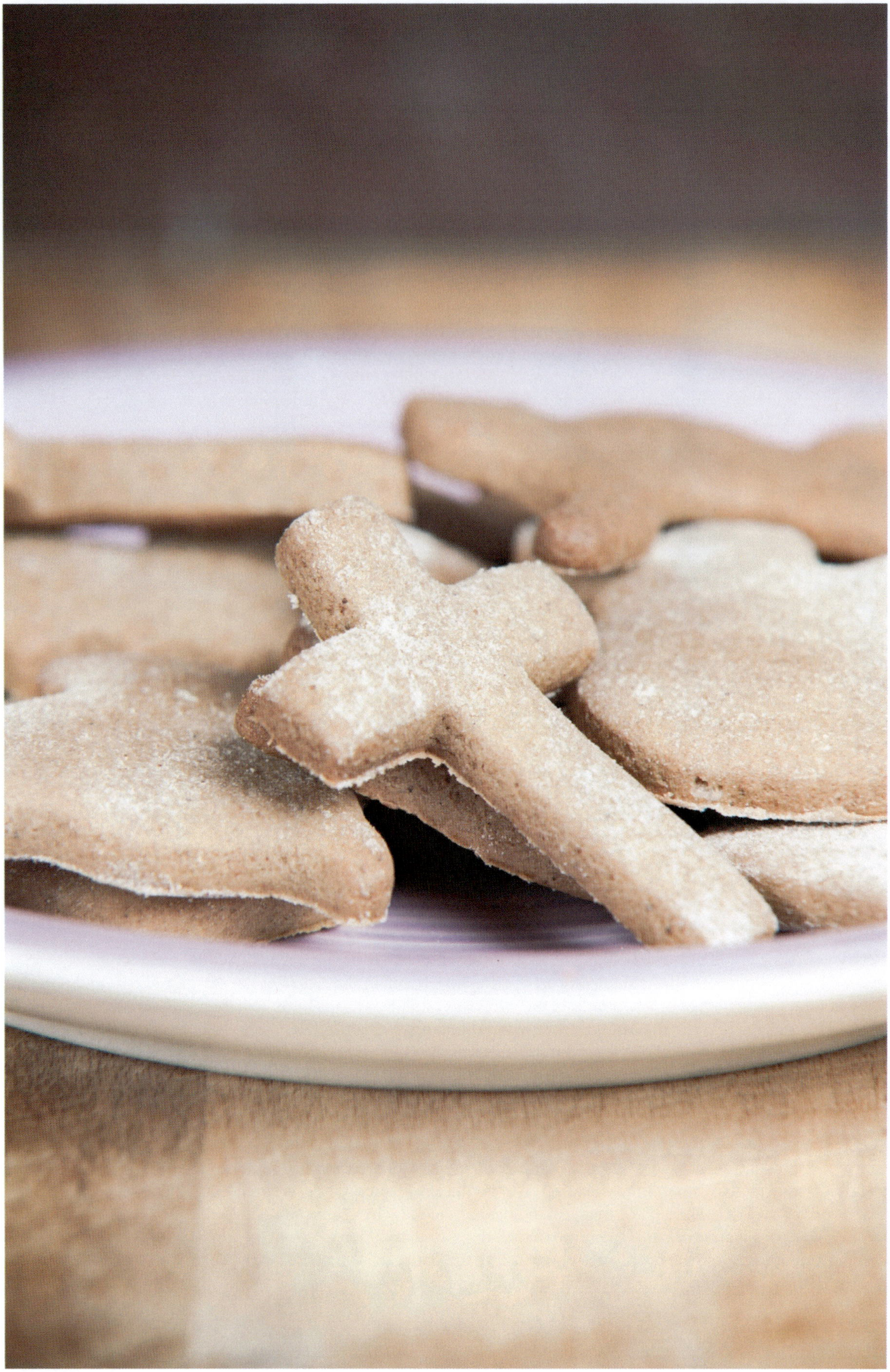

Spooky Halloween Gingerbread Biscuits

Curry-Spiced French Toast

I've been meaning to write this recipe for a while now. I first tried it about a year ago and instantly fell in love. It has been a go-to quick lunch ever since. I always use a hand whisk for the batter, but if you don't mind the extra washing up you can shove it all in a blender and get whizzing. If you *are* hand-whisking, then remember to add the water a little at a time. Make a thick batter first and then whisk out all the lumps before adding any more, otherwise you'll end up with a very lumpy mixture.

My main spice for this is hot madras curry powder mixed with a little turmeric, but if you have your own favourites then you can use those. The batter is completely gluten-free, though the bread I used in the picture was normal granary bread. Obviously just use your own gluten-free sliced bread if you are intolerant or coeliac. The batter will cover around 8-10 slices, so you can feed a couple of people with it. You want to dip the bread into the batter so that it is coated, but don't leave it in there for too long because only part of the bread will come back out in your hand! I've used coconut oil for frying, which complements it very well, but any oil you have to hand will serve just as well.

Prep time: 5 minutes. Cooking time: around 8 minutes per batch.
Easy to make gluten-free
Make 8-10 slices.

Ingredients:
150g gram (chickpea) flour
300ml water
3 tbsp plant-based yoghurt
1 tsp salt
¼ tsp ground black pepper
1 tsp ground turmeric
½ tsp ground ginger
1 ½ tbsp hot madras curry powder
2 tbsp tomato puree
1 tbsp golden syrup
Coconut oil (or any other oil) for frying
8-10 thick slices of bread (gluten-free or otherwise)

Method:
If you are using a blender, then you can throw all the ingredients, apart from the coconut oil and the bread, in together and then blend until completely smooth.

If you're old-fashioned like me, then put the flour into a mixing bowl and whisk in the water, a little at a time, until you have a smooth and reasonably thin batter. Add the rest of the ingredients, apart from the coconut oil and the bread, and then whisk it all together until fully incorporated.

Get a frying pan hot and then put in about ½ a tablespoon of coconut oil. Wait for it to completely melt. There should be a good heat to the oil for frying the bread. You can test this by dropping a little of the batter into the pan. If it immediately begins to sizzle, then you are good to go.

Dip a slice of bread into the batter mix, making sure it is fully coated. Let the excess drip back into the bowl, and then gently place into the frying pan. If you can fit two slices into your pan, then do so. Cook for about 3-4 minutes, until the bread is browned on the one side, then flip the slices over to cook the other side. When both sides are brown and crisp, they are ready. You can either serve each batch immediately or keep them warm in a low oven until you have finished cooking. Repeat the dipping and frying until all the batter has gone.

Serve the French toast with ketchup. It's really all you need!

Curry-Spiced French Toast

*****

Plaited Wholelmeal Bread

Wholemeal bread has always been one of those foods that's easier to buy than it is to make. Wholemeal flour is denser that its processed counterpart and, as such, is trickier to get a light bread from. I've long since given up the idea of 100% whole wheat in my breadmaking, so now I opt for about a quarter of strong white bread flour mixed in with the whole wheat batch. This 1:4 ratio is enough to get the gluten doing its job and give you the lift you need, at least when baking at home. Purists may scoff at my approach (though my wife is one such purist and she loves my bread), but this method works.

Other than this, I use all the same techniques for making this bread. I do give it longer to prove than I would with white bread, just to ensure that it has risen properly before baking it. The plaiting can be a little tricky if you haven't done it before. It had been a few years since I'd attempted it before making this one, so I had to undo it and start again. I'm sure if you're used to plaiting hair, then this will be a breeze. Just remember to tuck it in at each end to round it off before cooking. This recipe makes a large loaf, so you can always half the ingredients if you want something smaller.

Prep time: about 3 hours, most of which is proving time. Cooking time: 35 minutes.
Makes 1 large loaf.

Ingredients:
3 tsp (14g) dried yeast
1 tsp sugar
700-750ml tepid water
900g strong wholemeal flour
300g strong white bread flour
1 ½ tbsp salt
100g mixed seeds (hold some back to top the finished bread)

Groundnut oil for greasing

Method:
Put the yeast and sugar into a cup and add a little (about 50ml) of the tepid water. Stir with a spoon or fork until quite well blended, then leave aside for 15 minutes. During this time the yeast will activate and create a thick foam in the cup.

While the yeast is activating, put both flours, the salt and most of the mixed seeds into a large mixing bowl and combine with a spoon until fully amalgamated. Make a well in the centre and pour in the yeast foam. Add the water and then bring it all together using a table knife. Once it is sufficiently mixed, use your hands to knead it into a ball, then tip it out onto a floured surface and knead fully for about 10 minutes, until the dough has some elasticity.

Clean out the mixing bowl and line with a little of the groundnut oil, then put the dough in the bowl and cover with a towel. Put in a warm place and leave for about 2 hours, until it has doubled in size.

After this time, bring the dough back to the floured surface and knead all the air back out of it. Divide the dough into three and then roll each piece out into long sausage shapes (see picture).

Oil a baking sheet and tuck one end of each rolled dough together at the end of the sheet. Now plait them, one over the other, until all the dough it formed into plaits. Tuck in the other ends again so that you have a rounded shape at each end of the dough.

Brush oil over the finished dough and then sprinkle the remaining mixed seeds over the top. Cover lightly with the towel again and prove for the second time for about 40 minutes.

While the dough is proving preheat the oven to gas 6/200C/400F.

Remove the towel from the dough and gently place the tray in the middle of the oven. Cook for 35 minutes, or until it is risen and browned and sounds hollow when you tap the bottom.

Turn the cooked bread out onto a cooling rack and allow to cool before serving.

Plaited Wholelmeal Bread

Sweet French Toast with Forest Fruits and Banana

Not much beats French toast for breakfast, especially when the batter is sweetened and a little cooked fruit is added. It's a breakfast best suited to the weekend, when you have a little more time to create something special. This dish is a wonderful combination of hot and cold, and of soft and crunchy textures. With bursting berries and just-ripened banana, topped with maple syrup and a vegan crème fraiche, the flavours are divine. If you're not much of a breakfast eater, or the idea of working this hard on a Saturday morning is abhorrent to you, then this will also make an excellent dessert or even a late supper. The recipe for the batter and fruit topping is gluten free, so you just have to use your favourite gluten-free bread, whereas I used a regular artisan walnut bread for mine.

Prep time: 15 minutes. Cooking time: 20 minutes.
Easy to make gluten-free
Serves 2

Ingredients:
For the Batter:
1 ripe banana, mashed
250ml plant milk
A pinch of salt
1 tbsp 'No Egg' egg replacer
½ tsp ground cinnamon
A pinch of ground nutmeg
3 tbsp coconut nectar or maple syrup

For the Forest Fruit Topping:
1 tbsp coconut oil
250g frozen forest fruits
100g sugar
1 tsp vanilla extract

You will also need 4 slices of your favourite bread, plus more coconut oil for frying.

To Serve:
1 banana, cut into slices
2 heaped tablespoons vegan crème fraiche
2 tbsp maple syrup

Method:
First make the batter by putting all the batter ingredients into a mixing bowl and whisking until smooth. Set aside until needed.

Now make the forest fruit topping. Heat the tablespoon of coconut oil in a saucepan and add the forest fruits, sugar and vanilla extract. Bring to the boil and simmer for 10 minutes, until the berries are soft and the sauce slightly thickened. Set aside.

Heat another tablespoon of coconut oil in a frying pan and dip 2 slices of bread into the batter. Carry the batter over to the pan to avoid dripping, then place the two slices of bread into the pan. The oil should be hot enough that they sizzle immediately. Cook the bread for about 4 minutes each side, until browned and crisp, then keep warm in a low oven while you cook the next batch.

To serve, put two slices of the fried bread on a plate, place half the sliced banana on top, then add a couple of spoons of the forest fruit sauce. Top with a dollop of the vegan crème fraiche and a tablespoon of maple syrup.

Sweet French Toast with Forest Fruits and Banana

Warmer Climate Food

Tortilla Salad with Avocados and Red Chillies

Oven Roasted Figs with Vegan Blue Cheese

Basic Humous

Roasted Mediterranean Vegetables with Dried Dates and Clementines

Chilled Granola Peach Crumble

Sautéed New Potatoes with Kale and Figs

Aubergine and Sweet Potato Curry

Chickpea Flour Pancakes with Plantain

Baba Ghanoush

Pumpkin and Mango Curry

Richard's Homemade Hot Chilli Sauce

Poached Nectarines in Cardamom Syrup

Salad of Watermelon, Avocado and Vegan 'Greek Style' Cheese

Lemon and Ginger Cookies

Kale and Dill Wraps with Aubergine, Pineapple and Black Beans

Pancakes with Banana and Peaches

Aubergine and Cherry Tomato Bruschetta with Green Olive Tapenade

Peach and Frangipane Tart

Tortilla Salad with Avocados and Red Chillies

Prep time: 10 minutes. Cooking time: 15 minutes.
Easy to make gluten-free (just change wraps)
Serves 3-4

Ingredients:
2 tortilla wraps
2 tbsp oil
100g mixed salad leaves (pre mixed, or mix your own)
1 red onion, finely sliced
100g baby tomatoes, quartered
1 red chilli, finely sliced
2 ripe avocados, cut into 6 wedges each

For the Dressing:
Juice of 1 lime
50ml maple syrup
50ml olive oil
1 ½ tsp wholegrain mustard

Method:
Preheat the oven to gas 6/200C/400F.

Brush oil onto the two tortillas and cut them into halves, then quarters, then eights, so that you end up with 16 wedges in total. Put these wedges onto a baking sheet, then place in the middle of the oven for 10-15 minutes, stirring them around halfway through to ensure they cook evenly. Remove the wedges when they are golden but not too browned, then leave them aside to cool and firm up.

Put the mixed leaves into a mixing bowl, then add the onion, tomato and chilli.

To make the dressing, put all the dressing ingredients into a small bowl and whisk until completely combined. Pour the dressing over the salad.

Cut the avocados in half, take out the stone and remove the flesh with a spoon, so that the halves come out in tact (the avocados need to be ripe for this, and Has avocados work best). Cut each half into three wedges, so that you end up with 12 in total. Put them straight into the salad and mix to fully cover them in the dressing (this will stop them from going black).

When you are ready to serve, place some of the tortillas onto a plate and arrange the dressed salad on top. Serve immediately.

Tortilla Salad with Avocados and Red Chillies

Oven Roasted Figs with Vegan Blue Cheese

Remember the pineapple and cheese cubes on sticks we used to get at parties? Well think of this as the posh version. Your social cred will go up mega points if you serve these at your next bash, plus they take no time at all.

Prep time: 5 minutes. Cooking time: 12 minutes.
Gluten-Free
Serves 4-6

Ingredients:
12 ripe figs
2 tbsp olive oil
12 x 1 cm cubes vegan blue cheese.

Method:
Preheat the oven to gas mark 7/220C/425F.

Cut the stalk off the top of each fig and then cut a cross downwards from the top of each fig to about half way through. Put the figs into a bowl with the olive oil and then toss them around to coat them. Take each fig by the bottom and gently squeeze so that the cross you made opens up like a flower, then put one cube of cheese inside each opening. Place the stuffed figs on a baking tray and roast in the oven for 12 minutes, until the fruit is soft and the cheese is melted slightly. Serve hot or cold.

*****

Basic Humous

Prep time: 5 minutes. No cooking time.
Gluten-Free
Makes a large tubful.

Ingredients:
2 cans chickpeas, drained (reserve the liquid for one of the aquafaba recipes in this book)
3 tsp garlic paste
1 tsp Dijon Mustard
3 heaped tbsp tahini
1 tbsp liquid smoke
The juice from 1 lime
3 tbsp natural vegan yoghurt
½ tsp sea salt
A generous dash of black pepper
200ml sunflower oil

Method:
Simply put all of the ingredients into a food processor and blitz until smooth. Store in an air-tight container and keep in the fridge for up to 5 days.

*****

Roasted Mediterranean Vegetables with Dried Dates and Clementines

This is pretty much fruit and veg and not much else, only done in such a way as to be nothing short of divine. It is a dish for making an impression, for serving up on a big platter and sharing. It is your centre piece at the dinner table, with other, smaller dishes orbiting it like satellites. It is all colour and flavour, and the eyes of those nearby will be inevitably drawn to it in a dream-like gaze. You'll want to make sure you've got plenty of bread too, for all the leftover garlic oil.

Prep time: 20 minutes. Cooking time: about 55 minutes
Gluten Free
Serves 4-6

Ingredients:
For the Roasted Veg:
1 aubergine, cut into wedges
1 large courgette, cut the same
1 large red onion, large wedges
1 large red pepper and 1 large yellow pepper, cut into thick strips and those strips cut in half
5-6 cloves garlic, peeled and bashed with the flat of a knife
A large glug of olive oil (about 50ml)
Salt and pepper to taste

For the Dates and Clementines:
2 tbsp olive oil
2 tomatoes, cut into wedges
120g whole, pitted dates
1 large (or 3 small) spring onions, sliced
A handful of flaked almonds
2 clementines, peeled and segmented
A large handful of parsley leaves, roughly chopped
A squeeze of lemon juice
1 tbsp ground paprika

To Garnish:
A couple of spoons of vegan yoghurt
A couple of spoons of humous
A few chopped parsley leaves
A few almond flakes
A dusting of ground paprika

Method:
Preheat the oven to gas 7/220C/425F.

Put all of the ingredients for the roasted veg into a large mixing bowl and mix with your hands until everything is covered in the oil. Transfer to a large, lipped baking tray and roast near the top of the oven for about 45 minutes, stirring the veg a few times, until it is soft and slightly charred.

In the last 8-10 minutes of cooking, start cooking the dates and clementines. Heat the olive oil in a large frying pan or wok and cook the tomatoes and dates together in the pan for about 5 minutes. Add the spring onions and cook for another 2-3 minutes, then put in the almond flakes, the clementine segments and the parsley. Cook for 2 minutes more. Now stir in the lemon juice and the paprika and take off the heat.

To serve, arrange the roasted veg, along with the garlic and oil, around the edge of a large serving plate or platter. Spoon the clementine and date mix into the middle of the platter. Now top with the yoghurt and humous and sprinkle on the parsley, almonds and paprika.

Chilled Granola Peach Crumble

Crumble doesn't always have to be a lengthy process. You can make a fairly quick and easy crumble if you've got some granola lying around. For this recipe I've chosen peaches for the filling, which needed using up in my fridge, but you can use any fruit that you have available. The same with the granola, if you've got some shop bought in your cupboard, then use that. If you don't, or if you want to make your own, I have a recipe for it in my previous book, Going Vegan.

The only lengthy process to this is cooling down the fruit filling. If you can make this part the night before, then great. You will want to give it at least 2 hours in the fridge, however, to get it cold enough to serve.

Prep time: 10 minutes. Cooking time: 10 minutes, plus chilling time.
To guarantee Gluten Free, use gluten free oats (not always suitable for coeliacs).
Serves 4

Ingredients:
1 heaped tbsp vegan butter
4-5 peaches, stoned and cut into pieces
75g sugar
½ tsp ground cinnamon
¼ tsp ground nutmeg
Small pinch chilli powder
About 240g granola
About 150ml vegan cream

Method:
Melt the butter in a small saucepan and add the peaches, sugar and spices. Cook for 10 minutes on a good simmer, until the peaches are soft and covered in a thick sauce. Allow to cool, and then chill in the fridge for at least 2 hours, or overnight.

Put about 50g of granola into the bottom of a serving dish, spoon on a quarter of the chilled peaches, pour a quarter of the cream onto the peaches and then sprinkle a little more granola on top. Repeat this for 4 servings.

Sautéed New Potatoes with Kale and Figs

Not every vegan eats figs. Some consider them to not be vegan at all, due to the relationship between the wasp and the fig, a relationship that has existed for tens of millions of years. In a nutshell, the female fig wasp climbs inside the male fig flower to lay her eggs, this in turn pollinates the fig flower and the relationship is seen to be mutually beneficial. There are occasions when it is not, however, when concerning the dioecious fig, whose female flowers mimic the scent of male flowers to attract the female wasp, even though reproduction is impossible within the female flower. To cut a long (but rather interesting) story short, fig wasps spend their lives from birth to maturity inside the fig and many, of course, die inside the fig and are then consumed. It's easy to see why some people won't touch them, but I'm not one of them.

The brief appearance of fresh, in season, figs (which runs typically from August to October) on our shelves is, to me at least, a quintessential part of autumn. Their arrival is something I look forward to as much as the influx of pumpkins in early to mid-October. Their sweet, soft and vibrantly pink flesh, that is wonderful both as it is and cooked, fills me with excitement.
This dish is essentially a hot salad, where quartered figs are cooked for about 4 minutes at the end. The trick with figs is never to cook them for long, as you want them soft and warm, but not mushy.

Prep time: 10 minutes. Cooking time: 35 minutes.
Gluten-Free
Serves 3-4

Ingredients:
250g baby new potatoes
2 tbsp groundnut oil (or other flavourless oil)
5 black kale leaves, stalks removed and thinly sliced
A handful of pine nuts
4 ripe figs, cut into quarters
1 tsp garlic puree (or 1 chopped garlic clove)

For the Dressing:
50ml fresh orange juice
50ml olive oil
1 tsp Dijon mustard
¼ tsp harissa paste
2 tbsp maple syrup

To Serve:
A handful of pomegranate seeds

Method:
Bring a medium to large saucepan of water to the boil and put in the new potatoes. Boil the potatoes for 10-15 minutes, until they are tender (you can check this by piercing with a sharp knife). Drain and allow to dry.

Heat the oil in a large frying pan or wok and sauté the cooked potatoes for 8-10 minutes, until they are crisp and browned. Add the kale leaves and cook for 5-6 more minutes, stirring often, then throw in the pine nuts and give it 2 minutes more.

Now add the figs and cook for 3 more minutes, until they have started to soften. Be careful when moving them around the pan as they can mash up when soft. Add the teaspoon of garlic puree and give it all a final minute of cooking, then turn off the heat.

Now make the dressing by whisking all the dressing ingredients in a small bowl, until fully combined. Pour the dressing over the potatoes and figs while it is still in the pan and stir in to fully coat. Serve onto bowls or plates and sprinkle with pomegranate seeds.

*****

Aubergine and Sweet Potato Curry

This is a rich and spicy tomato-based curry, with aubergine and sweet potato. There is a good dose of chilli in this one, so if you prefer something milder, leave out the cayenne pepper and half the dried chillies. This dish uses garlic, onion and ginger that has been pureed prior to cooking to fully infuse the flavour into the sauce. If you don't have a blender or food-processor, just chop the onions and garlic up as small as you can. You can also use garlic puree instead of fresh, where you would allow a teaspoon per clove.

Prep Time: 15-20 minutes. Cooking time: about 1 hour.
Gluten Free
Serves 3-4

Ingredients:
2 onions, roughly cut
4 large garlic cloves, peeled and bashed with the flat of a knife
3 tsp ginger paste
75ml water
2 tbsp coconut oil
1 cinnamon stick
4-5 whole dried chillies
3 cardamom pods
1 tbsp coriander seeds
2 tsp cumin seeds
2 sweet potatoes, peeled and diced
1 aubergine, diced
10-12 cherry tomatoes, halved
1 tsp turmeric
1 tsp garam masala
3 tbsp tandoori masala spice mix (or other red curry powder blend)
¼ tsp ground black pepper
¼ tsp cayenne pepper
Juice of 1 lemon
2 tsp salt
2 cans chopped tomatoes
½ can water

Method:
To start, put the onions, garlic, ginger paste and 75ml of water into a blender and puree until completely smooth. Set aside.

Heat the coconut oil in a large saucepan or wok, then add the cinnamon stick, dried chillies, cardamom, coriander and cumin seeds and gently fry for 1 minute, until the seeds start to toast.

Add the sweet potato and aubergine and cook for 6-8 minutes, stirring often, until they start to brown and soften a little. Now put in the cherry tomatoes and cook for 2-3 more minutes.

Take your onion and garlic mix from the blender and add to the curry. Cook on a reasonably high heat for 5 minutes or so, stirring often to prevent sticking and burning.

Now add the rest of the spices and all the other ingredients. Bring to the boil and gently simmer for 40 minutes, until you have a thick and fragrant curry sauce.

Serve with rice.

*****

Chickpea Flour Pancakes with Plantain

Plantain is not something I have very often. I don't dislike it, it's just not in my regular repertoire. Sam and Charlotte love it though, and so they brought some home for me to cook. I admit that I tend to cook it the same way every time, and just vary the things around it. First, I slice it, then coat it in gram (chickpea) flour before shallow-frying it in a little oil.

The flour coating gives it a nice browned colour and a very slightly crisp outer shell. I don't stir them around, as this will break them up. Instead, I cook them on one side for a couple of minutes, and then turn them gently with a fork to do the other side. If you do it this way you might find that you want to brown the first side a little more. Just flip them back over gently and handle them as little as possible. When they are done, keep them on a plate while you do everything else. It doesn't matter if they go cold as they'll be placed inside the pancake later to warm back up.

The chickpea flour pancakes are something I discovered a little while ago and now I make as often as I can. All you do is fry the batter in a pan, just like a regular pancake, and you can stuff it with whatever filling you like. It's kind of like making a hot wrap, or a toasted sandwich. This recipe uses the plantain, as well as peppers, cheese and avocado. My favourite thing to do with them, however, is to make a big pot of chilli one evening, and then fill the pancakes with the leftovers from that. Then you've got two exciting meals out of one dish. If you haven't made these before, use this recipe as a starting point to get your batter mix and your technique. Once you have that down, there's a whole world of fillings open to you.

Prep time: 15 minutes. Cooking time: 12 minutes for the filling, then about 8 minutes per pancake.
Gluten Free.
Makes 6-8

Ingredients:
For the Pancake Batter:
250g chickpea flower
1 tsp baking powder
1 tbsp curry powder
1 tbsp ground coriander
1 tbsp ground paprika
1 tsp salt
Pinch of black pepper
400ml cold water

For the Filling:
100g gram (Chickpea) flour
A pinch of salt
2 ripe plantain, sliced
2-3 tbsp flavourless oil, such as groundnut
1 tbsp olive oil (or you can use same as above)
1 red onion, sliced
2 Romano (or other red peppers), sliced
Salt and pepper
Juice of 1 lime
2 avocados, sliced
About ½ can pineapple chunks (the chunks themselves will be too thick, so cut them in half. I did this to order while I was cooking them.)
150g vegan cheese, grated
Enough oil to fry the pancakes.

Method:
First make the batter. Put all the batter ingredients, apart from the water, into a large mixing bowl. Gradually add the water, whisking to make sure that no lumps form. If you begin whisking while the batter is very thick, you'll be able to get rid of the lumps before thinning it out with the rest of the water. Set the batter aside until it is needed.

Now fry the plantain: Put the chickpea flour and salt into another bowl and drop in the plantain (do this in batches if you need to), then shake off the excess flour. Heat the groundnut oil in a frying pan and fry half of the plantain at a time to not overcrowd the pan. Fry for about 3 minutes on one side, before gently turning them over with a fork and frying the other side. They are done when they are nicely browned, but not burnt. Set aside on a plate and then cook the other half of the plantain. Clean out the pan to use for the rest of the recipe.

To make the filling, first heat the olive oil in the pan and then fry the onions and peppers together for 4-5 minutes, until they have softened and slightly browned. Season with salt and pepper and then squeeze on the lime juice. Cook for a minute more and then transfer to a dish or bowl.

Now you can make and assemble your pancakes. Heat a little oil in the frying pan until quite hot, then pour about ¾ of a ladleful of the batter into the pan. Spread the batter around the pan, just as you would a normal pancake, and cook on the one side for a minute or two. It doesn't have to be fully browned, just make sure that it is cooked enough to be able to flip it over with a spatula.

Flip the pancake over as mentioned above, then start to add the filling. Keeping half of the pancake blank (have in mind that you are going to be folding it over at the end), place 4 slices of the plantain on the one half. Add a little of the peppers and onion mixture, then add about 4 slices of avocado. Put on a few of the pineapple chunks (remembering to cut them in half to make them thinner) and then top with a little of the vegan cheese. Now fold the other half of the pancake over and press down gently with the spatula. Once the pancake is crisp on the one side, turn it over to do the other side. Should take 3-4 minutes each side to be ready.

Once the pancake is ready, keep it warm in a low oven while you get on with the rest of them. If you only want to make a couple of these, then either halve the recipe, or store in containers in the fridge for another day.

Chickpea Flour Pancakes with Plantain

Baba Ghanoush

This Middle-Eastern aubergine dip has a distinctive smoky flavour, which is best achieved by roasting the aubergines whole on an open flame. You can do this on a barbecue, if the weather permits, or you can roast them over the flame of your gas stovetop. Do this using a pair of cooking tongs and keep turning the aubergine over, so that it blackens evenly over the entire surface area. Once I achieve a crisp, black skin, I like to then finish them off in the oven to ensure the aubergine is soft all the way through. You can cook the aubergines just in the oven if you prefer, but you will lose the smoky flavour that is so characteristic of baba ghanoush.

The dip will keep nicely in the fridge for a few days, so you can make it in advance if you like.

Prep time: 15 minutes. Cooking time: 30-35 minutes, plus chilling time.
Gluten-Free
Serves 4

Ingredients:
2 medium aubergines, whole
1 tbsp oil, for brushing
Juice of 1 small lemon
1 – 1 ½ cloves garlic, minced or grated on a micro plane
A small handful of flat-leaf parsley, chopped
3 tbsp natural vegan yoghurt
3 tbsp olive oil
Salt and pepper to taste

Method:
Preheat the oven to gas 6/200C/400F.

First you want to blacken your aubergines. Pierce both aubergines with a sharp knife in several places. Switch one of the burners of you gas stove onto a gentle heat and place one of the aubergines directly onto the flame. Cook for 10-15 minutes, turning often to make sure that the skin blackens around the whole surface of the aubergine. If you are confident with this, you can turn on a second burner and cook both aubergines at the same time. The skin will char and shrivel slightly when they are ready to remove.

Once they are done, place the aubergines on a baking sheet and brush them with the oil, then put them in the oven for another 15-20 minutes to cook all the way through. If you don't have a gas top, or don't feel confident doing this, then skip the first step and cook them in the oven for about 30-35 minutes (remember to pierce them first).

Once they are cooked through, allow the aubergines to cool enough to be able to handle them, then cut them in half lengthways. Pull the skin away, using either a spoon or a fork and chop the cooked aubergine flesh with a sharp knife. Put the flesh into a bowl.

Now add the lemon juice, garlic, parsley, yoghurt and olive oil and stir until fully combined. Season to taste with the salt and pepper, then cover and chill in the fridge until ready to use.

Baba Ghanoush

Pumpkin and Mango Curry

This dish combines some of my favourite ingredients, in particular pumpkin and mango, which I adore. I use coconut oil for making curries almost exclusively these days, as its subtle flavour lends itself really well to this kind of cooking. Whole spices are essential for this for their flavours to infuse without becoming overpowering. As a result, this curry is mild and sweet, yet incredibly robust.

If it's not pumpkin season and you haven't got any stored, then you can easily switch it with butternut squash for this recipe.

Prep time: 20 minutes: Cooking time: about 50 minutes
Gluten Free
Serves 3-4

Ingredients:
2 tbsp coconut oil
¼ large pumpkin, peeled, deseeded and diced (or one medium butternut squash)
Salt and pepper
3 whole dried chillies
1 cinnamon stick
1 tbsp coriander seeds
1 tsp cumin seeds
3 green cardamom pods
1 red onion, sliced
1 red pepper, diced
3 cloves garlic, chopped
2 tbsp mild curry powder
1 tsp ground turmeric
1 tbsp ground paprika
3 tbsp vegan yoghurt
1 ripe mango, peeled and diced
1 can coconut milk
Salt and pepper to taste

Method:
Heat half of the coconut oil in a large wok or saucepan and cook the pumpkin for 15-20 minutes, without a lid, until it is soft. Season with the salt and pepper about 5 minutes before the end of cooking. Once the pumpkin is cooked, remove it from the pan and set it aside.

Clean out your pan and heat the rest of the coconut oil in it, then add the chillies, cinnamon stick, coriander seeds, cumin seeds and cardamom. Cook for 2 minutes on a gentle heat, then add the onions and peppers and fry for 4-5 minutes, stirring often. Add the garlic and cook for another minute, then put in the rest of the spices and the yoghurt.

Stir thoroughly and then add the diced mango. Cook for 3 more minutes before putting the pumpkin back in the pan. Pour in the coconut milk, season to taste and simmer for 15-20 minutes, until you have a nice, thick sauce.

Serve with rice.

*****

Richard's Homemade Hot Chilli Sauce

With an endless variety of chilli sauces on the market, it's understandable to ask the question 'why bother making my own?' It's a perfectly reasonable question. There are a lot of really good chilli sauces out there that don't cost much more than a pound to buy, which is cheaper than buying the ingredients and doing it yourself.

The reason for making your own chilli sauce, for the most part at least, is because you have the passion to do so. I made this chilli sauce, not because I couldn't find one I liked, but because I really wanted to make this one. I also wanted to see how mine would hold up against the store-bought options.

As it turns out, I really like my chilli sauce recipe. It is hot without being overly so, and has a deliciously dense, fruity background flavour. Roasting the chilies, tomatoes, garlic and onions first really helps with the flavour. I'm sharing it with you here in the hope that you will also try it, and like it as much as I do. I will still be buying ready-made chilli sauces, just because it's more convenient, but I will also be making this from time to time.

This is quite a large batch, but I recommend making it all and freezing half of it. It'll last about 2 weeks in the fridge, so it is better to freeze what you think you're not going to use in that time. You could always portion it into 100ml batches and freeze them separately, or even use an ice cube tray.

Prep time: 20 minutes. Cooking time: 1 hour 25 minutes, plus cooling time.
Gluten Free
Makes 400ml

Ingredients:
12 medium red chillies, stalks removed and cut in half (no need to deseed them)
2 small onions, peeled and quartered
3 large cloves garlic, peeled and kept hole
6 medium tomatoes, quartered
2 tbsp sesame oil
1 tbsp olive oil
Large handful coriander leaves
Juice of 2 limes
100ml white wine or cider vinegar (I used white wine)
300ml red grape juice
145g golden caster sugar
3 tbsp tomato puree
1 tsp Dijon mustard
1 tbsp liquid smoke
1 ½ tsp salt

Method:
Preheat the oven to gas 6/200C/400F.

Put the chillies, onions, garlic and tomatoes into a mixing bowl and add the sesame and olive oils. Mix well and then spread the lot out onto a baking tray. Roast in the middle of the oven for 1 hour, or until the chillies have just started to blacken around the edges.

When they are done, allow them to cool slightly, then tip them into a blender. Add the coriander, lime juice and vinegar and puree twice, until completely smooth.

Tip the resulting liquid into a saucepan and mix in the rest of the ingredients. Bring to the boil and simmer, stirring from time to time, for 20 minutes. Add a little more salt if you need to, then pass the mixture through a sieve and into a bowl. The resulting thin liquid will trickle out into the bowl beneath the sieve. I found it helpful to use a large serving spoon to press the pulp into the sieve and get as much of the chilli sauce out as possible. When you are done, discard the pulp and allow the chilli sauce to completely cool. Store in the fridge for up to two weeks, or freeze in batches as mentioned above.

Richard's Homemade Hot Chilli Sauce

Poached Nectarines in Cardamom Syrup

Prep time: 15 minutes. Cooking time: 25 minutes, plus chilling time
Gluten-Free
Serves 4

Ingredients:
4 ripe nectarines
900ml water
300g sugar
2 cinnamon sticks
5 cardamom pods, opened and the seeds ground in a pestle and mortar

To serve:
8 tbsp plain dairy-free yoghurt
4 tbsp maple syrup
A little of the cardamom syrup

Method:
First you need to peel the nectarines. To do this, bring a pan of water to the boil, pop the nectarines in and simmer for 30 seconds to 1 minute. Take out of the water with a slotted spoon and plunge the nectarines straight into cold water. Leave them in the cold water for a minute, then use a small paring knife to peel them. You may need to do this twice for the skins to come off easily.

Now bring the 900ml water to the boil and pour in the sugar. Add the cinnamon and cardamom seeds and simmer for 5 minutes to dissolve the sugar.

Put the nectarines into the syrup, put a lid on the pan and gently simmer for 15-20 minutes, or until the fruit is tender. Allow to cool, and then chill in the fridge.

To serve, place a chilled nectarine into a dessert dish and pour over a little of the cooled cardamom syrup. Mix the maple syrup with the yoghurt and serve a quarter with each nectarine, either in the dish or on the side.

*****

Salad of Watermelon, Avocado and Vegan 'Greek Style' Cheese

The salads I grew up with had a very strict format: a few slices of ham and cheese. A boiled egg cut with one of those mechanical slicers that my sister and I used to ping with our nails like little guitar strings. A couple of dark, bland lettuce leaves placed on the side, and let's not forget the sliced, pickled beetroot. It's thin, runny liquid staining everything on the plate, giving the egg and cheese a strange purple hue, the lettuce almost black in parts. It's no surprise that I grew up with more than a mild distaste for the summer salad.

Things didn't change for me until I started making my own, where I became gradually aware of the huge breadth of food available. My interest in a not too pleasant childhood food grew rapidly. I began throwing anything and everything I could get my hands on into a bowl and mixing it together. Sometimes with disastrous results, other times I was able to create meals so intensely flavoured I couldn't help but go back for more. From apples and grapes to summer squash and quinoa. Hot food juxtaposed with cold on the same plate. There was no shortage of ingredients I could throw together. It was like cooking without rules and I loved it.

Years later, though my hand is a little more seasoned, I still take a similar approach to making salads. I play and I experiment. I use ingredients (for the most part) that are seasonal and readily available. It's often a case of banging things together and seeing what comes out. This Watermelon, Avocado and Vegan 'Greek Style' Cheese salad is the end result of one such experiment. Bursting both with flavour and colour, this recipe will get you excited about summer lunches in the garden.

Prep time: 15 minutes.
Gluten-Free
Serves 2-4.

Ingredients:
For the Salad:
½ bag ready-prepped mixed leaf salad
½ bag ready-prepped rocket, watercress and baby spinach mix (you can mix your own leaves if you prefer)
1 avocado, diced
2 medium tomatoes, cut into wedges
½ red onion, sliced
100g vegan Greek style cheese, cubed
300-300g watermelon, cut into large chunks.

For the Dressing:
50ml olive oil
3 tbsp white wine vinegar
1 tsp Dijon mustard
1 tbsp lemon juice
2 tbsp coconut nectar (maple syrup is also fine)
A sprinkle of chopped hazelnuts to garnish.

Method:
Put all the salad ingredients into a large bowl and mix around to evenly distribute them.

Put the dressing ingredients, apart from the hazelnuts, into a small bowl and whisk together until you have an emulsified dressing.

Pour the dressing over the salad and mix together again, then divide the salad onto plate and sprinkle over the chopped hazelnuts.

Salad of Watermelon, Avocado and Vegan 'Greek Style' Cheese

Lemon and Ginger Cookies

I love sweet things that taste of lemon. You can give them to me over chocolate any day of the week. Not that I don't love chocolate also (there's a whole chapter devoted to it at the end of this book), but that zesty tang has always been a favourite of mine. When I was a child, I chose lemon curd over everything else to spread on my toast, and my grandmother always kept a jar in her pantry for my weekend visits. Perhaps it's that childhood nostalgia that keeps me returning to that citrus flavour. Perhaps, to me at least, it tastes of weekends in the garden, climbing the apple tree and running around with my cousins. Or of Friday nights, tucked up in bed and being lovingly read to from comics that Nana would buy during the week for my sister and I. Taste and memory are mischievous allies: they lead each other down forgotten passageways and unlock dusty old doors.

So, with that yearning for familiar flavours, I set about creating this recipe. It's a basic vegan and gluten-free drop cookie mix, with a healthy dose of lemon zest and juice. I've also used stem ginger, the kind you get in a jar with syrup (you can put a little of the syrup in with it as well). The ginger gives the cookies a good base flavour and helps to balance out the lemon.

There's no real need to get out fancy equipment for this recipe, as you can mix all of this with a wooden spoon. Just make sure your bowl is big enough, so that you don't send cookie batter flying across the kitchen.

Prep time: 20 minutes or so. Cooking time: 20 minutes.
Gluten-Free
Makes about 24 cookies.

Ingredients:
Wet:
300g vegan margarine
300g unrefined caster sugar
1 tsp vanilla extract
Juice and zest of 2 lemons
3 tbsp golden syrup
75g (about 4 knobs) stem ginger in syrup, chopped into small pieces, plus a little of the syrup

Dry:
300g plain gluten-free flour
100g coconut flour
2 tsp baking powder
1 tsp bicarbonate of soda
1 tsp xanthan gum
2 tbsp chia seeds (optional)
½ tsp salt

100ml vegan single cream

Method:
Preheat the oven to gas 4/180C/350F and line a baking sheet with greaseproof paper.

Put the margarine and sugar in a bowl together and mix with a wooden spoon until you have a fluffy pale mixture (about 10 minutes). Add the vanilla extract and then grate the lemon zest, using the fine side of your grater, into the mixture. Squeeze the juice from the two lemons and then add the golden syrup. Mix until incorporated, then put in the chopped ginger pieces and a little of the syrup. Stir again to mix it all in.

In a separate bowl, combine the two flours, the baking powder, bicarb of soda, xanthan gum, chia seeds (if using) and salt. Mix it all together to incorporate.

Pour the dry ingredients into the wet and stir thoroughly. Pour in the vegan cream and mix again, then leave to stand for 10 minutes.

Now dollop a heaped tablespoon of the mixture at a time onto your lined baking sheet, leaving a good space in between them as they will spread out. I managed to get 6 at a time on my sheet, but I was probably a bit over generous with the portion size. Flatten them a little with the back of the spoon so that they are not too deep when cooked. It's actually easier to do this part with your hands, but it doesn't give that rocky finished look.

Put your tray in the middle of the oven and bake for 18-20 minutes, until crisp and golden. Turn the cookies out onto a cooling rack and leave to stand while you get on with the next batch. Continue until all the batter is gone.

Lemon and Ginger Cookies

Kale and Dill Wraps with Aubergine, Pineapple and Black Beans

These are the standard chickpea flour wraps, but with the addition of kale and dill to the batter to give it a green colour, and to get a few extra veggies in us. This is done by adding the kale, dill and some lime juice to water and blending together until completely smooth. That then becomes the water that you whisk into the chickpea flour to make your batter. I've chosen aubergine, pineapple and black beans, along with fresh, ripe tomatoes as the filling, but you can really use anything you like.

Prep time: 15 minutes. Cooking time: 20 minutes for the filling, plus about 6-8 minutes per wrap.
Gluten Free
Serves 4

Ingredients:
For the Batter:
2-3 black kale leaves, stalks removed and leaves torn into small pieces
A handful of fresh dill
Juice of 1 lime
450ml cold water
200g gram (chickpea) flour
2 tsp baking powder
2 tsp salt
¼ tsp black pepper
2 tsp mild chilli powder
1 tsp Dijon mustard

For the Filling:
2 tbsp olive oil
1 aubergine, sliced lengthways, the slices halved and then cut into batons
½ pineapple, sliced and then each slice cut into strips
1 can black beans, washed and drained
2 tsp garlic puree
3-4 medium tomatoes, cut into wedges
2 tsp harissa paste
3 tbsp tomato puree
4 tbsp tamari
50ml water
Vegetable oil for frying
150g vegan cheese, grated

Method:
To make the batter, first put the kale with the dill, lime juice and water into a blender and puree until it is completely smooth. Put the rest of the batter ingredients into a mixing bowl and gradually whisk in the kale water, making sure you get all the lumps out. Once you've achieved a smooth batter you can set it aside and make the filling.

Heat the olive oil in a large frying pan or wok. Cook the aubergine and pineapple together, on a high heat, for 6-8 minutes, until the moisture has evaporated and the strips have begun to soften and brown. Add the drained black beans and cook for another two minutes, then put in the garlic puree and fry for a minute more, stirring often.

Keep the same high heat going and throw in the tomato wedges. Continue cooking for 3-4 minutes, then stir in the harissa paste, tomato puree, tamari and water. Cook for 5 more minutes, or until most of the liquid has evaporated, then set aside.

Preheat the oven to gas 2/150C/300F.

In a clean, non-stick frying pan, heat a little of the vegetable oil, until quite hot, and then spoon a ladleful of the batter into the pan. Spread it around the pan, just like a pancake and allow to cook on the one side for about 2 minutes. Use a spatula to gently flip the wrap over to cook the other side. While that side is cooking, spoon about a quarter of the filling (or less if you prefer) onto one half of the wrap, leaving the other half empty, then sprinkle a quarter of the cheese on top. Use the spatula to fold the empty half of the wrap over the filling and then cook on both sides for a couple of minutes more, until they are browned and a little crisp.

Transfer to a baking tray and keep warm in the oven while you cook the remaining wraps. Serve with vegan sour cream and sriracha sauce.

Kale and Dill Wraps with Aubergine, Pineapple and Black Beans

*****

Pancakes with Banana and Peaches

If your store cupboard is anything like mine, you'll be able to make these pancakes without even having to go to the shop for ingredients. I made them intentionally out of things I had lying about the place: bananas, canned peaches, raisins and a bit of sugar. I also topped them with some vegan custard (and if you haven't got a stockpile of that stuff, then what's *wrong* with you?), just for something easy and delicious to soak into them. You can have these as a weekend breakfast, or you can do what I did this evening and just skip dinner altogether and go straight for the pudding!

These are the American style thick pancakes, which are my favourite kind, so the recipe is for a thick batter that you spoon into the pan. The trick with these is to make sure the oil is hot before putting the mixture into the pan, and also to make sure that the top, uncooked side starts to bubble before you turn them over. You want a good heat under them, but don't have it so high that you burn the outside of the pancakes before the middle is even cooked. Just have it slightly north of medium and you'll be fine.

Prep time: 5 minutes. Cooking time: 6-8 minutes per batch.

Serves 3

Ingredients:
300g self-raising flour
1 tsp baking powder
Pinch salt
50g unrefined sugar
400ml soya milk
60g raisins
Coconut oil for shallow frying
3 bananas, sliced
1 can peach slices, well drained
Couple of pinches of sugar
150ml vegan custard
A small handful of extra raisins to top

Method:

Put the flour, baking powder, salt and sugar into a mixing bowl, then gradually pour in the soya milk, whisking it as you go to remove any lumps. When you have a lump-free mixture, add the 60g of raisins and mix them into the batter.

Heat about half a tablespoon of the coconut oil in a non-stick frying pan or skillet. When it is hot enough, put about 2 large tablespoons of the pancake mixture into the pan and let it spread out for a moment. It should go to about 6-8 cm in diameter (about 4 inches). Put another two dollops of batter that are the same size in the pan, so that you are cooking three pancakes at a time. Turn them over when they start to bubble on the top (about 3 minutes in) and brown the other side. Turn them again for about 30 seconds on each side to make sure they are cooked through and then transfer to a low oven to keep warm while you make more batches. You should be able to get 9 or 10 out of the mix.

Once all the pancakes are cooked and are keeping warm, heat another tablespoon of coconut oil in the frying pan. Fry the bananas and peaches together in the pan for about 2 minutes (watch out for any spitting), until they are hot but before the bananas go mushy. Add the pinches of sugar and gently mix in. Warm the custard through (about 1 ½ minutes in the microwave).

Serve three pancakes to a plate, spoon a third of the fruit on top of each, pour on the custard and then top with more raisins.

Pancakes with Banana and Peaches

Aubergine and Cherry Tomato Bruschetta with Green Olive Tapenade

Bruschetta are a versatile lunch to have on a relaxing day. Toasted bread topped with just about anything you can imagine. What's not to love?

I've kept to a Mediterranean theme with mine: pan-fried aubergines and tomatoes with a little bit of salt and garlic, served on an olive tapenade and topped with rocket and pine nuts. Simple and delicious.

Try this recipe first, then you can expand it from there.

Prep time: 15 minutes. Cooking time: 15 minutes.
Gluten Free, with the right bread
Make 4-6

Ingredients:
For the Olive Tapenade:
100g pitted green olives
1 tbsp capers
Handful of fresh basil leaves
1 tsp garlic puree
½ tsp Dijon mustard
1 tbsp lime juice
30g pine nuts
150ml extra virgin olive oil

For the Topping:
2-3 tbsp olive oil
1 aubergine, sliced into rings
10 cherry tomatoes, halved
Pinch salt
½ tsp garlic puree

To Serve:
4-6 slices of your favourite bread.
Handful of fresh rocket leaves
A few pine nuts
A drizzle of olive oil.

Method:
First, put all of your tapenade ingredients into a blender and blend until fairly smooth but still with some consistency to it. Spoon into a container and set aside.

To make the topping, heat the olive oil in a pan and fry the aubergine, in two batches if necessary, until they are browned on both sides and soft, about 8 minutes. You may need to add more olive oil as you go along as aubergines suck it up like it's going out of style.

Set the aubergines aside and then add a touch more olive oil to the pan. Put the cherry tomatoes in and fry for about 3-4 minutes, flipping them from time to time. You want them softened slightly but not mushy. Add a pinch of salt and the garlic puree and fry for another minute, then turn the heat off the pan.

To serve, toast your bread and spread a couple of teaspoons of tapenade over one side. Top with 3-4 slices of aubergine and the same amount of cherry tomatoes on top of that. Put on a pinch of the rocket leaves, sprinkle on a few pine nuts and then drizzle with olive oil.

Aubergine and Cherry Tomato Bruschetta with Green Olive Tapenade

Peach and Frangipane Tart

I first came across a frangipane tart in my twenties and I was immediately awe-stricken by the firm, almond filling surrounding soft, delicious fruit. It stayed with me for some time and I made my first one a few years later from a recipe book. Despite the pleasure it gave me, I've only made it a few times since, and this is the first time I've put one together that's both vegan and gluten-free. This tart is best served chilled to allow the frangipane filling to really firm up before cutting into it. With that in mind, I would make it either in the morning, or the night before you want to eat it. A simple slice of this, served with a generous pouring of vegan cream, really is the most exquisite dessert.

You can use regular flour, instead of the gluten-free ones I have chosen here, if you have no problems with gluten. Just be aware that you will probably have to put less milk in the dough mixture, as the flours I have chosen here are quite absorbent and tend to need more liquid. You can also skip the whole process and just use a pre-made pastry to line your tart tin.

Prep time: about 30 minutes. Cooking time: about 90 minutes, plus chilling and setting time.
Gluten Free.
Makes 1 x 9 ½ inch (24cm) tart.

Ingredients:
For the Pastry:
300g buckwheat flour
100g coconut flour
100g vegan margarine, plus extra for greasing
½ tsp salt
3 tbsp sugar
250ml plant-based milk

For the Filling:
200g unrefined sugar
100g ground almonds
120g vegan margarine
Flesh of 1 ripe peach
100ml orange juice
1 tsp vanilla extract
50g buckwheat flour
4-5 saturn peaches (use 1 less if using larger peaches), stoned and quartered

For the Syrup:
100g sugar
50ml orange juice

You will also need a 9 ½ in (24cm) loose-bottomed tart tin.

Method:
Preheat the oven to gas 6/200C/400F and grease your tart tin with vegan margarine.

First make the pastry. Put the flour and margarine into a mixing bowl or food processor and either rub together or process, until you get a fine breadcrumb texture. Mix in the sugar and salt, then stir in the plant milk and knead into a dough. Roll out on a floured surface to about ½ cm thick and line your tart tin with the pastry. This pastry breaks up easily, so you may have to knit it together in the tin a little bit. Press into the corners and trim the edges, then put a sheet of greaseproof baking paper over the top, so that it covers all the pastry. Fill with baking beans or dry rice and bake in the middle of the oven for 15 minutes.

While the pastry is cooking, put all the filling ingredients, apart from the 4-5 peaches at the end, into a food processor and process until the mixture is light and fluffy. Scrape into a bowl and set aside.

When the pastry is done, allow to cool for 15 minutes or so, then remove the baking beans and paper and pour in the frangipane filling. Gently shake to make even, then push the quartered peaches into the filling. Put in as many as you can without the frangipane spilling over the edges of the pastry, but don't pack it so tightly that all you can see is peaches. Set aside.

Make the syrup by putting the sugar and orange juice together into a small saucepan and bringing it to the boil. Simmer for about 3 minutes, until you have a thick syrup that easily coats a spoon.

Spoon the syrup over the top of the tart, until all the filling is covered, then place the tart tin on top of a baking sheet for easy handling once it is cooked.

Turn the oven down to gas 4/180C/350F and put the tart in the middle of the oven. Cook for 1 hour to 1 hour 10 minutes, until risen slightly and golden brown. You can brown it off a little more by putting the tart at the top of the oven for the last 10 minutes of cooking. Allow to cool, then chill for at least 2-3 hours to fully set.

Peach and Frangipane Tart

Chocolate

Toffee Apples with Chocolate and Hazelnuts

Gluten-Free Chocolate Cake

Christmas chocolate Cookies

Chocolate Orange Cheesecake Tart

Chocolate and Peanut Butter Caramel Slices

Chocolate, Orange and Hazelnut Mousse

Vegan Chocolate Biscuits

Avocado Chocolate Cheesecake

Sticky Chocolate Pudding

Vegan Chocolate and Cherry Brownie

Toffee Apples with Chocolate and Hazelnuts

September 20th-23rd marks the autumn equinox. The nights draw in and we can sense, on some small level, the passing of summer. The children are going back to school and life is resuming its routine. Already, subtle changes are taking place. In my garden, unpicked pears, plums and apples are beginning to fall. You can hear the pears at the top of the tall tree as they break their hold on the branch. They tumble, hitting leaves as they go, until they crash to the ground with a small thud. The sound of their journey is like hurried footfalls through dense undergrowth.

Autumn does not mark the end, but really the beginning of an array of seasonal food. Chestnuts, damsons and walnuts come into their own this time of year, as do courgettes and other summer squashes. Later in the season, the hardier squashes will start to appear, and the stores will become like display windows for exciting colours and unusual shapes. Beetroot, kale and cauliflower become more abundant and the short-lived but greatly anticipated appearance of fresh, ripe figs adds a new dimension to our cooking. Autumn is life in full, glorious technicolour.

One of the great icons of autumn food is the toffee apple. Like pumpkin, the toffee apple is something we don't seem to have at any other time of year. We could. Apples are available all year round and toffee is easy enough to make, but we do not. I think it's because they are so symbolic to us. Toffee apples in the autumn are like cranberry sauce in December: it's just where they belong.

Making toffee is straight forward enough, but you do need to watch its temperature, as the outcome will vary depending on how hot you get it. A sugar thermometer is an invaluable asset when making toffee. I bought one for about £10 that clips to the side of the pan and has all the essential markings written on it. What you're looking for when coating apples is the hard-crack point. This is the point when the toffee will harden as it cools. It does this very quickly, so it is advisable to keep the toffee on a very low heat while you are dipping your apples to prevent it from hardening too quickly. If you don't have a sugar thermometer, it takes about 20 minutes of simmering to reach the hard crack point, and you can test it by dropping a little onto greaseproof paper. If it starts to harden straight away, and becomes stringy on your spoon, it is ready. Don't keep it boiling away past this as the toffee will burn, and you will taste it.

Another step you must take is to remove the wax from the apples so that the toffee will stick, in the same way you have to rub down a wall before painting it. You do this by dunking the apples into boiling water for 1 minute, before taking them out again and patting them dry. Once you've done this, your apples are ready for coating.

Prep time: 20 minutes. Cooking time: 20-25 minutes, plus setting time.
Gluten Free
Makes 6

Ingredients:
6 red apples

For the toffee:
500g unrefined sugar
250ml cold water
5 tbsp golden syrup
A pinch of salt

You Will Also Need:
6 toffee apple sticks
200g dark chocolate
100g vegan margarine
Chopped hazelnuts for dipping

Method:
Line a baking tray with greaseproof paper.

Bring a large pot of water to the boil. Gently put all 6 apples into the water and leave them there for 1 minute. Remove them with a slotted spoon and pat them dry once they are cold. Set aside.

Put all the toffee ingredients into a saucepan and bring to the boil. Simmer for about 20 minutes until you have reached the hard crack point (about 154 degrees C). Use a sugar thermometer for this if you can, or see instructions above to tell when it is ready.

Put the toffee apple sticks into the core of each apple and gently dip each one into the toffee, keeping it on a very low heat. Be very careful when doing this. After you have dipped each one, stand it on it's end on the greaseproof paper and allow to harden.

When the toffee has completely cooled, melt the chocolate and margarine and whisk them together to make a chocolate sauce. Arrange your hazelnuts into a suitable dipping bowl. Gently break off the toffee flats that have formed at the base of each apple, to allow for better dipping. Dip the base of each apple into the chocolate sauce, so that it comes about halfway up and then dip them into the hazelnuts. Leave on the greaseproof paper to completely set.

Toffee Apples with Chocolate and Hazelnuts

Gluten-Free Chocolate Cake

This is a basic gluten-free chocolate sandwich sponge recipe that you can use as your go-to cake for birthdays, or any occasion you like. It makes a standard two-layer cake that you place together like a regular sponge. I've also provided a filling and topping to go with it, but you can use your own if you prefer. Chia seeds are a great egg substitute for chocolate cakes as the black colour is hidden by the dark chocolate sponge. A light sponge cake will easily show the chia seeds, making the cake look speckled. You want to avoid this wherever possible, unless it is intentional.

Prep time: 20 minutes. Cooking time: 50 minutes to 1 hour.
Gluten-Free
Makes 1 x 8-inch (21cm) cake

Ingredients:
For the Sponge Cake:
1 tbsp chia seeds
4 tbsp water
400g sugar
400g vegan margarine
300g gluten-free self-raising flour
100g cocoa powder
1 tsp xanthan gum
2 tsp baking powder
1 tsp vanilla extract
100ml plant milk
4 tbsp plain vegan yoghurt
100g dark chocolate, chopped into pieces

For the Topping:
200g dark chocolate, broken into pieces
100g vegan margarine
100ml vegan cream
4 tbsp icing sugar

Method:
Preheat the oven to gas 4/180C/350F. Grease 2 loose-bottomed 8-inch cake tins and line the bottom of them with greaseproof paper. You will also want to cut 2 additional rounds of greaseproof paper to place on top of the cake during cooking.

To make the cake, first put the chia seeds and water into a small dish and mix together. Leave to stand for 10 minutes, until the mixture becomes gloopy.

Now put the sugar and margarine into a mixing bowl and cream together using an electric whisk, until you have a light and fluffy mixture (this takes about 5 minutes).

Add the flour, cocoa powder, xanthan gum and baking powder and mix well using a wooden spoon. Now pour in the vanilla extract, plant milk and yoghurt and stir until you get a thick batter. Mix in the chocolate pieces, then divide the batter between the two cake tins.

Place a circle of greaseproof paper on top of each cake and bake in the middle of the oven for 50 minutes to 1 hour, until the cakes have risen and a cocktail stick comes out clean when inserted.

Allow the cakes to cool in the tin for a few minutes, then turn them out on a cooling rack. Leave until completely cool.

To make the topping, melt the chocolate in the microwave (be careful not to overheat). Now mix in the margarine until fully combined, then let it cool a little before whisking in the vegan cream and the icing sugar.

Use a pallet knife to spread a third of the topping onto the top of one cake layer. Place the second cake layer on top of that and then spread the rest of the topping over the top and sides of the completed cake. Allow to cool for a couple of hours out of the fridge.

*****

Christmas chocolate Cookies

These are your standard Christmas cookies, but made gluten-free so that everyone can enjoy them. I've used buckwheat flour, which is a nice, firm flour for something like this. I think it also has more flavour to it than your usual gluten-free blend. Once the dough is made and chilled, it's time to get creative with your cookie cutters. We have quite a wide range at home that have been bought over the years, so there's plenty of variety. This is also a great recipe to get the kids involved in, as they just love pressing out the shapes and decorating the final cookies.

Prep time: 15 minutes. Chilling time: 1 hour. Cooking time: 15 minutes.
Gluten-Free
Makes about 40

Ingredients:
Dry Ingredients:
600g buckwheat flour
65g cocoa flour
2 tsp xanthan gum
2 tsp bicarbonate of soda
2 tsp baking powder
¾ tsp salt
2 tsp ground cinnamon
½ tsp mixed spice
2 tsp ground ginger
220g golden caster sugar

Wet Ingredients:
200g vegan margarine
1 ½ tsp vanilla extract
100g golden syrup
150ml plant milk

Method:
Put all of the dry ingredients into a bowl and mix together. Add the wet ingredients to the dry and mix with a wooden spoon to combine. Knead with your hands for about a minute to form a dough, then cover and chill in the fridge for 1 hour.

Once the dough has chilled and is ready to use, preheat the oven to gas 5/190C/375F. Break off pieces of the dough and roll out to about 5mm (¼ inch) thick. Cut out shapes using your cookie cutters and place onto a baking sheet lined with greaseproof paper. Bake in the middle of the oven for 10-15 minutes, until browned.

Allow to cool on the baking sheet for a minute or two and then turn them out onto a cooling rack. Repeat this until you have the desired amount of cookies. Decorate with icing when completely cooled.

*****

Chocolate Orange Cheesecake Tart

I've always loved chocolate and orange as a combination. Chocolate and mint is just fine but, for me, chocolate and orange will always win out. This, like all opinions on food, is highly subjective. Samantha, my wife, has a preference for the choc-mint combo, though she does like the orange as well.

This dessert makes use of fresh orange juice and zest, mixed with intense dark chocolate to give it that classic amalgamation. It is a cheesecake, of sorts, and its creamy taste and texture is as undeniable as it is rich. Yet it is also a deep-filled chocolate tart, baked in the oven on a low to medium heat to prevent it from rising too quickly and then sinking again.

The shortcrust pastry is cooked at the same time as the filling and not blind-baked beforehand. This sets the pastry just so, giving it a slight bite that is not too crispy or browned. For this to work your pastry must be thin. Too thick and you will have a squishy, undercooked dough supporting your chocolate centre. For this reason, I chose to use ready-rolled pastry, which is the prefect thickness for this kind of baking. It is a good idea, also, to leave it to cool for a while in the oven with the door slightly ajar. Again, this helps prevent the tart from sinking too quickly. Half an hour will be sufficient for this.

Cooling time aside, this is a very quick and easy dessert to make. The filling is blended, and then whisked. The pastry you just unroll and place into the tart tin, and all the chocolate can be melted in the microwave. Due to the pastry, this recipe is not gluten-free, but you can make your own easily enough. There are two recipes in this book (page 196 and 250).

Prep time: 20 minutes. Cooking time: 40 minutes, plus a couple of hours chilling time.
Serves 6-8

Ingredients:
For the Pastry:
Vegan margarine for greasing
1 x 320g sheet of ready rolled shortcrust pastry, at room temperature

For the Filling:
1 x 200g block of vegan cream cheese
150ml vegan cream
1 tsp vanilla extract
The juice and zest of one large orange
100g golden caster sugar
200g dark, dairy-free chocolate, melted

For the Topping:
100g dark, dairy-free chocolate, melted
25g vegan margarine, melted
100ml vegan cream
The zest of one orange (removed with a zester) to decorate.

Method:
Preheat the oven to gas 4/180C/350F and grease a loose-bottomed tart tin with the margarine.

Unroll the pastry and lay it into the greased tart tin. It won't cover the whole tin, but just cut off the excess and press it into the tin to cover the whole area, including up the sides. Prick a couple of times with a fork and set aside.

Put all of the filling ingredients, apart from the chocolate into a good quality blender and blend until completely smooth. Pour the batter into a mixing bowl then, making sure the melted chocolate has cooled slightly, whisk the chocolate in with the batter until fully incorporated. This will cause it to thicken a little.

Pour the chocolate filling into the pastry casing and bake at the bottom of the oven for 35-40 minutes, until the pastry is cooked, and the tart is set. Turn off the oven and leave the door ajar for 30 minutes to allow the tart to set further.

Once you have removed the tart from the oven you can make the topping. In a small bowl, whisk the melted margarine in with the melted chocolate until fully combined. Pour in the cream and then whisk again until you have a silky-smooth chocolate sauce. Pour this over the top of your tart and use a large spoon to spread it out to the edges. Allow this to cool for another 30 minutes before putting in the fridge to fully set, which will take up to two hours.
Once set, remove from the fridge and top with the orange zest, then cut into 6-8 slices and serve.

Chocolate Orange Cheesecake Tart

Chocolate and Peanut Butter Caramel Slices

I made these for a buffet we were having recently. The idea behind them was a soft chocolate filling on pastry with a caramel topping, all cut into small squares for people to pick at as and when they wanted them. This is not a quick dessert to make, but the results are worth the time you put in. It's entirely vegan and gluten free, but it does contain peanuts. If you have an allergy, the peanut butter is for flavour and can be omitted without affecting the recipe.

Prep time: about 40 minutes. Cooking time: about 1 hour 15 minutes, plus cooling and setting time.
Gluten Free
Makes 1 large tray.

Ingredients:
For the Pastry:
300g gluten-free, all-purpose flour
100g vegan butter
½ tsp salt
2 tbsp sugar
1 ½ tsp xanthan gum
100ml plant-based milk

For the Filling:
1 x 400g block firm tofu, drained
400ml plant-based milk
1 x 170g tub vegan cream cheese
1 tsp vanilla extract
4 heaped tbsp peanut butter
¼ tsp ground nutmeg
180g sugar
3 tbsp maple syrup
50g cocoa powder
200g dark chocolate, melted

For the Caramel Topping:
200ml vegan cream
50g vegan butter
250g soft, light brown sugar
2 tbsp peanut butter
1 tsp agar agar powder

To Decorate:
4 heaped tbsp icing sugar
1 tbsp water

Method:
First make the pastry. Put the flour and butter into a mixing bowl and crumb between your fingers to make a breadcrumb texture. Add the rest of the dry ingredients and thoroughly mix together, then pour in the plant milk. Bring together with your hands and knead into a dough. Cover and store in the fridge for at least 30 minutes before using.

Preheat the oven to gas 6/200C/400F and grease a large, rectangle baking tray with an approximately 1-inch lip.

When your pastry has chilled, roll it out to the size of your baking tray and line the bottom with it. Make sure the pastry goes to the edges of the tray but not up the sides. Prick the pastry with a fork and then cover with greaseproof paper, so that it goes up over the edges. Fill the paper with baking beans or dry rice and bake in the oven for 15-20 minutes, until just cooked. Remove from the oven and take out the beans and paper, then set aside to cool.

To make the filling, put all the filling ingredients, apart from the melted chocolate, into a blender and blend until completely smooth. You may need to scrape down the sides with a spatula to make sure everything is blended. Pour in the melted chocolate and blend again until fully incorporated.

Turn the oven down to gas 4/180C/350F.

Pour the filling out onto the pastry, you should have enough so that it fills the tray to about ¾ inch deep. Smooth out with your spatula and then cook in the middle of the oven for 45 minutes, until firm and browned. Let it cool in the oven for a while with the door ajar, then remove it and allow to completely cool.

While the tart is cooling you can make the caramel sauce. You also want this to be cool before pouring over the top of the tart to avoid it melting the tart and mixing in. Put all the ingredients, apart from the agar agar, into a saucepan and bring to the boil. Simmer gently for 5 minutes, whisking from time to time, then add the agar agar powder and whisk in. Simmer for 2 more minutes, then turn off the heat and allow to completely cool. It will thicken as it cools, so whisk from time to time to prevent a skin from forming and to keep it pourable.

When the tart and the caramel sauce have cooled, pour the sauce over the top of the tart and spread it all over with a spatula or pallet knife. Store in the fridge or freezer to completely set firm (2-3 hours).

To decorate, mix the icing sugar and water together and then drizzle over the top of the tart. You can cut the tart into either 12 large squares, or much small ones as in the picture.

Chocolate and Peanut Butter Caramel Slices

Chocolate, Orange and Hazelnut Mousse

Though this is a mousse with a lot of ingredients, it is still a very easy one to make as all you need to do is blend them until they are smooth. This is a great way to impress at a dinner party without going to too much effort. Put a chilled dish of this in front of each of your guests at the end of the meal and they'll be talking about it for ages! Make it at least two hours before you want to eat it, to allow it to fully set. You can make it the night before if you like, just remember to cover the dishes, or they will be dry on top when you come to use them. It is also best to garnish them right before serving, to prevent the garnish from wilting or going soft.

I used pre-chopped hazelnuts for the mousse itself and then crushed up whole nuts for the garnish. You can save some money by just buying the chopped hazelnuts and garnishing with those. Don't put whole hazelnuts into the mousse itself unless they have no skins on, as they won't process very well. If you don't have coconut nectar, you can make up the difference with more maple syrup, or even golden syrup will be fine. I put it in for variety of flavour (also because I have a lot of it in my cupboard and need to use more).

Prep time: 10 minutes. Chilling time: about 2 hours.
Gluten-Free
Serves 6-8

Ingredients:
1 x 400g block firm tofu, drained
250ml plan-based cream
250ml plant milk
Juice and zest of 1 large orange, reserve a little zest for garnish if you like, or get it from another orange (don't take too much from the recipe)
1 tsp vanilla extract
100ml maple syrup
50ml coconut nectar (or make it up with maple syrup)
75g chopped hazelnuts
A pinch of salt
A pinch of mild chilli powder
2 tbsp cacao powder
200g dark, dairy-free chocolate, melted and allowed to cool.
A handful of whole hazelnuts, crushed with the bottom of a heavy saucepan, for garnish (optional)

Method:
Put all the ingredients, apart from the melted chocolate, into a good quality blender and blend until completely smooth (you may have to do it a few times).

Pour in the slightly cooled, melted chocolate and blend again until fully incorporated. You may need to scrape down the sides with a spatula.

Pour the mixture into serving dishes and chill in the fridge for at least 2 hours, until fully set.
When you are ready to serve, garnish with a little orange zest and the crushed hazelnuts.

Chocolate, Orange and Hazelnut Mousse

Vegan Chocolate Biscuits

These are easy to make chocolate biscuits, that are similar in taste to the digestive biscuit here in the UK. They are made with oats that have been ground up in a food processor to a flour-like consistency, then blended with self-raising flour.

The biscuits are light and sweet all by themselves, so the extra step of coating them in chocolate is entirely optional. I have not tried these with a gluten-free flour, but I'm sure that if you switch over and add a teaspoon of xanthan gum to the mix, they will work out just fine. Remember to use gluten-free oats if you're doing that.

These biscuits are best eaten the same day, or at the latest the following day, as they tend to go soft after that. Don't worry though, friends and family will be eager to help you tuck in.

Prep time: 15-20 minutes. Cooking time: 15 minutes per batch.
Makes about 25 large biscuits (mine were very large).

Ingredients:
For the Biscuits:
100g oats
400g self-raising flour
1 tsp baking powder
½ tsp bicarbonate of soda
½ tsp ground ginger
½ tsp salt
225g unrefined sugar
150g vegan margarine
3 heaped tbsp golden syrup
100ml plant milk

For the Chocolate Topping:
1 carton of coconut cream, chilled for at least 2-3 hours, or overnight
150g chocolate, melted
50g vegan margarine
3 tbsp icing sugar
50ml vegan cream

Method:
Put the oats into a food-processor and blitz for a minute or so, until you get a flour-like consistency.

Put the ground oats and all the other biscuit ingredients, apart from the golden syrup and plant milk, into a large mixing bowl and rub between your fingers until you achieve a fine breadcrumb texture. Add the golden syrup and plant milk and stir with a table knife until large lumps form. Bring the dough together with your hands and shape into a ball. The dough will be quite moist, but will work perfectly for the biscuits. Cover and chill the dough for about 30 minutes.

Preheat the oven to gas 6/200C/400F and line a baking sheet with greaseproof paper.

Once the dough is chilled, roll it out onto a floured surface to a thickness of about 4mm (you may want to do this in two batches). Use a cookie-cutter to cut round shapes out of the dough (I used quite a large cutter, but you can use any size you like), then place the rounds onto the baking sheet. They won't spread much, so you can put them quite close together.

Once your sheet is full, bake them in the top of the oven for 15 minutes, or until golden brown. Transfer to a cooling rack and repeat the process until all the biscuit dough has gone. Allow the biscuits to completely cool.

Now make the chocolate topping. Drain the excess water from the coconut cream, which will be easy when the cream has chilled. Mix the margarine in with the melted chocolate (I always melt mine in the microwave). Make sure the chocolate has cooled quite a bit and then whisk in the coconut cream, icing sugar and vegan cream. It should all blend smoothly, but if it turns into a thick fudge instead of a smooth sauce just pop the mix in the microwave for 20 seconds or so. This will make it liquid again, so you will have to wait for it to cool and thicken to be able to spread it onto the biscuits.

When the chocolate is ready (i.e. it has a thick consistency), you can top your biscuits with it. Do this by picking up a biscuit in your hands and dunking it flat and face down into the chocolate, so that it covers the top half of the biscuit. Pull the biscuit out again and smooth off the top with a pallet knife, or other flat knife. Put the biscuit onto greaseproof paper to set and continue until all the biscuits are topped. They will be ready to eat in about 90 minutes. Consume within 24 hours.

Vegan Chocolate Biscuits

Avocado Chocolate Cheesecake

If you want to impress family and friends with a chocolate dessert, this one will do it. This rich and creamy, beautifully soft chocolate cheesecake has a chocolate oat biscuit base and a deep, firm chocolate layer on top. This dessert is so chocolatey that I was able to say chocolate three times in one sentence while describing it.

The base is made of oat biscuits that have been blended with some cocoa powder, and the filling uses a mixture of avocadoes, vegan crème fraiche and plant-based cream to give it a taste and appearance that will make you drool. The chocolate topping is poured on top after the filling has set, to give you a beautifully smooth layer. This is not a difficult cake to make and the only cooking involved is melting the chocolate (which I always do in the microwave). It is very important to allow the chocolate to cool for 10 minutes or so before adding it to anything. If the chocolate is too hot it will react with the other ingredients and seize up, becoming thick and fudgy instantly. Cooling the melted chocolate slowly, while having it remain pourable, is the way to prevent this from happening.

Prep time: 15-20 minutes. No cooking time. Chilling and setting time 4-5 hours.
Use gluten-free oats to guarantee gluten-free
Makes 1 x 9-inch (23 cm) cheesecake.

Ingredients:
For the Base:
300g oat biscuits
2 tbsp cocoa powder
50g vegan margarine, melted, plus extra for greasing

For the Filling:
The flesh of two avocadoes
1 tub vegan crème fraiche (200ml)
250ml vegan cream
200g macadamia nuts, soaked in hot water for 1 hour and then drained (cashew nuts are also fine)
250g unrefined sugar
3 tbsp cocoa powder
2 tsp vanilla extract
3 tbsp coconut nectar
75g vegan margarine
Small pinch of mild chilli powder
A pinch of salt
200g dark chocolate, melted and allowed to cool

For the Topping:
150g dark chocolate, melted and allowed to cool
75g vegan margarine
3 tbsp coconut nectar
1 tsp vanilla extract

Method:
Grease a 9-inch (23cm) spring-formed cake tin with a little margarine.

First make the base by blending the oat biscuits in a food processor until it is all crumbs. Transfer to a mixing bowl and add the cocoa powder and margarine. Stir until completely combined. Now transfer the mix to the cake tin and press down with your hands or a spoon, so that the base is covered and the crumbs aren't loose. If you get any crumbs sticking to the sides of the greased tin, just gently wipe around the edge with some kitchen paper. Chill the base in the fridge or freezer for up to 1 hour.

While it is setting you can make the filling, but do not add the chocolate. Put all of the filling ingredients, apart from the melted chocolate, into a blender and blend until completely smooth.

Once the base is set and ready for filling you can add the melted chocolate to the filling mix. Do not do this before the base is ready or it will set in the blender jug. Blend again until fully smooth and incorporated, then pour it into the cake tin, on top of the base. Give the tin a little shake to evenly distribute it and then cover and leave in the fridge to set for 3-4 hours.

Once the filling is completely set you can make your topping. Put all of the topping ingredients into a mixing bowl and stir together with a spoon to fully combine. The chocolate needs to cool enough to not react with any of the other ingredients, but still remain pourable. Now pour the chocolate topping over the cheesecake filling and gently turn the tin from side to side to allow the chocolate to spread evenly over the top. It should spread nicely and there should be no need to use any kind of spreading implement. Once this is done, leave it to set outside of the fridge for about 45 minutes, then cover again and store in the fridge until you are ready to cut and serve it.

Avocado Chocolate Cheesecake

Sticky Chocolate Pudding

I wanted to create something that was similar to a sticky toffee pudding, only with chocolate, and that was also vegan and gluten-free. This dessert was the result. Soft and moist in the centre, *extremely* chocolatey, with a chocolate sauce poured over the top. You can serve it cold, but it is much better when it is warm. You can do this in the microwave for about 40 seconds per serving, or just put the whole tray back in the oven for about 8 minutes.

I've used gluten-free self-raising flour, also buckwheat and coconut flour to add a little variety of flavour and texture. Gluten-free self-raising flour on its own will do just fine, and if you have no gluten issues then you can go for just ordinary self-raising flour. Leave out the xanthan gum if you are using ordinary flour.

Prep time: 20 minutes. Cooking time: 40-50 minutes, plus cooling time.
Gluten-Free
Makes 12.

Ingredients:
For the Pudding:
175g vegan margarine, softened, plus a little extra for greasing
175g soft brown sugar
2 tbsp black treacle
150g dates, soaked in hot water for 20 minutes
150g gluten-free self-raising flour
150g buckwheat flour
100g coconut flour
2 tsp baking powder
2 tsp xanthan gum
1 tsp bicarbonate of soda
½ tsp salt
350ml plant-based milk
200g dark chocolate, melted

For the Chocolate Sauce:
65g vegan margarine
150g soft brown sugar
200ml plant-based cream
150g dark chocolate, broken into pieces

Method:
Preheat the oven to Gas 4/180C/350F. Grease a large baking tray with margarine and line it with greaseproof paper.

To make the pudding, put the margarine and the sugar in a large mixing bowl and cream together, using either a wooden spoon or an electric whisk. It's ready when it is pale yellow and fluffy. Pour in the black treacle and mix. Now blend the dates, along with some of the soaking water (about 50ml), until you have a puree. Stir this in with the butter mixture until fully incorporated.

In a separate bowl add the flours, baking powder, xanthan gum, bicarb of soda and salt and mix together. Add this to the butter mixture and stir with a wooden spoon until fully mixed. Pour in the 350ml plant milk and stir to combine. Now mix in the melted chocolate and spoon the mixture straight into the baking tray. Do this right away as the chocolate will make the mixture become hard very quickly. You can either smooth the mixture out with a spatula at this point, or leave it a little rocky-looking as I did.

Place the baking tray in the middle of the oven and bake for 40-50 minutes, until risen and cooked, but not too dry.

When it's cooked, turn it out onto a rectangle cooling rack and allow to cool a little.
While it is cooling you can make the chocolate sauce:

Melt the margarine in a saucepan and add the brown sugar. Let this simmer for a couple of minutes then put the heat on minimum and add the cream. Simmer gently again for a minute or two more, then turn off the heat and stir in the chocolate pieces. The sauce is ready when the chocolate has melted and is fully mixed.

Put the pudding on a chopping board and cut into 12 even squares. Now put it back into the baking tray and pour the chocolate sauce over the top. Leave it to soak in for about an hour and then reheat a little to serve.

Sticky Chocolate Pudding

*****

Vegan Chocolate and Cherry Brownie

If you like brownies, you'll love this cherry version. It has rich and dark chocolate chunks, with juicy bites of whole cherry throughout. Serve it cold and get the delicious crunch of large chocolate pieces, juxtaposed with a tiny explosion of succulent cherry juice. Serve it hot, with just a splash of vegan cream, and get something wholly sensuous and utterly divine.

I've used frozen cherries for two reasons: because they're available all year round, and because they're already pitted, which means you just have to defrost, drain them and put them in the mix. It really couldn't be easier. I would recommend not chopping the chocolate up too fine either, that way you create either a good solid bite or a gooey explosion of chocolate, both of which are a taste sensation.

Prep time: 15 minutes. Cooking time: 20-25 minutes
Makes 12 large squares

Ingredients:
1 tbsp chia seeds
4 tbsp cold water

350g self-raising flour
75g cocoa powder
1 ½ tsp baking powder
200g unrefined sugar
75g vegan margarine, plus extra for greasing
2 tsp vanilla extract
400ml plant milk (I used oat)
4 tbsp coconut nectar (or maple syrup)
700g (2 packs) frozen cherries, defrosted and fully drained of liquid
200g dark chocolate, chopped into small pieces

Method:
Preheat the oven to gas 4/180C/350F and line a large, lipped baking tray with greaseproof paper.

Start by mixing the chia seeds and water together in a small bowl and leaving to rest for about 10 minutes, until the mixture turns quite gloopy.

Now sift together the flour, cocoa powder and baking powder into a large mixing bowl. Add the sugar and stir to fully combine the dry ingredients. Put in the margarine, vanilla extract, milk and coconut nectar and stir with a wooden spoon, until you have a thick, smooth batter. Finally, stir in the cherries and the chocolate pieces, so that everything is evenly distributed.

Pour the batter into the baking tray and bake in the middle of the oven for 20-25 minutes, until it is cooked but still moist.

Turn the brownie out onto a cooling rack and allow to completely cool, then cut into 12 squares.

Vegan Chocolate and Cherry Brownie

Vegan Quiche Lorraine, 9

Shredded Spring Greens with Red Kidney Beans and Teriyaki Sauce, 12

Spice-Marinated Tofu Curry, 12

BBQ Chickpeas with Braised Tofu, 13

Sweet Potato and Three Bean Nachos, 14

Smoked Tofu in Coconut Milk Soup with Rice Noodles, 16

Roasted Pumpkin with Lentils and Vegan Feta, 17

Braised Tofu Kebabs, 18

Mung Bean and Aubergine Dal, 19

Oven Roasted Kale with Spiced Lentils and Mango, 22

French-Style Aquafaba Omelette with Vegan Cheese and Tenderstem Broccoli, 23

Chickpeas with Lemon, Parsley and Vegan Feta, 25

Borlotti Bean Chilli with Rice, 27

15 Minute Thai-Style Lentils with Green Beans and Coconut Rice, 28

Fried Tofu with Rice Noodles and Black Bean Sauce, 29

Lentil, Spinach and Coconut Curry, 30

Aquafaba Mango Mousse with Raspberries, 31

Woodland Mushroom Tempura with Garlic and Lemon Mayo, 35

Cavolo Nero and Dill Falafel, 38

Sam's Vegan Rhubarb Crumble, 38

Summer Green Vegetable Quiche, 40

King Oyster Mushrooms with Tomatoes and Pesto, 42

Rhubarb and Red Onion Chutney, 42

BBQ Baked Spiced Apples, 45

Whole Wheat Mushroom and Kale Tartlets, 45

Braised White Cabbage with Sugar Snap Peas and Cherry Tomatoes, 48

Vegan Parsley Sauce, 48

King Oyster Mushroom and Black Bean Dumplings, 49

Rice Noodles with Portobello Mushrooms and Green Beans, 52

Creamy Vegan Mushroom Soup, 52

Cherry and Cranberry Pies, 54

Cajun Spiced Broccoli Bites, 57

Easy Chestnut Mushroom, New Potato and Leek Pie, 60

Carrot and Red Pepper Soup, 63

Vegan Leek and Cheese Parcels, 64

Pan Fried Cinnamon Pears, 67

Mulled Pears with Vegan Whipped Cream, 67

Blackberry Panna Cotta, 70

Caramelised Pear Crostini with Haloumi-Style Cheese, 72

Pan-Fried Pear Tart with Greek-Style Cheese and Redcurrant Jelly, 72

Deep-Filled Apple Pie, 75

Artichoke Risotto with Vegan Haloumi and Crispy Red Onions, 78

Awesome Spaghetti Sauce, 79

Black Bean Spaghetti with Garlic-Braised Cabbage and Peanuts, 79

Mac n Cheese with Asparagus and Tomato, 80

Quinoa with Broccoli and Cashew Nuts, 83

Brown, Red and Wild Rice with Courgettes, Peppers and Tomatoes, 83

Brown, Red and Wild Rice with Sugar Snap Peas and Woodland Mushrooms, 84

Creamy Kale Polenta with Roasted Tomatoes, 85

Beetroot Risotto, 88

Roasted Red Pepper and Aubergine Pasta Sauce, 88

Baked Spaghetti with Tomatoes and Parmesan, 89

Quinoa, Beetroot and Date Burgers, 90

Brown Rice Salad with Edamame Beans and Toasted Cashews, 93

Fettuccine with Mushrooms, Vegan Haloumi, Sundried Tomatoes and Pesto, 93

Red Lentil Pasta with Purple Sprouting Broccoli and Garlic Dressing, 94

Asparagus with Celeriac Mash, Mushrooms and Garlic Butter, 98

Sweet Potato and Carrot Soup, 98

Lemon and Garlic Roasted New Potatoes, 99

Garlic Braised Swede with Button Mushrooms, Rosemary and Tomatoes, 102

Sautéed Potatoes with Rosemary, 102

Pan-Fried Fennel with Olives, Garlic and Lemon Juice, 103

Dad's Potato Fritters, 105

Onion Bhajis with Cucumber Raita, 108

Baked Rhubarb with Sweet Potato, Swede and Crushed Hazelnuts, 110

Cumin Spiced Potatoes with Green Beans, 111

Sausage Pittas with Sweet Potato and Beetroot Yoghurt, 112

Roast Parsnip Soup with Cavolo Nero Dumplings and Toasted Cumin Seeds, 113

Roasted Oca Root with Artichoke Hearts and Parsley Pesto, 114

Pumpkin and Rice Cakes with Lemon Sauce, 117

Pumpkin Chilli Tacos, 119

Halloween Spiced Pumpkin Muffins, 120

Oven-Roasted Courgettes with Salsa Verde, 122

Butternut Squash and Carrot Burger, 124

Winter Squash Stew, 126

Courgettes in Garlic Sauce, 126

Butternut Squash and Celeriac Cakes, 127

Courgette Fritters with Basil and Dill Dressing, 128

Solstice Pie, 131

Roasted Butternut Squash Stuffed with Aubergine Curry, 131

Pumpkin and Lemon Drizzle Cake, 133

Pumpkin and Lentil Stew, 136

Very 'Meaty' Vegan Mozzarella Burgers, 138

Moroccan Style Vegan Sausages, 140

Spinach and Vegan Mince Koftas, 140

Vegan Sausages with Kale and Beans, 141

Vegan Chicken-Style Nuggets, 144

Apple and Red Onion No-Meatballs, 147

Vegan Tenders with Kale and Apple Slaw and Homemade Fries, 147

Vegan Cheese, Ham and Sundried Tomato Slices, 151

Cranberry and Raisin Granola Protein Bars, 155

Roasted Aubergine and Walnut Pesto, 157

Vegan Christmas Stuffing Balls, 158

Salad of Vegan Halloumi and Tomatoes with Cashews and Potato Bread, 160

Vegan Aubergine, Blue Cheese and Walnut Spring Rolls, 162

Christmas Fruit and Nut Roast Stuffed with Pears Mushrooms and Tomatoes, 164

Sweet and Spicy Almonds, 169

Vegan Lemon Tart, 169

Coffee, Banana and Walnut Pie, 172

No Bake Blueberry Tart, 175

Rosemary Flatbreads, 179

Classic Vegan 'Egg' Bread, 179

Vegan Scones and Homemade Strawberry Jam, 180

Five Ways with Pizza, 183

Oven-Roasted Tomato, Asparagus and Basil Pizza, 185

Potato, Onion and Rosemary Pizza, 186

Aubergine, Red Pepper and Rocket Pizza, 186

Wholewheat Pizza Dough, 189

Vegan Sausage and Mushroom Pizza, 189

Calzone Style Vegan Margarita Pizza, 191

Garlic Croutons, 193

Sundried Tomato and Black Olive Bread, 193

Sweet Gluten-Free Shortcrust Pastry, 196

Vegan and Gluten Free Yorkshire Puddings, 196

Vegan Toad in the Hole, 199

Tofu, Sweetcorn and Pineapple Quesadilla, 199

Buckwheat Raspberry Pancakes, 200

Spooky Halloween Gingerbread Biscuits, 203

Curry-Spiced French Toast, 206

Plaited Wholelmeal Bread, 207

Sweet French Toast with Forest Fruits and Banana, 210

Tortilla Salad with Avocados and Red Chillies, 213

Oven Roasted Figs with Vegan Blue Cheese, 215

Basic Humous, 215

Roasted Mediterranean Vegetables with Dried Dates and Clementines, 216

Chilled Granola Peach Crumble, 217

Sautéed New Potatoes with Kale and Figs, 218

Aubergine and Sweet Potato Curry, 219

Chickpea Flour Pancakes with Plantain, 220

Baba Ghanoush, 223

Pumpkin and Mango Curry, 225

Richard's Homemade Hot Chilli Sauce, 225

Poached Nectarines in Cardamom Syrup, 228

Salad of Watermelon, Avocado and Vegan 'Greek Style' Cheese, 228

Lemon and Ginger Cookies, 231

Kale and Dill Wraps with Aubergine, Pineapple and Black Beans, 234

Pancakes with Banana and Peaches, 235

Aubergine and Cherry Tomato Bruschetta with Green Olive Tapenade, 238

Peach and Frangipane Tart, 240

Toffee Apples with Chocolate and Hazelnuts, 243

Gluten-Free Chocolate Cake, 246

Christmas chocolate Cookies, 247

Chocolate Orange Cheesecake Tart, 247

Chocolate and Peanut Butter Caramel Slices, 250

Chocolate, Orange and Hazelnut Mousse, 253

Vegan Chocolate Biscuits, 255

Avocado Chocolate Cheesecake, 258

Sticky Chocolate Pudding, 261

Vegan Chocolate and Cherry Brownie, 262

Printed in Great Britain
by Amazon